Jean Leclercq

Memoirs

From Grace to Grace

FOREWORD BY
Inos Biffi

TRANSLATED BY
PAUL C. DUGGAN

ST. BEDE'S PUBLICATIONS
PETERSHAM, MASSACHUSETTS

FIRST EDITION
5   4   3   2   1

LIBRARY OF CONGRESS CATALOGING-IN-PUBLICATION DATA

Leclercq, Jean, 1911-
   [Di grazia a grazia. English]
   Memoirs: From grace to grace / Jean Leclercq ; foreword by Inos
Biffi; translated by Paul C. Duggan.
   Includes index.
   ISBN 1-879007-26-6 (pbk.)
   1. Leclercq, Jean, 1911-.   2 Benedictines—Biography.   I. Title.
BX4705.L4325 A3 2000
271'.102—dc21
[B]   00-028083

Published by   St. Bede's Publications
                 271 North Main Street
                 P.O. Box 545
                 Petersham, MA 01366-0545

Contents

Foreword to the Italian Edition

With some reluctance, Jean Leclercq yielded to the friendly insistence of those who invited him to write down his memoirs so that they might appear in Jaca Book's series, *Biblioteca di Cultura Medievale* after the biography of Gilson[1] which, drawing widely from his correspondence, shows itself in its turn to be largely a book of memoirs. Moreover, there is a close connection between Gilson and Leclercq: the latter provided an engaging profile of his admired former teacher at the Collège de France, later his friend and colleague in interests and studies, for the Italian edition of *La théologie mystique de Saint Bernard*,[2] defined by Leclercq himself as "the most beautiful book that has ever been written about the abbot of Clairvaux."[3] It was to Gilson that Leclercq owed his decisive choice of turning to the study of monastic authors. This choice turned out to be providential and fruitful not only for the history of spirituality but, also, just as much for the history and theory of theology. Gilson would be among those who correctly understood the significance of "monastic theology,"[4] "discovered" by Leclercq and destined immedi-

---

[1]L. K. Shook, *Étienne Gilson*, Introduzione di Inos Biffi, Milan, Jaca Book, 1991.

[2]*La teologia mistica di san Bernardo*, Introduzione di Jean Leclercq, a cura di Claudio Stercal, Milan, Jaca Book, 1987, pp. IX-XXI (Étienne Gilson, san Bernardo e la storia della spiritualità).

[3]*Ibid.*, p. IX.

[4]Leclercq had sent Gilson his *L'amour des lettres et le désir de Dieu*, which is his masterpiece. Gilson then wrote to him from Vermenton on July 24, 1957: "The young Benedictine monks have good taste. At one time they gained from St. Anselm the *Monologion*; now they have just gained from you this excellent introduction to the history of monastic ideas up to the end of the twelfth century. I have read it with intense pleasure and interest. There are so many things that I have learned in making my way through it! For, while your book is literary, as it had to be since you were celebrating the Letters, nonetheless what is found there is something else besides vain literature. You have earned the warmest congratulations." And except for the expression "monastic theology" about which Gilson stated a discreet reservation, he adds: "St. Thomas, St. Bonaventure, etc., were also monks. St. Thomas has always seemed to me to be a Benedictine-Dominican, more a man of Scripture than of Aristotle." And, when Fr. Leclercq sent him *St. Bernard et l'esprit cistercien*, Gilson again wrote on May 9, 1967 from Vermenton: "My reverend Father, your *St. Bernard et l'esprit cistercien* is, in my judgment, a masterpiece, since you have succeeded in writing the book that you wanted to write, and that, in these days, you alone could have written. Its merits will perhaps not be fully grasped except by those who, without knowing St. Bernard as well as you do, have become sufficiently familiar with him so that your

ately to draw upon itself prejudicial aversion, impassioned praise and thoughtful adherence.[5]

The reason for the section dedicated to the medievalists of our time in the *Biblioteca di Cultura Medievale* is readily apparent. Thanks to their research and to their methods the documents of the Middle Ages — which engendered western culture and marked it indelibly — come to light and are revived. An awareness of the life of a medievalist, as of any author, facilitates a better understanding of his or her works and clarifies

---

words might find a response in their personal experience of the saint and his teaching. In my view the book is perfect (*factum et perfectum*). I am completely in agreement with you. The pages in which you speak about his character, about his taste for animate nature, about his tastes as an artist, etc., draw nothing but approval from me. I doubt that any important revisions could be made on the monk and on the saint. The ones that could be done are of the kind that you yourself could do indefinitely, because of the infinite richness of his personality. I wonder if sometimes his theology of culture as *eloquentia* can be opposed to those of culture as *dialectica*. On the contrary, I think I see the latter always ready to blossom on the stem of the former. It also does so with a surprising and insuperable vigor. When he says (I am quoting from memory) that God is present in all things *causaliter non formaliter*, I believe, of course, that he is grasping once and for all the essence of Thomist theology. This feat of intellectual agility allowed him to leave behind all that Dionysian indeterminateness, which it would have been quite pardonable for him to have yielded to. The thought of this poet, a friend of symbols and metaphors, was, when necessary, doctrinally firm and precise in expression; these turn his symbolism into an utterly singular case. We surely have need of him. There is not only his dialectical theology, but his Thomistic as well! Those who do not have a taste for this undoubtedly have some reason for working with another of a different style, but it seems to me that their error is the idea that the truth of the word of God will be uncovered by philology rather than by dialectic. Bernard was an excellent grammarian, but his scriptural approach was not grammatical. The literal sense at the beginning, yes, as for Virgil or Cicero, but I believe it leads us astray when it invites us to limit ourselves to it, even when nourishing it with everything that archaeology can add to philology. Bernard is on the right path and in advance agreement with all that the great scholastics will say after him, precisely because the ones and the others are meditating on the same object: the truth of Scripture, which is neither that of philology nor that of dialectic." We also quote another excerpt from the same letter, indicating Gilson's regard for Leclercq: "In reading your valuable remarks on the saint's methods of literary composition, I believed I understood one of the reasons for the enthusiastic memory that your students in Toronto have kept of your teaching. Unless I am mistaken, there is no one today except yourself who knows these things: thank you for teaching them to us. Even when you do nothing else than tell us that you could teach them, you are rendering outstanding service."

[5]Cf. I Biffi, *La teologia monastica*, in "Teologia," 18 (1993), and also: *idem., Intelligenza e desiderio del mistero cristiano*, in J. Leclercq, *Esperienza spirituale e teologia. Alla scuola dei monaci medievali*, Milan, Jaca Book, 1990, pp. 9-23; *idem., Pubblicazioni su san Bernardo*, in "La Scuola Cattolica," 120 (1992), pp. 123-125; *idem., La cristologia di san Bernardo "pellegrino" in Terra Santa, ibid.*, p. 47. See also P. Zerbi, *"Teologia monastica" e "teologia scolastica,"* in *Medioevo e latinità in memoria di Ezio Franceschini*, Vita e Pensiero, Milan, 1993, pp. 479-494.

their paternity, the specific place of their birth and of their elaboration, and in some way their identity and features. Thus, after perusing the life of Gilson, the first medievalist in our series, one can understand and assimilate his books more deeply.

The same will surely happen with the books of Jean Leclercq: after reading his memoirs, we will be able to recognize the "occasions," the stimuli, the needs from which they arose, the circumstances that accompanied them, and thus we will perceive more immediately their spirit. However, in Leclercq's case, it is not a matter of a biography, nor of accounts by others about him—as was the work on Gilson, as narrated by Shook[6]—but of "memoirs," which moreover are neither a diary nor an autobiography with the chronological precision that those literary genres require, but a "gathering of memories," of events and of personages that were gradually impressed on Leclercq's soul. Now, after friendly and insistent pressure, they have reflowered to constitute a florilegium that will please both those who have met and liked Jean Leclercq and those who, after him and in the wake of his vast and tireless research, will advance in the field of those authors who, in a completely special way and in a singular form, have cultivated the love for letters and, even before that, desired God—the monastic authors, especially the medieval ones.

As Leclercq writes in the Preface, at first he resisted and then was hesitant to satisfy the demand for these memoirs, until Father de Lubac (who had dedicated to him the first volume of his renowned *Exégèse médiévale* for the help he gained from his knowledge and friendship) told him that these recollections were a duty, with the admonition: "Do it, before you lose your memory."

Still, the anxiety did not leave him totally. Just a few weeks before they appeared in the Italian edition, which was their first, he confided to those who had pressed him to continue and bring the work to its end: "The closer the publication of my memoirs comes, the greater the apprehension and confusion I feel over the idea of talking about

---

[6]On Jean Leclercq—biographies and works—see, among others: L. Leloir, *Dom Jean Leclercq*, in *Bernard de Clairvaux*. Studies presented to Dom Jean Leclercq, Cistercian Publications, Washington, DC, Consortium Press, 1973, pp. 1-17; volume 16 of "Monastic Studies," 1985; E. Jeauneau-M. Sheehan, "Hommage à dom Jean Leclercq," in *Studia Monastica*, 33 (1991), pp. 379-388; A. Limage Conde, "Dom Jean Leclercq y las letras monásticas," in *Studia Monastica*, 32 (1992), pp. 315-359 (with the bibliography there cited). For the bibliography of Leclercq until 1988, see below Note of the Italian translator of these memoirs.

myself. But those who are publishing it are the judges and are taking responsibility for it. Especially after Gilson's broad and rich biography!"

Clearly Leclercq does talk about himself, but not to tarry over himself. He calls his life a succession of graces. Graces granted to him, certainly, but through him we can admire the graces given to the Church: "My memory has been marked by the phases of the Church's life that it has been given to me to traverse."

The journey begins with the "joys of a beginning" at Clervaux. It brings us to the "Roman walks," to the "Parisian paradise," to medieval encounters, to the discovery of St Bernard, taking us to countries and to monasteries abroad and, in the end, bringing us back to where the long journey had begun.

The early years at Clervaux are important. Against a background of a nature rich in gifts and of a cultivated and refined adolescence, ready for joy and enjoyment, there appears the young Jean Leclercq presenting himself to monastic life. He began there with passion and liveliness; with commitment, not lacking in humor nor in the ability to be entertained and to entertain; with listening to masters, whom he would always distinguish from professors; and with his first basic contacts with the great texts of the Christian tradition assimilated deeply together with the most instructive expressions of contemporary spirituality. Leclercq would thus open himself to the procedure and enjoyment of *lectio divina* (sacred reading) — after methodical prayer failed for him — and to the living knowledge of the Fathers of the Church. All this would lay the foundation and be the remote origin of the "discovery" of that other theology that would make Jean Leclercq renowned and also controversial: the theology that, following the suggestion of a Dominican, he would call "monastic."

From another viewpoint, the aim of these studies was not the achievement of an intellectual monachism: "I wanted to be a monk, and nothing more.... I did not want to study, or to become a priest.... I became one, without the vocation, because of institutional chance." Later on, not without resistance, he would explain and gain re-acceptance for the "type" of the simple monk, without the addition of the priesthood. As far as his not wanting to study, fortunately his intentions were not heeded or perhaps not fulfilled, except in the sense that Leclercq never was a pure scholar with a manuscript for a heart. It was also in the same sense that he read rapidly — "God made me fast" — something of everything, satisfying the exuberance and curiosity, in the best sense, of his nature, inclined in any event to knowing, but not towards anything ending in the abstract. His predisposition to aesthetics and his cultivation of music—which in liturgy he distinguished clearly from pomp—would make him into a peerless guide in understanding and illustrating the beauty of the works of St Bernard. It would also make him into a writer of refined and radiant pages, and entire books. Finally, it honed his unique flair for bringing rediscovered authors to new life, quickly, with a marvelous finesse, and in editions produced under unimaginable conditions. He wrote, "Philosophy never satisfied my hunger." It would be satisfied by other sources, by other "beautiful things in the world" (Valéry), including literature, poetry, and theater. No wonder, then, that there is a sense of completeness and variety to be found in him and in his writings.

It could be said that, as is apparent in the memories of the early years, Leclercq's formation consisted in a process of interior liberation, of discernment between the essential and the contingent; from these proceeded his seriousness and joviality, his sharing and smiling, his lack of sourness, and the disappointments and diversions which distinguished him. He spent much time during his many years among books, but never renounced life and its events; in these he shared intensely, moving through them easily and often with amused whimsy. He stated that, until his discovery of St Bernard, at the age of thirty-five, his studies "were never determined by purely historical, intellectual or academic concerns, but by life and the problems that it aroused." This would also be true in later life.

This could be seen in his intervals in uniform, in his "Roman walks," and in the school of theology at Sant'Anselmo: there he was trained not by manuals but by the reading of the great works, such as those of Newman. He was taught by the genial Benedictine, Anselm Stolz, who did not repeat theology but rather drew it from its sources.

And always with the distinction between professors and masters, and in the school of the latter, Leclercq's years in Paris were decisive: those were intense years of scientific preparation, of direct knowledge of the manuscripts in the Bibliothèque Nationale, of his first essays and of his thesis. In Paris he had the opportunity and the leisure for numerous relationships and events at the École des Hautes-Études, at the Institut Catholique, and at the Collège de France. He would meet Bloch, Lavelle, Valéry, Le Bras, Lebreton, de Lubac, de Montcheuil, Maritain and, especially, Gilson. It was Gilson who, beginning with the documentary material, "brought men back to life"—as Leclercq in his turn was able to do—and who is impressively portrayed in these memoirs. Gilson was also to be, as we have already mentioned, the inspirer of Leclercq's choice of a field of study, namely, medieval monastic literature. During his time in

Paris those lucid profiles began to emerge that have yet to lose their fascination: on Pierre de Celle, Jean de Fécamp, followed by Peter the Venerable and an early St Bernard. Gilson deserves much recognition for the guidance that he gave to the young scholar, since on that account we have been able to recover and admire a world largely unknown or disregarded, left to us precisely by the union of the "love of letters" and the "desire for God." Perhaps unconsciously, Leclercq's multi-layered culture was, from the start, oriented in that direction, happily aligned with his inclinations; little by little he was receiving "grace upon grace," including the "images of St. Thérèse" and the period of time he spent as a non-combatant soldier, sharing in sincere communion the serious and sometimes comical situations of his mates.

His colorful account of the "discovery of St Bernard," with its adventures and misadventures, makes for very enjoyable reading; there was nothing in Leclercq to indicate that he would become the editor of the works of St Bernard, about whom he knew very little before he was thirty-five, a circumstance showing that Shakespeare was right: "There's a divinity that shapes our ends, rough-hew them how we will" (*Hamlet* V, ii). For this thirty-year task, Leclercq traveled up and down Europe; the result was eight volumes of the critical edition and an impressive number of learned and impressive analytical essays. If this edition can be improved in one point or another, it will probably be several decades before it can be surpassed. Leclercq thus became the world's specialist in Bernard. Thanks to him, the figure of the Abbot of Clairvaux has become universally accessible, more historically true, even more attractive in his humanity and in his "mystery," and an exemplar of monastic theology.

In untiring contact with Bernard and with innumerable other monks both ancient and modern, Leclercq was able to become the competent authority on monasticism and on its meaning in the Church. His writings, lessons and conferences multiplied, and his teaching – free and "practical," rather than academic and doctoral – with the journeys and the exchanges that it involved, have rendered him a respected and in some ways ever more indispensable point of reference on the monastic question; though he has not gone unchallenged. This is partly due to his style of frankness and freedom – in the innate distinction that habitually avoided the harshness of polemics – that always characterize his contributions and his criticism. Leclercq thus for decades fully applied the program delineated by St Thomas: *aliis contemplata tradere* (to bring to others what one has contemplated). The result was an ever-clearer outline of the specific and singular quality of the ecclesial experience of monastic contemplation in which, supported by the knowledge of historical experts, he could identify its proper and permanent features that belong to the definition of monasticism, as well as the more contingent and recent forms. This was a valuable and needed condition for formulating and issuing basic judgments, and especially for pointing out wise and enlightened lines of renewal, and motivating prudent and courageous new experiments. This is what Jean Leclercq was called to do, thus becoming "the most traveled monk in history," with visits to at least fifty-five countries. This fact will not fail to arouse some perplexity among those who attribute to St Benedict *stabilitas loci* [stability of place].

The second part of this book, "Memories from Overseas," takes up his journeys. An extensive account could not be expected; these are only notes, but they reveal once again Leclercq's concern for being in contact with life—often dramatic and painful—and with "monasticism in motion." Without bias, ready to see, to hear, to learn, to study local texts and documents, to compile dossiers, to enjoy, to be entertained, to evaluate with discretion and a lucid competence derived from an accumulation of knowledge both historical—especially but not only as a medievalist—and of monastic practice. It is hard to keep up with him in his "listening to America," in his journey from Morocco to Madagascar, in his travels through Asia, Latin America, and the southern hemisphere. Monasteries are discovered that are old and traditional, and others that are about to be founded and taking on indigenous forms. It was a matter of carrying on and being renewed; of comparing other monastic experiences—non-christian ones—of being present to them and, to a certain extent, of being culturalized, without losing identity and originality, whether Christian or monastic. These are the two concerns and constants that will be found in these pages of Leclercq. He is undoubtedly open, attentive, and ready, but he is also well-rooted and explicit in what is original and unalterable in Christian monasticism. He writes, "Doctrinal problems are what count. Do not faith in God and the revelation that Jesus Christ has given us perhaps constitute the difference between Christianity and the other religions" and consequently other forms of monasticism?

However, it should not be thought that Leclercq's scholarly activity was paralyzed by these journeys. Throughout his whole life, he knew extraordinarily well how to combine travel with study, and had an exceptional capacity for work and concentration. His last great effort was the centenary of St Bernard's birth in 1990. His presence had the weight of a witness: to think now of St Bernard is to think of Jean Leclercq, for he learned everything about that abbot of the "giant personality," even though at the end he asked whether "his mystery is within the reach of the historian."

After entering into the "order of octogenarians," he returned to Clervaux; although he no longer traveled, Jean Leclercq did not remain idle, if by idle one understands a sterile and pointless waste of time. He continued to cultivate friendships, always near to his heart as it was to medieval monks; moreover, he did not stop working. Indeed we can read with delight his *Regards monastiques sur le Christ au Moyen Age* (Monastic Views on Christ in the Middle Ages). Thus it can no longer be said that the infancy, passion, humility and humanity of the God-Man were not uncovered before St Francis. Leclercq calls these *regards* a "kind of testament by an eighty-year-old." But his swan song soon began and was repeated more than once.

Yet, finally, this is not as important as the "monastic mystery" — as he has called it — made visible by him. He has written in the memoirs: "At times I have been reproached — and this still is happening — for this faith in the contemplative life. Yet it is not something I can deny, for it has its roots in my primordial experience and in the fervor of the ambiance that introduced me into what I later called 'the monastic mystery'.... The objection would be legitimate if there were talk about a theory of monastic 'life,' whereas it...is a *praxis* and nothing else. There are tens of thousands of us in the world who believe in the value of the life of prayer."

"I think that I will no longer be able to travel," he wrote shortly before he died, "except for the great Journey toward God.... May the Lord grant me strength while I await the End.... It is time to go to SEE, to see him." Meanwhile he assured us that he was "growing old in the Lord" toward whom so many monks yesterday and today have turned their gaze. Yet what else is monastic contemplation if not "gazing upon Christ"? He has taught us this throughout his life and his memoirs. These are a story of graces that will ignite desire for them not only in monks but in every Christian who, by definition, is one who turns to gaze at Jesus Christ.

Inos Biffi
Milan, Easter 1993

Italian Translator's Note

In one of the many letters that he sent to me in November of 1991, Dom Jean Leclercq stated, in one of his typical *plaisanteries*, that he had changed his monastic order: from then on he belonged to the O.O., the *Ordo Octogenariorum*. Now, two years later, here is *Di grazia in grazia*.

In translating this last work (or "task," as the author himself defines it), I have found a freshness and an enthusiasm which reveal no octogenarian wrinkle. Rather, all the recollections flow smoothly and brilliantly before the reader's eyes. After *San Bernardo. La vita, Umanesimo e cultura monastica, Esperienza spirituale e teologia* and *Pietro il Venerabile* (as well as *La figura della donna nel medioevo*), it has for me been an honor and a pleasure to provide the first version of this collection of memoirs. This is not the place to illustrate the meaning of the thousand experiences narrated here by Dom Leclercq, because this has already been done in the enlightening Foreword to this volume. My only wish is to express here the acknowledgment by a modest but fond translator who, after six works (rather, small but edifying services), has discovered even more deeply everything behind and within the words and studies of this extraordinary Benedictine monk. And his "final plans" lead us to hope that after some years he will again change Orders.

It seems opportune to me to inform the reader that the various chapters — or blocks of chapters — are given specific dates in the original text: the first chapter goes back to May 8, 1983 (Clark's Summit); the second, third and fourth are dated June 24, 1984 (Vichy); the fifth and sixth, January 21, 1984 (St. Paul's outside the Walls); the seventh, July 7, 1984 (Vichy). The whole second part (chs. 8-13) was written beginning in Lent 1992 and finished in July of that year. In particular, it is noted that in the seventh chapter, dedicated to "Polish Interludes," the author often makes reference to episodes and situations that are no longer current after the fall of the communist regime. Nonetheless, in the translation the original chronological order has been maintained.

Moreover, we want to specify that the titles of the works and articles in French of Leclercq and other authors cited here have been left in the original language, while the remainder have been translated into Italian. For the catalogs of the bibliography relevant to the author, see: R. Grégoire, *Bibliographie de Dom Jean Leclercq, I (1939-1968)*, in "Studia Monastica" 10 (1968), pp. 331-359; Idem, *Bibliographie de Dom Jean Leclercq, II (1968-1977)*, ibid. 20 (1978), pp. 409-423; A. M. Altermatt, *Bibliographie de Dom Jean Leclercq, III (1978-1988)*, ibid. 30 (1988), pp. 417-440.

Antonio Tombolini, 1993

Preface

These memoirs do not constitute a journal or an autobiography, with the chronological precision required by those genres. They are simply a collection of memories that different people have asked me to put into writing. For a long time I resisted this request, then I hesitated to fulfill it, until the day that Father de Lubac, whom I consulted, not only told me that this was a duty, but also added this admonition: "Do it before you lose your memory!"

Here is the result: not an apology for a strangely conducted monastic life, nor for poorly accomplished tasks, but a thanksgiving. The title imposed itself gradually.

It will not always be easy—or useful—to discern in what order the facts occurred that are recalled here. My memory has been marked especially by the phases of the Church's life that it has been given to me to traverse. A florilegium of anecdotes could have been added to each chapter. Yet these small matters count little when compared to the constant attitude that has emerged: thanksgiving.

Clervaux
October 1992

Part One

European Horizons

1

Monasticism and a Sense of the Church
(1927-1932)

1. THE JOYS OF A BEGINNING

I entered the Abbey of Clervaux toward the end of August 1928 at the age of seventeen. Two years earlier, I had decided to become a monk, but did not know where. A priest at the school of Saint Pierre de Fourmies, where I was a boarder, told me that he knew a certain Father Salmon at a monastery in Luxembourg. In September 1927, on the feast of St. Maurice, patron of that monastery, I went to visit him and asked to be admitted. I was told to wait yet another year and to come back after I had passed the second part of my baccalaureate. This I did, and then I was accepted.

I did not notify my parents until the end of Christmas vacation that year. I took my father and my mother aside and told them brutally, without any preparation: "In six months I am becoming a monk." This statement aroused all kinds of grim ideas in them, especially in my mother, who had read quite a bit. They began to raise objections, based on my shortcomings that were well known to my family. Without further ado, however, I answered them, "I am not asking you, I am telling you." Later I learned that my father approached the school's headmaster, asking him to dissuade me, but he answered him, "If Jean has decided to do this, he will do it." Thereafter no one brought the matter up with me again. When graduation came around in July, my schoolmates showed their surprise, but there was nothing to say about it, so nothing was said.

In the meantime, my father one day took up the offensive again in my room. I collected books, and I loved beautiful bindings, whether old or recent. My mother had acquired for me, from a woman reduced to poverty, a series of seventeenth-century volumes: they were volumes of every kind, among which was an edition of the *Treatise on Divine Love* by St. Francis de Sales and a copy of the *Imitation of Christ*. Reading these was not alien to the call that I one day felt to serve God. My parents had

3

also given me a bookcase. I recall having bought and read, among others, Taine's *Histoire de la littérature anglaise*. My father pointed out that I would have to leave all that behind. My answer was, "At Clervaux I will have 60,000 volumes." And that was that.

During Easter vacation in 1928, with my parents' permission, and no longer without their knowledge, I made a brief visit to Clervaux, and they themselves came to take me back by car. They met Father Abbot, the master of novices, and the guestmaster, and they were impressed by everyone's kindness. I was impatient to realize my monastic dream, and I would have preferred to start it right after graduation. However, my parents made Father Abbot of Clervaux aware that the family wished to spend one last vacation with me. In July, as in every year, I went for thermal treatment at a sulfur baths spa (since childhood I had a non-painful condition in my throat and nose). My two brothers and my twin sister, informed at the beginning of July about my entry into the novitiate, came with my parents to join me at Challes-les-Eaux, in Savoy, and we took, as in every year, a fine auto tour for one week, in the northern Alps. That year I had chosen Challes over Cauterets and over Uriage, where I had gone earlier, since this spa was not far from the Abbey of Hautecombe. One day I went there with my mother on an excursion. I could not stop myself from telling the monk who was showing us the church that I was going to become a Benedictine at Clervaux. "Why not here?" he asked, and he granted me the privilege of entering the cloister in order to show me how charming it was.

Earlier, during the preceding spring, at Carnival time, I went to Paris as I usually did once or twice a year. Normally I would just go to concert halls, theaters, museums, and fine restaurants. This time, I had the aim of visiting as well the Abbey of Rue de la Source, which I had heard about. There too I was approached about joining, but it was too late. I had chosen Clervaux by chance, and I have never regretted it.

Toward the end of August, then, I left for Clervaux. On the morning of the trip, I was suddenly struck with a violent toothache. The idea occurred to me that this was perhaps the devil attempting to block my way. However, I promptly went to a kind dentist whose treatment enabled me to continue on my trip. My father had decided to drive me there by car. My older brother was then working in Nancy. He had gotten off work for that afternoon and the next day—it might have been a weekend. And since this would be the last good meal that I would have in my life, they took me to one of the best-known restaurants at the time in Nancy, the Thiers. When we arrived at Clervaux that afternoon, I was suffering from indigestion and asked to go immediately to lie down. The Master of Novices was edified: "It is his emotions," he declared.

The next day, during midday recreation, I was introduced to the novitiate. There were twenty-seven of us, of various ages and backgrounds. Father Master was a very good man. A former professor of mathematics in a seminary who had become a monk at, I believe, the age of forty-seven, he believed in "methods." Since he also believed in prayer, he presented it, at least to beginners, as methodical. He tried to initiate me into it but because all this only gave me headaches, he dispensed me from the method. I gladly gave myself over to the practice of *lectio divina*, about which I later would write a great deal.

At my previous visit to Clervaux, and then at my entry, I had asked to be admitted as a lay brother, for I wanted to be a monk, nothing more, or, according to a formula that became common later on, *sine addito*. I did not want to study or to become a priest. However, Father Master told me each time "to consider that idea as a bad thought." I readily adjusted to this without making any problems for myself or for others. The fact remains that I had no desire to be a priest, but that I became one, without the calling, because of institutional chance. Later on, I would study the problem and would devote part of my activity to showing that this nearly automatic identification between monasticism and the priesthood was not the only form of monastic life attested by history. This separation is now widely admitted and is accepted in legislation.

A novitiate that large needed its own structures. Father Master was assisted by a Father Zelator (Counselor), also an extremely good man. He was Fr. Pierre Gsell, an Alsatian professed at Solesmes, who had a brother who was a monk at Beuron. They were bilingual, and the one at Solesmes had come to Clervaux to be the tutor of Prince Otto of Hapsburg, who did his early studies there. When he left for higher studies in Louvain, Fr. Gsell remained at Clervaux for several more years. Now and then Prince Otto would come back to Clervaux, and I cherish some memories of him, as well as the image of his mother, the Empress Zita, who sometimes came to see him.

Several of the young professed and novices held various posts among us. The most important was that of Master of Ceremonies, who initiated us into every ritual. At that time it was Fr. Robert Weber, a former seminarian in Strasbourg who was quite studious and who later was to make a name for himself by his publications dealing with biblical and Latin patristic tradition. One of the means used for forming postulants and novices in humility consisted in making "observations" about them.

Some of the Fathers thought that we should do something about these "faults" and did not refrain from suggesting as much to the Father Counselor. Since we were always exposed to the Fathers' scrutiny, a word comes to mind in this connection: "Behold, I am sending you like sheep in the midst of wolves."

I was an easy target for such surveillance because of my casualness, and also because of my delicate health, doubtlessly the result of privations suffered during World War I, as well as of an extreme gluttony that, far from being combated, was rather encouraged in my family. Thus, like the others, I could not take offense at the observations. Still, we often received graces of generosity and ready acceptance of everything for love of the Lord. Those in whom a critical spirit prevailed were eliminated bit by bit. Others came in their place. We shared in each other's joy, suffering and surprises. And life was very joyful.

One of the strong personalities in the novitiate was Fr. Suhr, then a young professed, who seemed like a patriarch to me because he was thirty-three. A Dane, he had led an adventurous life in the Pampas of Argentina before converting from a lukewarm Protestantism to Catholicism. He had been baptized, I believe, at Assisi, and his godfather, Johannes Jorgensen, a famous writer of the time, had introduced him to Pius XI. Twelve years later the pope would remember him and send him on an apostolic visit to Denmark. Seeing the good results, he appointed him bishop of Copenhagen. I formed a solid friendship with him back then which we still share.

Father Suhr contributed to the seriousness and at the same time to the joy of our rowdy group. Every Thursday, during our walk, he would take one of us aside and ask, "Now, tell me about your conversion." It had not been so eventful for most of us as it had been for him. He overflowed with humor. For example, when Father Master assigned all of us to read a book by a Carthusian entitled *La vie intérieure simplifiée et ramenée à son fondement* [*The Interior Life Simplified and Restored to its Foundations*], he advised us that it was about "the interior life complicated and removed from its foundations." One day, a rich person from his country, a convert like him, sent a huge candle with a candlestick, both richly decorated, to be set before the altar of St. Ansgar, the apostle of the Scandinavians. But the whole thing was so ugly that it was never placed there. And Fr. Suhr thanked the donor by writing him that "St. Ansgar never saw such a candle burning before his altar."

2. BEGINNINGS

The first community member whom I met was Fr. Pierre Salmon, since he had been the companion, at the French Seminary in Rome, of the priest with whom I had spoken about my desire for the monastic life. The latter loved to tell me about the time that the two of them went to the Palace of St. Callixtus, where the Commission established by Pius X was then located, which included Benedictine monks from several countries, in order to work on the "restitution" of the text of the Latin Bible, the Vulgate. Fr. Salmon had been moved by this blending of a life of prayer with that of study. My friend believed that this encounter with the community at St. Callixtus was the origin of Fr. Salmon's Benedictine vocation, never suspecting that, ten years later, Fr. Salmon would become the abbot of the Monastery of San Gerolamo (St. Jerome), founded by Pius XI to continue the work of the Commission at St. Callixtus, and would remain there for thirty years. There was also a marvelous continuity in the life of this man of the Church. Even after he became a bishop, he did not cease working on biblical and liturgical manuscripts, those of the Vatican Library and elsewhere, until the time of his return to Clervaux where he died in 1981.

During my two visits in the abbey's guest quarters, from my window over-looking the cloister, I could see, through the windows of the library building which faced me, Fr. Salmon handling various volumes. He was then arranging our books in the classification system they still have today. His reading covered a vast range. Shortly after my entry into the novitiate, while he was our Counselor, he was named Prior. Shortly after, he also became Procurator. At that time, he had a friend come from Luxembourg who was an accountant, and with his advice, he set up a modern organization for the monastery's material administration. He was skilled in business. From time to time, he would return to the novitiate to give us a talk on some unannounced topic. Usually he would come with a newly issued book; he would present it to us, and we would read some excerpts from it. I still remember the strong impression made on me in this manner by a small book, newly published at that time, by Maritain entitled *Religion et culture*, and the one by Guardini on *L'Esprit de la liturgie*. It was especially by broadening our culture that he contributed to our formation.

Above all, he was a "liturgist," still a relatively rare competence in those days, outside of a small erudite circle. For the purposes of his conferences as Counselor to the novitiate, he had written a history of the Divine Office and a history of the Mass that deserved to be printed before Jungmann published his history of the Mass. As for his knowledge about the Divine Office, it later became part of the works that he wrote on that topic. He studied the sources in the Greek and Latin Patrologies of Migne, and drew from them whatever related to his subject.

This became evident to me when I asked him to lend me his notes when he was no longer teaching liturgy to the novitiate. I copied them myself almost entirely, and was deeply grateful to him for them. He had been singled out at the Gregorian University by Fr. de la Taille, whose *Mysterium fidei* had engendered an entire field of literature. We were in the years when Fr. Lepin and others were writing on "the essence of the sacrifice of the Mass," and that placed us at the very heart of the liturgy, beyond aesthetic forms to which, especially in Benedictine circles, some people attached great importance.

He was also the one who initiated me into *lectio divina* after my block in methodical prayer. He suggested that I read the Fathers in chronological order, beginning with the Apostolic Fathers. The Letters of St. Ignatius of Antioch, of St. Clement, then the Epistles of St. Cyprian to the Christians suffering persecution, filled me with enthusiasm. Then he offered me the Sermons of St. Leo, which are very dense and profound. Later, after the first meeting in which Frs. de Lubac and Daniélou talked about a project that became *"Sources chrétiennes,"* I immediately planned to write an Introduction to the Sermons of St. Leo, which I did. For thirty years, Fr. Dolle, my former novitiate companion who became Procurator, found great enjoyment, in the leisure time that his responsibilities left him, by producing an accurate and harmonious translation of those *Sermons*, which took up four volumes of *Sources chrétiennes*. At first the intention was to give the series the simple name of *Sources*, but I pointed out the fact that the Bibliothèque Nationale, where I was then working, was about to launch a magazine with that title, of which only some issues were to appear.

I then read the treatises of St. Augustine on the Gospel of John with so much enthusiasm that, right afterwards, I began the reading of the treatises on the Epistles of St. John. Then I went on to the commentary of St. Cyril of Alexandria on St. John, and to other doctrinal texts. They nourished me interiorly more than Cassian or other works on moral perfection and even on prayer.

At the beginning of my novitiate, Father Master gave me *Les voies de l'oraison mentale* [*The Ways of Mental Prayer*] by Dom Lehodey. He then went away for a week. Upon his return, he asked me what point I had reached: "I am at mystical marriage and transforming prayer." "I didn't think you would go so far or so fast," he retorted with an air of some alarm. "I thought you would still be in discursive prayer." "What do you expect?" I said. "God made me fast." I finished that reading which, in fact, did me no harm. But it was the last book of that kind that I tried. Later, I was to discover—without studying them—the methods of "speed reading" that were very much in favor in the United States; it was in that country that I gave a conference on "Prayer and Speed: Spirituality for the People of Today."

In reading the Fathers, I did not go so fast. I even savored them slowly. It took me six months to finish St. Augustine's writings on St. John. But when one spends half an hour a day or more in the company of such an author, sharing in the experiences of which he was a part, reacting to them by praying, one is no longer entirely the same. Something of his own reactions to the mystery of God passes into us.

Another important member of the community was Fr. Fohl. He was from an aristocratic Luxembourg family, but of a tendency termed "liberal" at a time when Christian social ideas—and Christian worker unionism—were beginning to spread in his country. Trained in law at the University of Fribourg in Switzerland, he had become a canonist. At Sant'Anselmo's in Rome, he had admired the teaching of his compatriot, Fr. Joseph Gredt, the author of a dense *Manual of Aristotelico-Thomistic Philosophy*, written, to be sure, in Latin. All this yielded an astounding mixture of intelligence in the manner of approaching all problems of existence, but also with a rigorous application of law. His critiques could be incisive, with regard to anyone holding authority. It was not until later that I discovered this aspect of his personality. I took note of it, without ever losing his friendship nor ceasing to profit from his advice. It was to him that I owed—without having requested or foreseen it—being sent to Sant'Anselmo's to do my theological studies there. After the war, which he spent as master of novices at the Abbey of St. Paul Outside the Walls in Rome, he was passing through France for the first time and asked me to arrange a visit for him at the broadcast facility of Radio-Paris, just as television was in its early phases. He anticipated the interest that this means of mass communication would someday offer as a possible instrument for the spread of Christianity. He was able to foresee developments well. Soon he was assigned by the Holy See to work at "federating" many religious communities that were unified by no organic bond. He always tried to respect the legitimate wishes of all, even though he himself would act energetically. Thanks to his firm tenacity, he was able to settle certain situations that had long awaited a solution.

The one who dominated the whole spiritual and psychological atmosphere of Clervaux in those days was in reality Father Abbot. He

9

was extremely kind, which I had admired during the visits that I had with him during my first two brief stays at Clervaux. I kept up correspondence with him. He manifested a similar affection for me up to the last conversation I had with him just before the War. We still corresponded afterwards, while he was in a monastery in Spain. He would disappear from the monastic scene without becoming talked about, during the War, in circumstances that remain mysterious to everyone. Perhaps those who were least close to him were the ones to judge him most harshly. Even though at times I became annoyed by his conduct, I hold nothing but good memories about him, and my gratitude to him is undying. At the time of my first sojourn in Spain, in 1947, at the monastery of Estibaliz in Navarre, where he had taken refuge for several months, many people asked me for news about him. They were still full of admiration for his deep religious spirit.

He had received scarcely any intellectual training, which was not his fault, yet he was intelligent. He showed this by appointing, as his Prior and Sub-prior, two men as gifted and educated as Fr. Salmon and Fr. Fohl, whom he knew were better than he was in many fields and whose influence he perceived as outstanding. He had been chosen by the General Chapter of the Benedictine Congregation of France as the First Assistant to the Abbot of Solesmes. He knew his limits, and he was skilled at getting help, for example, in asking someone, as happened to me, to draft a text for him that he was to deliver in public. He inspired confidence. On occasion he was warmly eloquent, even though his French was not always correct.

Once, in one of the monasteries that I visited before entering Clervaux, when I declined their offer to join because my choice was settled, the response I heard was: "Over there the Abbot is the one doing the recruiting." This was partially true. At times he had the tendency to encourage people to become monks who really would have done better not to. The fact remains that this contributed to the prosperity of Clervaux. Soon it became necessary to think about a foundation.

At first, thought was given to Denmark, with which the abbey had maintained relations ever since the preceding abbot, Fr. Renaudin, had received approval from the Holy See for a prayer association, centered at Clervaux, "for the return to unity of the Scandinavian peoples." Dom Renaudin had become blind and had to seek refuge in Fribourg, Switzerland, where he continued to work in promoting the doctrine of the Assumption of Mary. He produced various publications on this subject and others, and received an honorary doctorate from the University of Fribourg. I had the joy of spending a brief visit with him. His successor always showed him great esteem and often went to see him, particularly whenever his health gave cause for alarm.

Father Abbot had made a visit to Denmark, and he related to us an anecdote concerning Msgr. Baudrillart, who seemed to give rise to stories everywhere he went. Yet the idea of a foundation in that country had to be abandoned when Pius XI asked the abbot of Clervaux to start a foundation in Rome, which will soon be described below. Father Abbot then made a clandestine visit to the Eternal City. Emotional and easily influenced, he was not well prepared for dealing with the prelates of the Curia.

For us simple monks, these relations with Rome and the visits we received from the Nuncio in Brussels, and once from the one in Paris, contributed to cultivating in Clervaux a "sense of the Church" that was to leave a definitive mark upon many of us. At that time, the spiritual life there was intense and the liturgy never ceased to amaze me. I discovered the Psalms and, more than fifty years later, I cannot recite some verse or another without recalling the strong impression that they made upon me then. The Gregorian melodies enchanted me. The antiphons of the first feast celebrated after my entry into the novitiate seemed to me to be a peak. I knew them by heart, and I later experienced the same joy with respect to all the other chants, even though they undoubtedly were not performed to perfection. However, that did not prevent me from easily falling asleep in choir. After the office of Compline, when we would kneel to recite some prayers or litanies—now suppressed—I would immediately bow my head deeply. I know that the Fathers noticed this and smiled over it, but no one ever mentioned it except to tease me. At Matins and Lauds, every morning, I even learned to stand up and bow at the end of each psalm, for the *Glory Be*, without waking up. But what I did perceive during my liturgical somnolence, and during the offices of the day, aroused wonder in me.

I had only one fear, that was my only real suffering: that my state of health might not allow the community to admit me to profession. For many years I had wanted to be a monk. During the trips I used to make with my family, in Brittany and elsewhere, my sister shared with us an idea she had picked up from the nuns where she was a boarder: when one enters a church for the first time, if one asks God for three favors, they surely will be granted. My one wish was the one that I spoke of to no one: to enter Clervaux. What would happen if I had to leave? I shared my anxiety with the Master of Novices. To combat it, he had me read the book by Dom Lehodey on *L'abandon à la divine providence*. Grace acted.

Since then I have practiced this abandonment, and I can only thank God for it.

One occasion for arousing my apprehension came when, for the first time, I had to pass, as was said, through the Chapter of Faults. Twice a week, after the office of Prime, one by one in order of seniority, each one would accuse himself of some infractions of which the novitiate *Ceremonial* contained long lists. I had found one that fit me perfectly, and I began to recite it: "I accuse myself of letting myself fall asleep during the offices." But as soon as I had uttered these words, it all seemed so funny to me that I was seized by a fit of uncontrollable laughter. It was contagious and the whole novitiate was swept into it. I did not know what to do. Father Abbot put me at ease and said to me with a smile, "You can go out." During the morning, I went to him to offer my apologies. I expected to be dismissed politely. "Quite the contrary," he said, "that is a very good sign." It was commonly said that uncontrollable laughter by a novice was a sign of a vocation. Later, when I had to research (for the article *Noviciat* in an encyclopedia) the phenomenon of de-structuring and restructuring that this sort of life change involves, I understood that this uncontrollable laughter was the mark of a certain psychological tension destined to be reabsorbed little by little, which was truly the case.

Two deep convictions were communicated to the whole novitiate by Father Abbot and the Novice Master. The first consisted in a solid faith in the worth of the contemplative aspect of monastic life. The active clergy then would often reproach monks for being useless, or of enjoying a religious aestheticism that was a form of selfishness. During my novitiate I had encountered, both by letter and verbally, attacks of this sort by certain priests whom I had known earlier. But what was sometimes called "the monastic creed" was not just, even at first, a means of defense. We felt that it was being shared with us in a vital way, by those who were forming us, by their example and their words. The basic doctrine that we were taught was to come from Dom Delatte whose works were carefully read. Yet these concepts were also a part of our experience. I absorbed them without restraint, all the more willingly as they corresponded with my own aspirations, which they justified: the value of a life of prayer for the whole Church. Later on, I was to reflect still more on this mystery, and to speak about it in many monasteries during retreats or conferences, as well as at meetings of contemplatives in France, in Canada, in the United States, in the Philippines, and elsewhere. This message found its way into many books which stated what I had been saying.

At times I was reproached — and this still happens — for this faith in the contemplative life. But I am not about to renounce it, because it has its roots in my early experience and in the fervor of the setting that introduced me into what I would later call "the monastic mystery." This expression also was challenged, nor is it a matter of "a way of life." The objection would have had merit if it were a matter of a "theory" of monastic life, whereas this, it was said very reasonably, was but a *praxis* and nothing more. There are tens of thousands of us in the world who believe in the value of the prayer life. Recently, when I had to write an introduction to a compilation of texts by Paul VI delivered to monks and nuns, I was very glad to find in them all my basic convictions. I also like to respond that John Paul II, on each of his journeys, finds the means to give a discourse in the same vein. This faith in the prayer life is part of an ecclesiology: it places monasticism in the organic totality of the Body of Christ. It is also tied to a Christology: it presupposes that the prayer of a Christian is a sharing in that of the Lord Jesus, who saved us not only by preaching and doing good but, above all, by prayer and self-offering.

This confidence in the contemplative life went against the current, as I have mentioned, of a then widely-held tendency. It was the time of the pontificate of Pius XI, "the Pope of the Missions," "the Pope of Catholic Action." Action was needed on all fronts. Thus in monastic circles we did not fail to cite the unconditional praise that the Pope had made of the "hidden life" in his solemn document addressed to the Carthusians, and the importance that he attributed to the message of St. Thérèse of Lisieux, "the Patroness of the Missions." The contemplative conviction was inseparable from what was called "the sense of the Church": an attitude difficult to define and to analyze but which is easily identified with the lived faith of the mystery of the "Communion of Saints." Religion was not individual but rather communitarian and universal. All this was shared among us. Father Abbot sometimes reacted against this elitism which could tend, in each religious institute, in each realization of Christian existence, not to esteem others. For this purpose he would refer to Dom Guéranger. It was certainly to him that we were indebted for this desire never to lose sight of the entire Church, and the service by all to all.

The Church is communion. It is also an institution whose visible center is the Pope, "the Vicar of Christ," according to an expression then widely used. Because of Pius XI's personal prestige, because of the great initiatives that characterized his pontificate, and of the attacks by certain Catholics which he endured, this faith in Roman Catholicism tended to evolve into what was called "devotion to the pope." This was less an

13

affectionate attachment to the person of the pontiff than it was devotedness to the Holy See and to all the causes that it strove to promote. I participated very vigorously, intensely and personally in this whole mentality of fidelity to Rome. It was within this psychological and spiritual context that we were present at the foundation of the Abbey of San Gerolamo's in Rome by the abbot and monks of Clervaux.

This foundation was brought about, apparently, by chance. Some members of the Benedictine commission for the restoration of the Vulgate left St. Callixtus each summer in order to spend their vacation at Clervaux where the welcome was proverbial. The most active participant on this commission, Dom Henri Quentin, was acquainted with Clervaux and its flourishing recruitment of new members. The idea took hold in the mind of Pius XI, and in Dom Quentin, to replace this commission with a homogeneous and permanent monastic community in which all the members would come from the same abbey, thus ensuring its continued growth. Dom Quentin had made the acquaintance of Pius XI when the latter was Prefect of the Ambrosian Library of Milan. Later, during Pius XI's pontificate, Dom Quentin had been given assignments which brought him into frequent contact with the Pope. He would tell us that, assigned to direct the preparation of a liturgical office of the Sacred Heart that would be more biblical and more doctrinal than the preceding one, he had spent long evening sessions with the Pope who discussed and judged every text. In the first conference he gave us at San Gerolamo's, he recalled that, on the evening of his election, Cardinal Ratti, now Pius XI, had called him to tell him that one of the major projects of his pontificate would be to conduct the revision of the Vulgate.

When one of Pius XI's plans was fulfilled — the "conciliation" of the Holy See with the Italian State — and he had gained ample restitution of earlier alienated assets, he set out to make good use of them by building a number of edifices, in Vatican City and in Rome. The Abbey of San Gerolamo was one of these. Like so many other buildings, it was constructed in the specific style by which the Pope aimed at leaving his stamp on the Eternal City. A Milanese architect, Castelli, found himself entrusted with the entire enterprise. He created a style that was designated "Lombard," which was debatable, but not bereft of harmony: it made much use of light-colored brick and stone, adding a note of cheerfulness to dignity.

One day Father Abbot left for Rome, where he had been summoned, without telling us the reason for his trip. Had Dom Quentin made him aware of the project relating to the Vulgate? At any rate, when he returned, he announced to the community that Pius XI had asked him to found a monastery in Rome. According to a common refrain then, one that has not entirely disappeared, "a wish of His Holiness was a command." It was not disputed. Was it opportune or normal to consult the Chapter of Clervaux and to submit the project to a vote? At that point the majority of us did not even think of it. The regret that this was not done was not expressed until later, and then only by a few scattered voices. Besides, was not the Pope the supreme authority? Did not his will, within the limits of his power—which is vast!—dispense with minor formalities? We welcomed gladly and fervently the idea of a foundation in Rome, with the possibility that any one of us could be sent there for it. This seemed to us to be a service rendered to the Church, and therefore to Christ, in perfect conformity with the requirements of our vocation.

We followed from afar the stages of construction of the new monastery. Father Abbot made a few more brief trips to Rome. Once the decision was taken, all the rest followed its course. There was room, of course, for different motives on the part of different people, which only God can judge. We were not told of them. Enough for us was our ecclesial enthusiasm. Only the spiritual climate explains this whole adventure— San Gerolamo's was founded not by a sin of ambition but by an act of faith in the Church.

The building was completed in 1933, and I was among the first groups of monks who, beginning in September of that year, were sent to Rome. I went there as a student, others as collaborators on the Vulgate project. Shortly beforehand, Father Abbot had received the foundation document, a bull *"sub plumbo"* (apparently this formality added to the solemnity), which I had a chance to examine. Professional canonists did not refrain from studying and, indeed, from criticizing this decree. It conformed entirely to the law; its drafters, in the Roman Curia, and Dom Quentin and the Pope himself, were assured of this. Still, it was singular: for the first time in the history of Benedictine life, an abbey termed "pontifical," dependent directly on the pope, was governed by an abbot appointed by him and staffed by monks who continued to belong to their monastery of profession but who, during their stay in that foundation, constituted its conventual chapter. In one of the first courses given to us at Sant'Anselmo's, the professor of Canon Law, Fr. Gérard Oesterlé—as renowned as he was entertaining—analyzed this bull, showing both its innovative character and its legality.

San Gerolamo's was solemnly inaugurated on December 7, 1933, the vigil of the canonization of St. Bernadette Soubirous. In addition to cardinals and prelates of the Curia, the French bishops came for the ceremony of the following day. Soon Pius XI granted us an audience in which he spoke of San Gerolamo's as "our monastery." At that time, much weight was accorded to these formulas of approval and protection. Then the Pope appointed Dom Quentin as Abbot. One morning soon afterwards, he was found dead in his bed following a heart attack. Fr. Salmon was then called from Clervaux to succeed him.

Today, fifty years later, the task assigned to San Gerolamo's is almost finished: the critical edition of the entire Old Testament is almost completed. Many scholarly publications have accompanied and commented on it. Some editions of a "practical" character have been issued; this is especially the case of a one-volume edition, with limited notes, achieved by Fr. Weber and published by the Biblical Society of Stuttgart, and of the "Neo-Vulgate," the text of which has been incorporated into the liturgical books promulgated after the Second Vatican Council. Several monks from San Gerolamo's very actively contributed to it, especially Fr. Mallet of Solesmes and Fr. Gribomont. Fr. Henri de Sainte-Marie (another novitiate companion of mine) was called by Fr. Salmon to be Prior of San Gerolamo's. He also provided a very erudite edition of the Psalter of St. Jerome "*Iuxta Hebraeos.*" It is rare in history that this sort of team of scholars has accomplished, in half a century, such a work. Without doubt, only the Bollandists provide a comparable example. Standing at the origin of this great accomplishment is a set of persons and circumstances that it is good to remember. God knows that all of this was built on the love of the Church and of monastic life.

Life in the novitiate of Clervaux proceeded agreeably. One would remain there for four years: a year of postulancy (which for me lasted ten months), a year of novitiate, then two more years after first profession. The first thing that I was taught was how to use a broom, something that I had never done. We cleaned the monastery in the afternoon; it was one of the forms of manual labor. Others consisted in helping with picking fruits, beets and potatoes, and at the harvest.

Four years later, when I arrived at the barracks for my military service, I already knew how to sweep, which was not true for everyone. Is it perhaps because of this experience that one day I would revive my interest in brooms? In some Buddhist monasteries in Japan, I discovered that one of the spiritual exercises, called *samu*, consisted in plying long brooms rhythmically. At the National Museum in Tokyo, I found ancient images that illustrated this observance. I then began to compile iconography on this tool, and even to collect some examples of it in the Shaker villages of the United States and elsewhere. When I was asked to contribute to the volume of *Mélanges* offered to Cardinal Daniélou, I chose for my theme "The Broom in the Bible and the Liturgy." There was a light irony in some of the cited patristic texts, however, His Eminence took it well and thanked me kindly.

We entertained ourselves intensely during recreations. From time to time, one of the most senior and venerated members of the community, Fr. Édouard du Coëtbosquet, used to come and "hold conversation." He was a man of ancient nobility, of whom it was said that one of his ancestors had fought in the Crusades. He had been a superior and the first Abbot of Saint-Maur de Glanfeuil, restored by Dom Couturier and some monks from Solesmes. Long since retired, he at first resided at the International College of Sant'Anselmo in Rome. There he was told that he would have to leave because he had made some remarks with regard to *Action française* that differed from Pius XI's intentions. At Clervaux, he was a model of self-effacement and he kept mostly to himself. Someone said that he "always looked like he was excusing himself from living." He died very peacefully at Solesmes during the war.

At one time he had a little argument with Claudel during one of the latter's visits to Clervaux while he was ambassador to Brussels. Claudel loved to spend Holy Week there, being present at all the offices and fasting seriously. On a Holy Saturday evening, he said, "Tomorrow I am resting." But on the morning of Easter Sunday, at twenty minutes to four, when he heard the bells pealing, he could not restrain himself. He wrote his poem, *"Les cloches de Pâques"* [*The Bells of Easter*], and went to Matins. Upon his arrival, he asked for a concordance of the Latin Bible. When Fr. Salmon had him visit the library for the first time, foreseeing that he might look in the card file to see if we had his works, he told him prudently, "We especially have religious works." He replied tartly, "Are not all my works religious?" It was in the same tone that he reacted when Fr. du Coëtbosquet lamented the good old days of the monarchy: "The normal regime of humanity has been tyranny tempered by assassination," he responded.

Is it because of these old memories that I was drawn to Claudel's work, which I read extensively with the help of Jacques Madaule's *Introductions*? I liked everything about him: his poetry, a cheerfulness so abundant that it sometimes passed into bad taste. I found something of philosophy in *Connaissance de l'Est*, *L'art poétique*, the *Grandes odes*, a doctrine of love in *Le partage de Midi*, *Le soulier de satin*, and everywhere a theology of communion, a sense of catholicity that corresponded to that "sense of the Church" which penetrates us. Later I had occasion to correspond a little with him and to hear his warm voice. When I was discharged in 1940, I went to Gallimard and, with my discharge pay, bought everything that was still for sale of Claudel and of Péguy, and enjoyed them thoroughly. One detected in Claudel that he actually delved into certain Fathers of the Church. One could tell at what period he discovered Rhabanus Maurus or some other. Thus, when I had to conclude an international congress at "Les Fontaines" cultural center in 1982 on St. Gregory the Great, it was a pleasure to show that Claudel's *Journal* revealed several citations, sometimes amusing, of this very pastoral and human Doctor.

I had read the *Homilies* of St. Gregory on the Gospels during my novitiate. Just as Fr. Salmon had done—whose example carried much weight in my eyes—I had chosen him as my patron of profession, taking his name as my name in religion, as was the custom then. I have never ceased talking about him admiringly in my teaching, whether at Sant'Anselmo's, at the Gregorian, at Fordham and, in more recent days, at the State University of New York (SUNY) at Binghamton. I know that many people have discovered his value for our times. When Henri-Irenée Marrou asked me to serve at the Sorbonne on the jury for the thesis of Fr. Claude Dagens, he was amused by the experience I related of one of my students. I cited him as an example of the difficulty people sometime have in reading a great spiritual writer who always talks about the same two realities: God and union with him. It involved a young religious in Rome to whom I had suggested that he take up the *Exposition of Job* as a "regular" and therefore obligatory reading during Lent. I left Rome, and he later wrote me, "If I persevere in this reading, it is only because this is Lent." He began to like it, and then wrote me that he was continuing "from Lent into Eastertide."

Finally, another element of continuity throughout my monastic life, for which I thank the Lord, has been a kind of ease in facing the mystery of death. On the day of my entry into the novitiate, after having recited the rosary in the afternoon, as we did every day, I went, as was customary, to the cemetery. A historian monk was being buried there, Fr. L'Huillier, who at one time had gained some renown. He was quite elderly. There also rested Dom Pothier, the former Abbot of Saint-Wandrille, who had earned a name for himself in Gregorian chant; Fr. Baillet, a friend of Péguy and known because of him; but also younger ones, victims of the First World War. I calculated that the average lifetime of a Clervaux monk was forty-nine years. So I still had twenty-seven left to live there. Today, that time frame has long since been surpassed, but the thought of death has not left me. Before speaking at a Congress on Death in the Middle Ages, organized at the University of Manchester in England, before people were inundated with macabre images and lugubrious texts, I thought it opportune to relax their minds by telling them about *The Joy of Dying According to St. Bernard of Clairvaux*: "the joy of newness," of an adventure not yet experienced and infinitely surprising, the joy of penetrating into God with an "eternal curiosity." Since my first steps in the monastic life, I began to perceive that, even before heaven, this would lead me from discovery to discovery.

Clark's Summit, Pennsylvania
May 8, 1983

2

Grace Upon Grace

1. EMPIRICAL HUMANISM

The first problem to be posed was that of how to reconcile an ideal of contemplative life with the need for studying. Fifteen years later, in connection with Pierre de Celle, I was to propose the solution that tradition had taught me. In the meantime, I had to discover it personally and put it to the test.

I had never wanted to be assigned to studies, and I had not expected to. I was amused when, during one of my family's first visits to me at Clervaux, my father told me the story about the offer that a businessman with whom he dealt made to him. (The man was a Jew, but during the Great War he had saved the life of a young officer with a fine future. Later he was adopted as a son into the family, a member of which was the Bishop of Versailles.) The man said to my father: "I have heard that your son has entered into Orders. If you wish, I can intervene with an influential bishop so that he can have a fine ecclesiastical career."

A work was read to us and commented upon that was entitled *Du bonheur d'un simple religieux*, by a seventeenth-century Maurist; it was pointed out that the subject was *only* a religious. The life of a monk who has no important post and who is vested with no dignity was also to be realized in me. The real danger seems to lie in doing something other than what one's function requires, if one has a function. When I discovered in the Middle Ages the case of many "abbots who were just abbots," this designation pleased a number of people.

The contemplative tendency became branded by what some would call anti-intellectualism. There was mistrust toward those who knew things, could compare them, judge them, and then criticize them. Fortunately some monks, who had received a good formation, were able to maintain a correct balance. Each one of us had to find at least his own way in this latent — but fruitful — conflict.

I never had the desire to be a priest. In my last year of secondary school, I had adopted as my motto three letters which served as the initials for an advertising slogan for a make of automobiles: S.S.S., namely, "Simple, Supple, Silent." "Rapidly and silently it runs. It's a Samson." To be nothing but a monk. Nonetheless, it was necessary to become a priest, and to be prepared to do so. I consented without a fuss. However, later on, I was to expend a good bit of energy in struggling against this obligatory and automatic identification of monasticism with the priesthood. Now the cause is won.

My studies were those being done at that time in seminaries in preparation for the priesthood. I remember having designated them as "little studies," as compared to the ones that a novitiate confrere told me about: he had been sent after profession to the Benedictine International College of Sant'Anselmo in Rome. The philosophical training was given in conformity with the manual of *Aristotelico-Thomistic Philosophy* by Fr. Gredt. It was very clear but I never succeeded in finding it convincing. It was a philosophy of theologians for future students of theology. The speculative problems that would one day be posed to them in theology were resolved in advance.

Before entering the monastery, I had read a lot, ranging from books that were somewhat epicurean, such as the *Physiologie du goût* [*Physiology of Taste*] by Brillat-Savarin, to very serious and voluminous works by Pierre Termier (at the time, a renowned geologist), *La joie de connaître, À la gloire de la terre* [*The Joy of Knowing, The Glory of the Earth*], on the reconciliation of science and faith. At the monastery we had free access to the library and I took advantage of it. Under the influence of one of our professors of philosophy, many works were acquired that dealt with what was then called experimental psychology, to distinguish it from scholastic psychology which was highly theoretical. I devoured several of them. A confrere asked me one day, "Why do you work so much?" Another, an American student at Sant'Anselmo's, was to ask me point-blank, "Jean, why do you think so much?" Without doubt, my superiors had good reason not to leave me in ignorance. I would read while taking notes, which I never re-read. This procedure at least obliged one to some slowness in assimilation, all the more because Fr. Salmon had re-introduced — out of love for poverty, or for archaeology? — the use of goose quills, which constantly had to be trimmed and then dipped into ink.

At the same time, the contemplative was not forgotten. Just before my first visit to Clervaux, in 1927, I bought the *Commentaire de la Règle de S. Benoît* by Dom Delatte. I brought it with me and, besides, there was a copy of it in each novitiate cell. Philosophy did not satisfy my hunger: it required putting faith and hope in parentheses, and nourished intelligence but not love. Fortunately, the reading of the Fathers of the Church reestablished the balance, as did reading the *Année liturgique* of Dom Guéranger, which I had already begun, almost clandestinely, in my last year in secondary school. It was recommended reading, not obligatory, except for the sections which were read every day in common, but not on the days when, for some reason, the lector found a note saying, "This evening, please do not read Guéranger."

The idea arose to add to the two-year program of philosophy a course in apologetics. We then began to study the *Tract on the Church* in a totally classic way. Yet the mystery was so fascinating, and matched my aspirations so much, that I plunged into the reading of everything that I could find on the Church. It was my joy. Now, the sense of the Church was constantly put to the test. Even in our monastic circumstances, the agitation provoked by the crisis over *Action Française* disturbed some minds. Once again, it was important to remain free and, if one were to adhere to one or the other side of the issues, to know why one was doing so. In any event, what the defenders of the condemned newspaper kept repeating prepared us to recognize, fifty years later, many things that the integrists were saying after Vatican II; the resources of the human imagination are limited.

Since my youth, in my family and at school, I had come to know older men, who could be role-models, and professors belonging to both parties. There were intelligent people on both sides. But those of the extreme right, as they were called, were slaves of the slogans imposed by those who controlled their minds. I understood that they were not free. I decided not to let myself be influenced, and thus I was considered from then on as "on the left." I had been wounded by an insult that, in my early childhood, some street kid had hurled at me: "Rich scum!" I became sensitive to the plight of the poor. At home, I always undertook the defense of the domestic help. It reached the point that I was treated like a communist. At school, for two years, I spent all my free afternoons in busying myself with workers' children, getting them to play and teaching them the catechism. At the monastery this whole "social" past revived; it had to find its place within the contemplative vocation.

The liturgy, as it was celebrated then, was not performed without certain problems arising. At the beginning of my experience, it appeared above all as a form of aesthetics. At school, I had discovered that the poetry of the texts in the Missal equaled the beauty of the ones I was studying in class. I played the piano a lot (and badly), but well enough to be affected by the music. My preferred composers were modern: Debussy, Fauré, Ravel, Franck; or the romantics like Mendelssohn and, above all, Chopin, whom I had discovered beginning with the *Nocturnes* – I played at sight many of his other works. Inside myself, I constantly sang their melodies and sometimes, without being aware of it, I would hum them. In school, I was admonished for doing it *mezza voce* during times of silence. After several days in the novitiate, a novice in a neighboring cell asked me, "Do you like Ravel, Fauré, Chopin?" "How did you know?" I asked him. "You are continually singing them!" I took this seriously, and since then I have never touched a keyboard. It took me several years to learn how to listen to music without extreme emotion. I had been able to listen to a great deal of music, of all eras, on records and at concerts, thanks to my two brothers, who both loved beautiful music. Mozart was to become my model for music as I dreamed it would be in heaven. In this field, having seen the narrowness of judgment on the part of those who "love" this music but not that, I had decided not to choose. It is true that I have had to make no effort in this, for any music, whatever it might be and without exception, fascinates me. It goes without saying that Gregorian pieces enrich this interior repertoire.

To the aesthetic aspect of the liturgy there now began to be added research into its history. Dom Salmon had encouraged me to study sources, beginning with those of all the rituals and especially of the Commemoration of the Dedication of Churches. Once again, the mystery of the Church! The essentials were there, but the forms of pomp that adorned the solemnities sometimes risked pushing them into the background. At the conclusion of certain pontifical offices, when the organ was playing loudly, when a procession of brightly-colored vestments – and not always in the best taste – advanced under blinding lights, one had the urge to applaud, as if at the end of a spectacular revue. One feast day evening, after such a Vespers, I let myself go and spontaneously wrote a note on the place that the absurd had in liturgy. I never re-read it, but it helped me accept, once and for all, the relativity of everything that is not the mystery itself. It needs expression but, after all, it matters little if it conforms to history or aesthetics. God is not an aesthete. The majority of Christians have come to God, and continue to do so, through the ugly. What is the point of reasoning about it all, of having absolute canons about it? Nothing matters except God.

Our spirituality was greatly nourished during retreats, preached by spiritual authors well-known at the time. Fr. Petitot was a Dominican who had written on St. Thomas, St. Teresa of Avila, St. John of the Cross, and St. Thérèse of Lisieux. He knew how to reconcile St. Thomas' doctrine with the experience of the others. He insisted on the role of the body, and on the usefulness of images. The result was what he called an "integral spirituality," positive and encouraging. This made us smile when, later, we would hear it said that the Church had always been pessimistic and negative, centered on "scorn for the world." I never shared that mentality. Nor would there be any need to discover the value of "earthly realities."

The diffuse humanism that we breathed without even knowing its name accompanied our everyday human relations. We witnessed the growth, then the joyous departure of our older brethren. One of them, having received the last sacraments, yet still hoping to go for a convalescent thermal cure, asked that someone bring him, on his deathbed, a railroad timetable. That was the last thing he read.

My health was still delicate. Just as St. Romanus had done at Subiaco for St. Benedict, Father Master had eggs given to me secretly. One confrere, a former infantry officer, had me do gymnastics. He was vigorous and solemn. He was heard one day, during a session of this kind, to say to young Prince Otto: "Straighten up, my Lord." All the humor was in the tone. How many other anecdotes, provocative or charming, could also be recalled! An unshakable confidence in Divine Providence helped us to overcome all obstacles. Already at school I had learned to use the response that Joseph Cottolengo used to give to those who asked him what drew him out of each day's difficulties: "Ma, c'è la divina Providenza!" [Divine Providence, of course.] These words remained in my ear and in my heart.

Don Cardijn had just founded the *Jeunesse Ouvrière Chrétienne* [Young Christian Workers], the J.O.C. No one in Belgium understood him. Some, before approving it, were waiting to see if he would succeed. Our community, international in character and located in Luxembourg, welcomed him cordially, him and the young people or the chaplains whom he brought there for retreats or conferences, enlivened by Fr. Fohl. Cardijn spoke to us, and could not leave us indifferent. I was enthusiastic about his ideas and his work, and I had the opportunity to see him again and to hear him in Rome. One of the first articles that I was to write, in 1939, was entitled *"Des stations romaines au Missel Jociste"*: it was a hymn to the convergence of the popular character of the ancient Roman liturgy and of this first book of the Mass, all in French, illustrated with photos taken from everyday worker life, a very new genre; joy over this harmony between archaeology and current events.

24

During my early years as a student, a friendship developed, and still exists, with Pastor Skydsgaard, a Danish Lutheran who was then working on a thesis on St. Thomas, whom he admired. He sometimes stayed at Clervaux and, in the library, engaged us in lively conversation, especially about the Church and the authority of bishops and of the pope. These conversations were very enlightening on the possibility and the difficulty of an ecumenical dialogue. Skydsgaard later became dean of a faculty of theology in his country, and a Lutheran observer at Vatican Council II. We have had many occasions to see each other again at Clervaux, Rome and, most recently, Copenhagen.

One of the problems on which existence itself led me to reflect was that of obedience and the exercise of authority. How could one remain dedicated, ready for everything, seeing everything, accepting everything, and keep one's freedom of judgment, the capacity and right to criticize without grumbling, and without losing joy? I have kept many notes of lectures given on this point in those years. Later, I often had occasion to broach the subject. In fact one day, toward the end of the fifties, in Rome, the Father General of the Jesuits asked me to speak on obedience before the assembly of all the major superiors of religious orders. No one would have wanted to risk addressing such an audience on this subject. I accepted without hesitation. It is true that I dealt above all with the obedience of superiors, yet this light piece was welcomed and published. Such is the privilege of never having been anyone's superior!

2. INTERLUDE IN UNIFORM (1932-1933)

After two years of profession, at the age of twenty-one, from the spring of 1931 to that of 1932, I was summoned, like every French citizen, to do my military service. It was a joyful year. I had accepted the necessity of it spiritedly, but I had not foreseen that it would be so amusing. I had been sent as a second-class soldier — a "gunner," as it is called — in an anti-aircraft defense artillery battery. It seems to be an elite weapon, and its advanced equipment required skilled handling. In compensation, we were transported on gunnery trucks — we never had to march. The regiment was stationed at Metz, in one of the casernes that the Germans had built in Gothic style. The corridors resembled cloisters. Indeed, soon I was to make the acquaintance of a monk serving a term as a reservist, who first got the inspiration for his vocation while living within these cloistered buildings.

Everything was new. I was discovering a peasant and especially a worker world, about which I had some notion, but which I had never really experienced. It was worth more than I had imagined it to be. Not skilled with my hands and somewhat frail, I cut an incapable figure. My comrades were friendly, indulgent and a bit sorry for me. I helped them write to their fiancées and listened to them if the separation caused some of them to feel melancholy. I had never found so many fools gathered together as there were in the lower ranks, whether young or older career soldiers, as I saw and heard then. The others, whom I never met, should not have ignored the mediocrity, the lack of respect for a man, with which they treated us. Each of us was a number, each one called a serial number. Above all, they tried to break our resistance to what they called discipline. Everything gave the impression of an institution that survived the last war badly and foresaw nothing of the next one. The future was to confirm this view which all of us had more or less formed. They did not forgive me for the irony that this inspired in me.

Amusing anecdotes, bizarre gossip, and the most unexpected blunders filled our days. My memory is still fresh with them and I could fill pages with them. We hardly did anything except kill time. This idleness bothered me. Even for the few things that we had to do, they hardly knew how to put us to use. In the beginning, they kept us occupied by having us learn and recite the "theory" on discipline. They showed us the operation of the mechanized artillery. They even had us fire rifles without having taught us how. My handwriting was so bad and I was so poor in arithmetic that I could not even be a secretary. I had a series of jobs: bicycle guard, bicycle orderly (in charge of making runs into town), mess dishwasher, "batman," cleaning the rooms of non-commissioned officers. At least this last function, like all the others, left me some free time so that I could spend it alone in a room, reading.

After four years of cloistered life, it was normal that I should have a little crisis of vocation. I recovered my balance by reading, under those conditions, a highly penetrating book to which I had no access earlier: Le monachisme bénédictin by Dom Cuthbert Butler. I had to borrow it from one of my friends whom I would meet in town every evening and every Sunday, for one of my few principles of conduct was to be outside of the caserne as often and as long as possible. At the soldiers' club and among the families to whom I had been recommended, I made lasting friendships. One of the graces of that year was that, during a period of maneuvers in a field of lice-ridden Champagne, I made the acquaintance of a young Jesuit, Fr. L.—he too was doing reserve duty—whose kind influence was decisive for me.

There too I could read. The little that we would do consisted in launching shells without powder toward a wind sock that an airplane was pulling by a cord from a long distance. So that the pilot might always know where our battery was located, its emplacement was signaled to him by a large white sheet. In order to prevent it from flying away, four men were told to stay seated on its four corners. It did not bother me to be picked for this "sheet team," whose work was among the most contemplative. Amid the fictitious bombardment sessions, I had long conversations with Fr. L. He had finished his novitiate and his tertianship and was now starting his philosophy. We exchanged our views on the institutions to which we belonged. A cultured musician, he had a leaning toward Gregorian aesthetics, but he knew nothing about Benedictine life, and I had never spoken with a Jesuit. The discovery was reciprocal. Our friendship lasted and grew deeper up until his death some fifteen years later. Providence saw to it that we met again often, and we wrote to each other frequently.

During my leaves, then after military service, he invited me to go see him in the main study centers of the Society of Jesus, beginning in Vals, where the *Archives de Philosophie* were and are still published. In this journal, I had admired a long article by Fr. Jousse; it had helped me understand psychological and somatic processes at work in the creation and then in the recension of texts of the Old and especially of the New Testaments, and in *lectio divina* as it was practiced in our surroundings. Fr. L. introduced me to Fr. Gaston Fessard and many other Jesuits, already teachers or still students, who would leave their mark on the upcoming generation. It was then that he started telling me about Teilhard de Chardin. He lent me texts by this author as they were being circulated, bit by bit, in mimeographed form, under the table, among the young Jesuits, some fifteen years before they were published. Later on, I twice had occasion to go and pray at the tomb of Teilhard de Chardin in the United States.

Thanks to his teachers, Fr. L. was very informed about the post-Blondelian philosophical current called existentialism which was expressed in the collection *Philosophie de l'esprit*, directed by Le Senne. Gabriel Marcel, Louis Lavelle and others wrote in it; I began to read their works, as well as those of Max Scheler. During that whole year, I had the experience of friendship: these thinkers presented a justification and analyzed the content of this reality, beginning with the notions of person and communion. The personalism of Mounier was oriented toward practical applications, especially in the social order. Thanks to all these encounters and readings of this kind, my military year thus turned out to be, in many respects, a time of formation, for which I never cease to thank God. I received a foretaste and an experience of so many of the riches that later I would discover slowly in theology, then in the monastic authors of the Middle Ages.

3. ROMAN WALKS (1933-1937)

This expression comes to mind spontaneously to characterize the four years I spent in the Eternal City, after my return from the caserne. I was sent to finish my theological studies at Sant'Anselmo's—a priceless experience for someone who is young and curious. It took place on two levels, that of existence and that of knowledge.

The legendary charm of Italy was then clothed with the form of the Fascist comedy. I had left with a group of monks who were entering the community of San Gerolamo's. Right after we passed the border station, in the middle of the night, a man in uniform, holding a large muzzled dog on a leash, took an empty seat in the compartment. He claimed to have been one of those who made the "march on Rome" with Mussolini. He spoke French better than any of us spoke Italian. He questioned us kindly. Imprudently, I asked him how the police were behaving. That morning, in Genoa, we took a taxi to go visit a famous cemetery—the Campo Santo—and other tourist sites. It was one of the numerous Fascist holidays. Seeing the abundance of uniforms, I naively asked our driver if everybody was Fascist. "O per amore o per forza" [Either out of love or out of compulsion], he replied. My confreres suggested that I put a stop to my insinuations. I did not run any other risks except for once when, out of curiosity, I went to the Piazza Venezia to be present at one of the appearances that, after a long wait, Il Duce used to grant from the balcony on high. I was unable to hold back a light display of mockery. "Careful," my neighbor told me in a low voice, "you're being watched." I took him seriously. Yet it was evident that this cult of authority could only lead, sooner or later, to oppression and to catastrophic political decisions.

When the train arrived at the Termini Station, Fr. Quentin was waiting for us. We went to give him an embrace as monks do, but he kept his distance, since the obligatory morality forbade any form of embracing in public. It was evening and it was raining. Yet when the taxi arrived before St. Peter's, a flash of lightning illumined the façade, the colonnade, and the whole square. This unexpected sound-and-light show was marvelous. The next day, our discovery of this prodigious city began with a visit to the tomb of St. Peter. That priority was obligatory and it made much sense. How many times have I asked, while there, to be able to do something for the Church!

For four years I was able to visit, with a guidebook in hand and after preparatory readings, basilicas, catacombs, museums, and palaces, and to learn in the streets more of the history of the Church and of Mediterranean civilization than several professors could have taught me about them. The whole religious culture within which the Roman liturgy took shape came to life. I succeeded in slipping into a French group which, every Thursday afternoon, would make a visit to a site under the guidance of an archaeologist. Little by little, I also went to see the outskirts of the city, and later all of Italy. This taste for such walks—which were not wasted time—was not understood by everybody. Yet I never regretted it.

In Rome, I had a profound experience of catholic life—the encounter with Christians of all races, the consciousness of being in deep communion with everyone, and especially with the pope (despite all the jokes concerning the Holy See and its personnel, which one begins to hear before long). These are part of Catholic tradition and education, well before the times when, beginning with the Renaissance, the old mutilated statue of Pasquino became the daily repository of epigrams and satires. I read a collection of *Five Hundred Pasquinades*; this too is a means for learning about the history of the Church, and to keep a healthy faith in the midst of all the forms of adulation that threaten a strong and centralized power. There we find a proof of vitality that is far from being depleted. Roman humor at times inclines toward mockery; it does not always avoid nastiness. Yet among Catholics it never becomes destructive sarcasm.

The quality of the Roman experience in those years, when I first encountered it at the end of 1933, came precisely from the personality of the currently reigning pope, as was commonly said. It was a time in which great initiatives were being made in all fields: religion, missions, and creation of indigenous bishoprics; politics, the resolution of the Roman question; doctrine, and the elimination of fear in the face of history, criticism, and science. Fr. Quentin used to visit Pope Ratti, whom he had known as librarian. He spoke to us about him freely. These informal observations mitigated the authoritarian character that the pope's public image gave. We discovered, for example, the intelligent piety of a Bishop of Rome who would spend whole evenings personally revising all the parts of a new Office of the Sacred Heart in order to make it more biblical and, at the same time, more theological. He also had decided to "return" (his words) to the Biblical Commission a decree that exegesis no longer confirmed. This vigor of thought and this freedom gave us confidence.

Pius XI had proclaimed a great Jubilee of the Redemption for 1933. He would speak about it on every occasion. He likewise inaugurated collective audiences reserved for groups of young married couples. He canonized or beatified many people. At every papal Mass, Sant' Anselmo's would provide the Gregorian chant, which assured us of excellent seats for those sumptuous spectacles. These occasions were archaic and anachronistic in many respects, yet they were laden with meaning. The air that we breathed favored idealism and fervor, as long as we kept away from pettiness, present everywhere a court exists—and the Roman Curia is no exception.

The Church had had its martyrs in Mexico and in Russia. It was beginning to have them in Germany. Those in Mexico had died crying, "Long live Christ the King." This title given to the Lord, the devotion that it inspired, and the feast that celebrated him then penetrated our life of faith and our piety. During that period, a young American poet by the name of Thomas Merton was converted after having seen the mosaics of Christ in majesty in the churches of Rome where they could be found. Ten years later, he dedicated to Christ the King his autobiography, *The Seven Storey Mountain*, which helped so many others find the truth.

At Sant'Anselmo's, a hundred or so Benedictines from around the world, interns or externs, lived very fraternally. Friendships were formed that were to endure beyond borders and through the vicissitudes of an already menacing future, and about which many were unconcerned. During the vacation that followed the beginning of the civil war in Spain, one of our young confreres was killed. The professor of Hebrew, also a monk from Montserrat, never returned. Many of our companions were preparing, unwittingly, to spend part of their lives in jails of the East. A young Czech, soon elected abbot, communicated to us the joy that he felt at the independence of his country; I saw him again later, matured by twenty years in prison. An Englishman would state the widespread opinion that, if Great Britain were to withdraw from India, that country would fall into misery and anarchy. A new world was coming about, and the majority of us scarcely realized it. Every day, during the hour of recreation, I would hold a conversation with a colleague of a different nationality. Thus we could gain practice in foreign languages and, at the same time, learn about many situations.

Occasions arose for meeting with great scholars such as Fr. Meersseman, then a member of the Dominican Historical Commission; Fr. André Wilmart, likable but reserved; Fr. Quentin, member of the

Curia, destined for a career which was interrupted by an embolism — he was as confident about textual criticism as he was mistrustful of every form of theology. Professor Josi taught archaeology with a fervor that made him lose none of his critical sense; he sometimes told us that "the Apostle Thomas is the patron of archaeologists, because he doubted." Some of the intellectuals, more erudite than cultivated, could have been role-models for us to imitate but I resolved never to become like this one or that one among them, including the one who stated, "in order to work one must be a bear." Is helping young researchers at the risk of writing one less article a waste of time?

At Sant'Anselmo's, the schedule was laden with more than twenty hours of classes per week. That did not prevent anyone who wanted to from reading widely and I did not deprive myself. The history of art and archaeology, Roman impressions of so many men of letters, some of them geniuses, prepared me for the walks. We were provided with many German bibliographies. I absorbed a large portion of the material produced by Maria Laach. All of Newman's works were in the library, and I benefited greatly from them. Each weekend, at San Gerolamo's, I took something of what I had read to Fr. Suhr and we exchanged views on everything; as a mature adult he added a living dimension to all the bookish material. From time to time, large public conferences in the city, as well as concerts, allowed us to hear leading international personages. Also, at that time, Cardinal Pacelli, the Secretary of State, delivered a series of panegyrics on the saints, each lasting more than an hour, but I never had the opportunity to attend even one.

The professor of history at Sant'Anselmo's was a Fr. Poulet, a talented popularizer, author of a manual, working from secondary sources, but well enough that he never lacked for a publisher. We had been born in the same small town, and I had known his parents. We became friends. He was an admirer of Mauriac and used to read one novel of his after another. He would then pass them on to me, and I became part of the same school. I also read Mauriac's more doctrinal works, so to speak, on *Bonheur et souffrance du chrétien* [*The Christian's Happiness and Suffering*], on Pascal and Jansenism. In these works, as in his novels, he always dealt with sin and grace, but with the latter always having the last word: a deep perception of the human condition and invincible Christian optimism. The little that I ever knew about moral theology, I owe to Fr. Poulet. Later I would have occasion to hear his husky voice and to meet him again, stricken and in pain, lucid yet confident. He lived not far from the monastery on the Rue de la Source. He sometimes came there for Mass.

At Sant'Anselmo's there was a teacher well worth hearing: Fr. Anselm Stolz, a young theologian about thirty years old. He was a trail-blazer but was to die, at age forty-two, from an infection contracted during the war while he was hearing the confessions of badly-wounded people. Providence willed that he should start with the tract *On the Church* as I began my theological studies. He directly passed over all apologetics and immersed us in the great dogmatic problems that were discussed by St. Paul and all the New Testament authors, as well as the Greek and Latin Fathers. For each topic we soon came, according to chronological order and the development of doctrines, to St. Thomas, then to Vatican Council I. Fr. Stolz made great use of the patristic "themes," at once poetic and rich in content. He was anticipating what, in the following generation, Daniélou and others would reintroduce into common theology. We rose beyond the erudition of specialists who were only patrologists, beyond the artificial "theses" of Thomists who were nothing more than scholastics. Teaching of his kind was truly contemplative, and I was not the only one to leave the classroom in a state of prayer. Every Sunday, I would do my *lectio divina* quietly on the notes that I had taken during those lectures. Moreover, he insisted on the fact that, according to St. Thomas, theology is not a science like the others, and the problem of knowing if, in what measure, and in what sense it could be called a science would stay with me forever. I had always believed that theology would be much more than a science, even though we act as if it were one by using scientific methods to study it.

Nonetheless, the great dogmatic problems raised in class were those posed by current reality: among them, the position, in relation to Christ, of the Jews being persecuted in Germany. I was even present at the arrest of a young Catholic of Jewish descent from that country when he was captured in an Italian monastery where he had been hidden. The Church as mystery, as the People and Temple of God, the relations between the bishops and the papacy; everything that one day would be discussed at Vatican Council II was already in sight. The points of view of Scheeben, Franzelin and Newman were added to those of Scripture and of patristics. I was decisively influenced by this approach. Fr. Stolz treated me as a friend and in 1937 I published a translation of one of his articles. We kept in contact by letters, through clandestine channels, even during the War. When I was asked to compile a volume of my patristic and liturgical essays dating from those years for the series *Lex orandi*, I dedicated them to the memory of Anselm Stolz, whose methods had inspired them. He also gave us, in the form of special courses, material that he prepared for the retreats that he preached at Chevetogne; those texts were published and have been reissued.

He made great use of what was then the best in German "philology," as it was then being presented by Erik Peterson. This historian of ancient religions, a Lutheran who converted to Catholicism, had lost his university chair. He had had to leave Germany and found refuge on the Aventine, near Sant'Anselmo's. Later, he became a professor at the Pontifical Institute of Christian Archaeology, and Pius XII gave him asylum in Vatican City. We often saw him at Sant'Anselmo's and could easily approach him, either there or at his residence, where I would go to see him again at a later time. He influenced some of us, both through Fr. Stolz as intermediary and through his books, of which several considered the relation of faith and politics in the patristic age. His commentary on the chapters of the Letter to the Romans concerning the mystery of the Jews and the nations was very timely. His book on the martyrs — *Témoins de la vérité* [*Witnesses to the Truth*] — was of the same tenor. I devoured his *Livre des anges* [*Book of Angels*] and everything that he wrote. He and Fr. Stolz drew our attention to the importance of words and the history of their meanings. This concern never left me, and it appeared in my two volumes in the *Studia Anselmiana* dedicated to the monastic vocabulary of the Middle Ages. Recently, on the occasion of a conference in Turin, I was moved upon seeing all his files there, acquired by an institute that now bears his name in the university of that city.

Toward the end of my third year of theology, the time had come to think about a subject for my doctoral thesis. I spoke about it to Fr. Poulet. He was interested in the political theories of the Middle Ages, and he pointed out to me that an important treatise by a certain Jean Quidort of Paris, a Dominican and partisan of Philip the Fair against Boniface VIII, deserved to be the object of study and of a critical edition. He suggested that I speak about it with François Xavier Arquillière of the Institut Catholique in Paris; he had founded and directed a collection of works on "Church and State in the Middle Ages." This proposal fit perfectly with my continued interest in ecclesiology. I saw Arquillière in Paris at the beginning of the following vacation, and he immediately offered to publish the thesis that I was intending to write and defend in Rome.

Accordingly, during my fourth year, at the same time as I was studying for the examination for my licentiate, I started going to look over some manuscripts of Jean de Paris [Jean Quidort] and of others in the Vatican Library and in other libraries in Rome. I spent my free mornings and many of my afternoons there. I discovered with much interest all that history had to offer on the theme of the kingship of Christ, from the earliest centuries—my first article on the subject dealt with St. Justin—up to the encyclical *Quas primas* of Pius XI, of which I knew some of the formulas by heart. I set about a plan for writing this history, of which one part appeared at first in the form of articles; the ones among them that related to the Middle Ages were gathered, at Fr. Congar's request, in a volume of the collection *Unam sanctam* which he edited. This gave me the opportunity to examine, from this point of view, the entire corpus of St. Thomas' writings and discover an unpublished sermon of his.

These years in Rome were punctuated by holidays in different resort spots. Frascati, near ancient Tusculum, from where the view extended over Rome and the whole countryside, was in particular the ideal setting for reading the letters on friendship by Cicero, the *Divine Comedy*, Manzoni, and so many other masterpieces. A literary friend of mine, a Latinist, had the gift of bringing ancient texts to life, re-read at Ostia or Hadrian's villa. However, this pleasurable and useful leisure began to be overshadowed by current events and the menaces of the future. A press campaign had prepared public opinion for the conquest of Ethiopia by Italy. After the country's first and easy victories, Pius XI blessed this war policy publicly. After having pushed for the decolonization of the missions, he imposed on that part of Africa an episcopacy that originated from the conquering power. An empire was proclaimed. The only true victor was Hitler. I remember one day having come upon the retinue of Goering, and another time that of Horthy, the Regent of Hungary, on their way to the Quirinal. All this seemed very transitory. But for someone who was the only Frenchman among the students at Sant'Anselmo's, it was better to display the least possible skepticism.

I did not spend much time in preparing for examinations, which I passed anyway, with undistinguished grades, but high enough to earn the degrees of bachelor and then of licentiate. The ordinary ambition, considered as normal, was to earn the most praiseworthy grades. But to what purpose? The attraction of manuscripts and libraries was stronger. Frequenting public libraries, even that of the Vatican, was considered unusual and even dangerous. In saying good-bye to the Primate of Monte Cassino, at the beginning of July 1936, I told him about my thesis project, which he told me pleased him.

This "Anselmian adventure" ended well. At his return from the celebration on July 11 of the centenary of Solesmes, where he had met with the Abbot Primate, my abbot told me that my presence at Sant'Anselmo's was no longer welcome. I was stunned: no one had given me any inkling of this. The reason that had been given, he told me, was that it was dangerous for me to remain outside of my cloister. Father Abbot—I learned this only later—got his information from Fr. Salmon and Fr. Fohl, who were present at Solesmes, and who had seen me living in Rome. At his return, he proposed to send me to Paris. This was unexpected. I asked to reflect on it. I sought advice and accepted the next day. This was a new and unforeseen grace. There I would find teachers, environment, and means of training thanks to which the experience in Rome, having been very deep, would be expanded.

3

Relocations and Encounters

1. PARISIUS-PARADISUS (1937-1938)

At Paris the program for the fifth year of theology comprised few courses so as to allow free time for the thesis and other works. As elsewhere, there were a certain number of good professors and some masters. Outside of our program, we could only choose from among the latter. They did not have to teach us for long in order to leave their mark on us, to show what their thinking was, to communicate a method to us and to give us a share in their experience. The personal contacts we had with them were as beneficial as their courses. Arquillière, a specialist on Gregory VII, directed a seminar of practical studies in medieval ecclesiology and once a week would gather in his house all those who were taking part in it. In a course on the history of Christian-Jewish relations, Fr. Bonsirven spoke of the vicissitudes of the people of Israel with such benevolence that some thought that he came from an immigrant Jewish family from abroad; in fact, he came from the South of France. The historical information that he provided completed the theological notions of Stolz and Peterson. It was always useful later to return to them.

During one semester, Fr. Yves de Montcheuil gave a course on marriage in the work of St. Augustine or, more accurately, in connection with that work; indeed, his thought was very personal. It was around that time that a book by Doms, a German theologian, had just been published on the ends of marriage that was critical of the total subordination of a secondary end of marriage — love — to a primary end, procreation. Fr. de Montcheuil presented this view enthusiastically. After the semester, we learned that a decree of the Holy Office had ordered that the book be withdrawn from sale, though his ideas were to become accepted later on. What de Montcheuil had to say about friendship, marriage, love and St. Augustine left an indelible imprint on me. We remained in friendly contact until he was killed amid the partisans of

Vercors in 1944. He did not have enough time to publish very much, but several courses and conferences given by him circulated in duplicate form; I had them all.

Outside of the program, at the Sorbonne and at other educational facilities, we could choose to attend classes only given by the masters. At the École de Chartes, Alain de Bouärd was professor of paleography; all his experience as an archivist came to life when discussing the facsimiles of documents that he would read, embellished by maxims such as: "Paleography is not a science, but rather a set of conjectures," and, "Believe nothing, not even what I tell you." I would maintain a long-lasting bond with him. At the École des Hautes-Études, Charles Samaran taught paleography with the same method — which consisted in deciphering texts, in dating their writing, in establishing the regions they came from — but with another style. I owed much to him. He always showed great loyalty toward the students whom he had encouraged and whom he treated as friends. He would die a centenarian.

The same must be said about Louis Halphen, also at the École des Hautes-Études. He held a seminar on the letters of Fulbert of Chartres. He was famous, and attracted to his seminars more students than he wanted, but he was skilled in dissuading a large number of them in the early sessions. He selected others and helped them; thus he arranged that year for the publication in the *Revue historique du droit français et étranger* of the text of one of my contributions to the seminar. We would become very close friends in the painful future that awaited him. Among those I had occasion to meet privately or to hear speaking in public, the names and the images emerge of Marc Bloch, Louis Lavelle, Paul Valéry, Gabriel Le Bras, Fr. Lebreton, Fr. de Lubac, and especially Jacques Maritain and Étienne Gilson. At the Manuscript Department of the Bibliothèque Nationale, I made the acquaintance of various scholars who would come there regularly; among them was Glorieux. Others worked there permanently, like Canon Victor Leroquais.

Our place of residence was the abbey of Sainte-Marie, known as "La Source," where the *bey* Ghica resided, where Fr. de Monléon was publishing spiritual books that enjoyed great success, and where a group of young monks maintained intense vitality. Many texts of the Maurists and unpublished conferences of Dom Delatte on the contemplative monastic life were heard in public readings. The writing of my thesis progressed, in large part thanks to the documentation that I had compiled in Rome. To it was added the boundless resources in manuscripts, printed books and journals found in the libraries of Paris.

During that period, a modest apostolic activity began among youth groups—students, scouts and others—who came on Sundays for retreats. It also happened that I was asked to give talks in some of the secondary schools in Paris and the suburbs. Beginning around that time, there were two main orientations. First of all, the traditional way of praying in monasticism proved to be accessible to all, and useful in the context of Catholic Action; furthermore, conjugal love appeared as one of the main realities of lay Christian life. Under the influence of the JOC and of the work of German theologians such as Dietrich von Hildebrand, a spirituality of marriage was developed during that period. Abbé Caffarel, the future founder of the magazine *L'anneau d'or*, frequented La Source. After a talk that I held one Sunday for a student group, he asked me for the text so as to publish it in a pamphlet; a printed sample of the cover was made, dated 1937. Its title would have been *L'idéal de l'amour dans le mariage chrétien*, but my abbot thought that, at twenty-five, I was too young to get involved in that particular field. Nothing more was said of it, and so I closed a parenthesis in my life that was to be reopened thirty years later in Oxford.

In Rome, Fr. Stolz loved to recall the patristic theme of paradise. In the thirteenth century, some papal decretals had shown, in the Catholic university of the Church which was then being founded in Paris, a new paradise—*Parisius, paradisus*—where, after the transfer of studies—the *translatio studii*—the four rivers of knowledge then ran. This new image of paradise completed the first one, and it was of the former that I had the most vivid memory when I returned to Clervaux.

2. CLOISTER PARENTHESIS (1938-1939)

A few weeks after the beginning of vacation, Halphen and Samaran wrote to my abbot, asking him to send me again to Paris for a year of studies. It was a question of vocation. This sort of request flattered Father Abbot, who was inclined to grant it. I answered that I had not entered the monastery in order to do studies, nor to become a scholar, nor to write books, and I refused. Then I was given the post of teaching dogmatic theology to the group of fifteen students at Clervaux at that time. My memories of it are good, all the more because I formed bonds of friendship with several of them. In keeping with the teaching that I had assimilated, friendship was becoming important in my life or, more accurately, friendships were multiplying; as diverse as they were one from another, they did not exclude one another, but rather reciprocally complemented each other. I was especially encouraged by a monk from Kergonan, Fr. Landry, who lived at Clervaux. I submitted to him some essays I had written in periods of enthusiasm; he urged me to present them to *La vie spirituelle*, and that put me into contact with its editor, Fr. Bernardot. Another Benedictine from Kergonan came to spend a long sojourn with us: a modest and reserved man, he worked in the book-bindery. No one could foresee that this Fr. Le Saux would go to India to join Fr. Monchanin, that there he would become Swami Abhishiktananda and, before dying, would write extremely deep books on the relations between Christianity and Hinduism. There still exist Abhishiktananda Societies in Italy, Switzerland and India. The remembrance of this then-hidden genius helps in understanding that great destinies are prepared in the obscurity of prayer and silence, of life in community and in fraternal charity. Later, and even recently, I was to encounter on my own path the work and the works of Fr. Le Saux. A while ago, a congress was held in Milan on some aspects of his message.

Meanwhile, with the aid of the microfilms of some manuscripts, I was preparing a few articles on questions that were not new to me. Above all, they dealt with the notion of theology as a science according to unpublished texts of the generation following St. Thomas: if theology is not a science, then, it was asked in these texts, "can it be taught?" Moreover, the question of the relations between politics and religion, between the Church and the temporal power, remained current and could be clarified in the light of the theories — and the errors — of the Middle Ages. The reading of the *City of God* by St. Augustine helped to interpret our era, in which the temporal and the spiritual were confronting each other more and more sharply, as were the politics and the religion of those witnesses of God who were the Jews and the Christians. We were even more aware of this at Clervaux, because the monastery, located along the borders of Germany, France and Belgium, had become a kind of refuge. Very soon, the Nazi regime would make it pay dearly for this. Had anyone been imprudent? The risks of charity are worth running. Thus, among the guests were two Spanish monks who each supported a different party in the bloody struggle going on in their country. It was good to listen to the two "bells" and to foster harmony between them.

On the occasion of the two major international alarms that marked the years 1937 and 1938, at the order of the French embassy in Luxembourg, all Frenchmen who could be mobilized had to get ready to rejoin the army. Our life in peace was then interrupted by two stopovers in my home town of Avesnes in the north of France, near my center of mobilization. During the first one, in one of the days leading up to the

Munich Agreement, while facing the prospect of dying in war, I was tempted to renounce any future. I fled to the church and I recall exactly the moment, the place and the way in which I received the grace of consenting to this call. After that I felt free, forever.

3. NON-COMBATANT SOLDIER (1939-1940)

At the end of August 1939, we were really called to arms. I was assigned to an anti-aircraft battery that, after a period in Douai, was moved to the center of the mining region, not far from the abbey of Anchin, at one time illustrious; its manuscripts would keep me very busy later on. Since a blitzkrieg was awaiting us, in order to be able to carry out a speedy mobilization, recruitment was organized on a local level: all men were called in the immediate environs of the places where they lived. The result was that, since a blitzkrieg did not happen, everyone was tempted to go back home often and, if they could, every evening. Almost everybody worked in the region's mines, often "in the pit," as they would say. Accustomed to a hard life, they were generous and ready to help one another. I was a simple soldier, but they all knew that I was a priest: the term "monk" meant nothing to them, yet they showed indifference mixed with curiosity toward religion and its ministers. I met again Fr. L., who had become a non-commissioned officer; there was also a Dominican and two likable seminarians. Our mates showed no hostility toward all these clerics, but rather sympathy and sometimes trust, which continued to increase. We managed that the three of us who were priests should be assigned to three different batteries, so that one of us would be in each one, and I remained alone with the two seminarians. Nonetheless I often saw Fr. L., and whether at the residence of the Jesuits in Douai or at the school of Saint-Jean of that same city, in the evening I often met eminent personages.

We lived in shelters dug in the black soil in that carboniferous zone. It was extremely humid there. The men had to be there, ready to take their posts at the cannons or by the sighting equipment. Free time enabled reading, for the few of us who had the ability and the desire, and conversation. I lived in the shelter that served as an office with a comrade, married and the father of a child, who worked as secretary in a garage. We got along well. He was the one who typed the notes for my thesis, not without gross errors in the many Latin citations and numerous references to the works of St. Thomas and other medieval writers. I finished the manuscript of an article on *La théologie comme science d'après la littérature quodlibétique* [Theology as a Science According to the

Quodlibetical Literature] — every word in the title sounded strange to lay ears. These pages had to pass through military censorship at all levels, even to the highest. At the lowest, my lieutenant had to see it without reading it; after writing "approved" in the margin, he sent it back to my office comrade saying, "Luckily there are some imbeciles who will read this stuff!"

Since there were three of us priests, we provided Sunday Mass in turn. For the first time in my life I had to preach, but not without having sought the advice of my two confreres. One of them had been trained in sacred eloquence by Fr. Pinard de la Boullaye, preacher at Notre Dame, and the other by Fr. Sertillanges. One of the seminarians, Gérard, was a poet and philosopher, fortunately without knowing it. Delicate and sickly, he would suffer intensely during imprisonment. Nevertheless he lived a long time: he was an ardent admirer of Pierre Emmanuel and a great reader of Nietzsche. He finished his life while humbly serving the Church as secretary to Msgr. Daniel Pézeril in Paris, to whom he had introduced me. He suffered and died quietly. We saw each other often; Gérard was one of the nicest people I ever met. With him we cultivated then, in our battery, a "friendship group" in order to bring a bit of joy to all those men separated from their wives and families. Within a few weeks, the atmosphere did in fact change. I was given the nickname "Smiley" and the trust that was placed in me was not lost upon the battery commander. He was in no way jealous, and his job was certainly harder than mine. I did what I could to help him. Although he was notoriously anticlerical, on some afternoons he would say to me, "Father, use your influence so that enough men stay on the field this evening in order that our cannons can fire if the alarm is sounded." This mode of cultivating friendship became a new method that we discussed during meetings of mobilized priests, the greater number of whom had been involved in Catholic Action. I was also called to other batteries.

Everything that I had read and learned about friendship and about the person being made for communion thus found direct usefulness, and for many became a font of joy. I became fond of these comrades who became part of my life. The habit grew of smiling each time one crossed oneself. True, not everything was charity and moderation in our battery any more than it was in others. But the atmosphere certainly was not sad. One evening the sergeants tried to get me drunk, but I knew when to stop and everything ended well.

As the harshest weeks of that very cold winter were beginning, I was summoned to Arras to report to a military discharge center with all those who had health problems. An otolaryngologist briskly examined my throat, asked me to say "ah" as he put an overheated mirror in my mouth, allowing me only to say "eh." He scolded me for not knowing the difference between one letter and another. When the results were reported, I learned that I was being sent for observation to an army neuropsychiatric center. I thought I had been taken for illiterate or mentally ill. I found our later that one of the medical officers, convinced that I was wasting time in that battery, had tried to have me discharged and sent back to a more useful life. However, the attempt failed, and I really would never have tried to escape an obligation common to all. So I went to the neuropsychiatric center, situated in the most luxurious hotel in Torquet-Paris Plage. The ambiance was very entertaining, filled with neurotics of all kinds, and with fakers who nonetheless found it hard to keep up their act for very long. I was used as an interpreter for some English soldiers stricken with amnesia after they were found frozen or burned-out by alcohol. I began to organize a library.

On the day of my arrival, a nurse led me to a lovely hotel room transformed into a three-bed dormitory room. The two soldiers occupying the other two beds looked anxiously at the nurse; she gave them assurances (I soon found out that, the night before, the one whose place I took had had a raving attack of madness). They were afraid of a repetition. Two doctors, who in civilian life worked at the university, questioned me, one after the other, while a stenographer wrote down everything that I said, in order to be able to compare the two statements; they were on guard for fakers. When some extracts from a scholarly article came to me, I provided them to the medical officer "to aid his diagnosis." He had to realize that there had been some mistake. During an alarm that aroused fear of an invasion, room had to be made in that hospital as in others for receiving the most seriously wounded. I was given the choice of being transferred to a psychiatric center in Brittany or to go back to my battery after a convalescent leave. I chose the second option.

The day on which I was to defend my thesis had been set by the authorities of the Institut Catholique for May 10, 1940. I had postponed until that time the ten-day leave that I was entitled to, and that everyone else had taken earlier. In the afternoon, on the day of the defense, I took a nap and did not wake up on time: thus I arrived late. Fr. Lebreton, the dean, and all the members of the commission were waiting politely. Since the title of the volume that they were about to judge contained the name of Jean Quidort ("he who sleeps"), I imagine that they joked about it. When I showed up in the uniform of a second-class artilleryman, I was entitled to their indulgence. The next day, as I took the train to rejoin my battery, the German invasion was just starting. The railroad lines had already been bombed. I could get no further than Laon. I had wanted to be near my comrades in those hours that were turning out to be so hard. All of them were taken prisoners; some died en route to a camp in northern Germany, and others contracted illnesses from which they were never healed, as happened to Fr. L. and Gérard. After they came back to France, many of them told me that I surely would not have withstood the rigors of the journey, of field life, of the climate, of the labor, of the forced marches at the time of the slow liberation in 1945. I was spared all of this by the decision of a thesis commission that could never have foreseen any such thing.

4. MONASTERIES-SHELTERS (1940-1941)

From Laon I was transferred from caserne to caserne. In the one in Beauvais I discovered that my neighbor, on the straw that served as a dormitory, was Fr. Deman, a Dominican famous for his studies on the history of moral theology. I would see him again thereafter, more than once, at the University of Fribourg in Switzerland, before he died prematurely. These unplanned moves seemed to be truly blessed by Providence. Passing through Clermont-Ferrand, where I knew that the major seminary of Strasbourg had taken refuge, I made an appointment to meet Professor Jean Rivière. The author of a book on the political controversy in which Jean de Paris had taken a stand, he had advised and encouraged me; moreover, he had accepted a manuscript for the *Revue de sciences religieuses* which he edited. When I showed up in my uniform, it took him a moment to recognize me since he had thought I was a scholar of advanced years. I thought he was going to give the article back to me, but he recovered himself and began a cordial conversation.

This long journey through invaded France did not lack intense experiences. In particular, when we had to stretch out on the ground because of an enemy flight or bombardment, each of us was aware of facing possible death. Then fear and the instinct for preservation took precedence over all convictions. It came to me to pray that the projectiles might land on someone else. I was left profoundly humiliated by this visceral selfishness when the alarm ended and danger had been temporarily avoided. It is one thing to accept death ahead of time — lucidly, feeling well and in full possession of oneself — and another to grasp that one could soon be killed at any minute or, worse yet, could be left forever bodily injured or mentally debilitated. There was certainly no lack of occasions for reflection and for examination of conscience before

God. The analysis of existential situations in the manner of Gabriel Marcel helped me stay lucid during that period.

I ended up in a village in the South of France, not far from the wonderful city of Cahors. I was lodging in a private home. I asked the parish priest for a room; he was a poet, a *félibre* (a Provençal writer) who wrote for the *Jeux Floraux* (Floral Games). His company was delightful, as was that of my new comrades among whom, without glory and apparently by chance, my service in the army in wartime came to an end.

While I was demobilized in the zone called "free," that is, not occupied, Clervaux, like all of Luxembourg, had been annexed to the thousand-year Reich. I then sought refuge in the one monastery of our congregation not in occupied territory: the abbey of Hautecombe, on the banks of Lake Bourget in Savoy. There I found some fifteen monks who were unable to return to their own community. It was a very pleasant setting where new friendships sprang up. The abbot informed me, with great solicitude, that my younger brother Robert, to whom I was very close, had been killed at the Somme front. I could not hold back a reaction of rebellion against God: why had this disaster happened to my mother, to me, and not to someone else among those who were with me? Why Robert, young and engaged—his wedding was supposed to have been celebrated on the very day on which he was killed—and not me, when I had nothing special to do in this life? Little by little, thanks to the charity and the prayers of my confreres, I recovered peace. The time had come to share it with others. I then also learned that my older brother and my brother-in-law were prisoners, that my mother, my sister and her son had taken refuge in Brittany and that the home of my birth had been abandoned to looting.

Since there was no hope of returning any time soon to Clervaux, I and another of my confreres decided—to reduce the burden on Hautecombe—to become chaplains in a military school. I was sent to the one that had a dozen sites in the Black Mountain, a region in which the Benedictine abbey of En Calcat was located. Contingents from an officers' school and from a military medical school had been assigned there. The several hundred students made for a difficult, demanding and critical environment. They were discouraged over the events which were the cause of their presence in those places and intolerant of the manner in which the old soldiers attempted to train them. "We want to be treated like young men and not children," one of them said.

I had the task of starting a newspaper, and to this end I recruited a group of students from the École Normale Supérieure who were very intelligent and full of ideas. I conversed with them at length, reflecting on what was true youth, that of God. This too was the source of friendships that enriched me. I also benefited from the readings of these students. Later on I saw some of them again, and they had me meet their own teachers. I even wrote a book with one of them. One day one of them asked me, "Are you a Stoic?" Seeing my surprise, he responded that many of the things that I was telling him made him think. I told him, "I have read something of Lavelle." He always carried the *Manual* of Epictetus and found convergences between his master of thought and my masters.

Among these young men, I took up pastoral activities that my position as chaplain involved, with all the joys and disappointments it brought. In addition to the religious services, I held meetings of "friendship groups," just as I had done in the artillery battery. In order to come to accept a situation or separations that were not caused by us, we sought to reflect, after the manner of Gabriel Marcel, starting with concrete and daily experiences, with existential situations, to become aware of the love of which each one of us is capable and, in one way or another, experiences.

At En Calcat, where I often went, I definitively completed the manuscript of my thesis with the aim of publishing it. There I met Fr. Denis Martin, who one day would call me to Morocco and then to black Africa. An unknown future continued to prepare itself in an unexpected present. In the next village, Dourgne, lived Isabelle Rivière. I had just finished reading a novel of hers, *Le bouquet de roses rouges* [The Bouquet of Red Roses], the one on her life. She loved to evoke the remembrances of her husband, Jacques Rivière, of her brother, Alain-Fournier, of Péguy, of Gide and of others whom she had known.

I took advantage of the nearness of Lourdes to make a pilgrimage there, and this too was a return to my origins. Indeed, in 1917 I spent several months there, when my family took refuge there after we were able to leave the invaded North. This "repatriation," as it was called, allowed me to make my first long journey, for it was impossible to traverse the two hundred kilometers that separated us from Paris: the "front," the lines of combat, lay there. We then needed eight days and eight nights to travel, in deep winter, on a train of repatriates, through Belgium, Holland and Germany and to arrive in Geneva, where the Red Cross reserved for us a generous welcome, which compensated for the harshness and privations of the journey that was nonetheless instructive and at times entertaining. I have retained precise memories of it. At Lourdes an elderly cousin, a very devout Christian woman, had us take part in services with sermons that seemed interminable to me. So, at the age of five, I was led to associate the idea of religion with that of boredom. I returned to Lourdes a number of times afterwards without experiencing the same impression. Yet the reading of *Les foules de Lourdes* [The Throngs at Lourdes] by Huysmans definitively instilled in me a sense of compassion for the human ugliness streaming through there.

When I returned there, during a new world war, I could not help but say in a prayer, "Lord, what have we done to you, that we should treat you this way?" Nonetheless, at Clervaux I had understood the relativity of what is considered to be beautiful or ugly. Now, the immense misery that poured through there and the faith that transformed it made one forget all the rest. Some prisoners of war recently repatriated, after too many sufferings and privations, languished pale and dragged themselves rather than walked. Many of these seriously ill people, victims of imprisonment and then of exile, were Poles. Before the grotto where Mary had appeared, people prayed not for temporal goods, which had been lost, but for the true goods. Joy and serenity were granted to us.

After spending some months on Black Mountain, it did not seem that the situation at Clervaux could change; I left that camp and went to seek the hospitality of the Benedictine abbey of Ligugé, situated in the occupied zone of France. Memories from my childhood tied me to Ligugé, from when I had read Huysmans before entering Clervaux.

At that time *L'Oblat* had colored my vocation with a kind of romanticism. Moreover, I had known this monastery through its publications on the Middle Ages, the *Revue Mabillon* and the *Archives de la France monastique*. The abbot was Dom Basset, an intelligent and cultured man. The library was excellent. I formed new friendships; the one with Dom Basset lasted, on this earth, until he learned in 1953 that cancer would take him within three months; he then summoned his friends one after another. The remembrance of this farewell conversation and of all those that led up to it are infinitely dear to me; the Paschal Mystery lay at the center of all his colloquies. He loved to recall the visit that Claudel had made to Ligugé, just before the adventure that befell him which became the subject of his *Le partage de Midi*. His confessor had required him to remove the book from sale, but there was a copy of it at the Bibliothèque de l'Arsenal, which I had on microfilm. The other preserved copy, in which he had written a dedication, was at Ligugé. When the work was reprinted, Claudel added a new dedication to it: this profound inner drama had found its lyrical solution in *Le soulier de satin*.

Ligugé was situated near the line of demarcation between France's occupied zone and the free zone. Thus people were aided in crossing it clandestinely. This was the case with Robert Schumann after escaping from a Nazi concentration camp; he then brought to the apostolic nuncio a dossier on what had taken place there. He lived incognito in a novitiate cell: "the most solitary of the novices," he would say when, in the post of prime minister after the war, he went back to Ligugé in order to decorate Dom Basset with the Legion of Honor. I was invited to the ceremony, and after it I had occasion to see Schumann again at the Quai d'Orsay.

Life at Ligugé went on in this somewhat dangerous but studious atmosphere. I was expecting to stay in that monastery until the end of the war, which appeared to be some time away. I had been there for a few weeks when I received a letter from the administrator of the Bibliothèque Nationale; in it, he asked me to come there and continue a work begun by Dom Wilmart. He had found it necessary to leave Italy because of the war, and had started to compile a catalogue of Latin manuscripts of patristics and theology. He took advantage of his fine state of health to undergo an operation, which was successful, but he died of the aftereffects. Since I could not reach my superior, I asked Dom Basset for his advice, and he urged me to accept—a new separation, due to completely unforeseeable circumstances. After finding kind hospitality at Hautecombe, En Calcat, and Ligugé, I joyfully returned to live at La Source. My ties to Ligugé remained strong.

4

Medievalism and the Life of the Church

1. WAR YEARS

The decade that was beginning was to be a period of intense vitality for the Church. The years of the war (1941-1945) were to prepare, even amidst great hardship, a postwar period extremely fruitful in initiatives. We are still living on that thrust.

I agreed to work at the Bibliothèque Nationale—the B.N., as we called it—on the staff of the Centre National de la Recherche Scientifique (CNRS), and not as part of the personnel of the library staff. In that way I was taking no one's place, and I remained free with respect to the regime then in power, as well as to its ideas. The curator of the department of manuscripts was Jean Porcher, an eminent historian of miniature painting, with whom I soon established a deep and lasting friendship, so much so that he introduced me to his family. The work, which consisted in analyzing manuscripts and writing a descriptive note about each one, amounted to a fine schooling: I was dealing with the most varied texts, and gained much information about them. A group of refined collaborators, men and women, was assigned to the Latin Catalogue, and among them there was perfect understanding.

In the next office, a task force of librarians and scholars, in uniform, were "occupying" the Department of Manuscripts. It was said that others, in another room, were working on some plans of London with a view to its reconstruction after the war, once it had been razed to the ground. One day, one of these "*messieurs*," as they were called, after learning that I could read German, had a note in that language delivered to me, seeking some information. I answered in Latin, and that put an end to our contact. One morning I was summoned to the headquarters of the Gestapo, without knowing why. In case I would not be coming back, I asked my brother to accompany me as far as the site. They had me pass through a number of doors that were all locked with a key behind me and the soldier accompanying me. In the office where we finally arrived, it was only a matter of giving me a response, from Fr. Alban Dold of the abbey of Beuron, to a question that I had posed him concerning a manuscript. He had chosen the official way for responding. We would have preferred others.

The required work left ample time for other personal activities. I yielded to the temptation to publish various unedited texts. Among the scholars working at the Department of Manuscripts, were some—like Leroquais—who were always available to answer the questions of younger researchers. We helped each other a great deal. A Dominican, an editor of scholastic texts, confessed to me one day his bewilderment over a marginal note that abbreviated an author's name with the letters BO FOR. I then remembered Alain de Bouärd's maxim: paleography is a set of conjectures. I thus took a risk with "Bonae Fortunae." And indeed it was of St. Bonaventure. One morning this scholar said goodbye to us. He had sent a note to the Historical Commission to which he belonged, with these words: "Every age has its pleasures. I am entering La Trappe." Later I did see him in a Cistercian habit.

My thesis on Jean de Paris had been presented by Halphen and Samaran for the Diplôme des Hautes-Études, and it gained me the title of member of the École Française. Not that this meant going to live in the Palazzo Farnese, but at least we met together among comrades, with new degrees, Farnesians and Laureates of the Villa Medici. Once a week we gathered for a meal; the conversations revolved above all around ancient and contemporary art. I learned much and once again became aware of the subjectivity of judgments in the area of aesthetics.

At Gilson's advice, Joseph Vrin had agreed to publish my thesis, but no one had taught me how to correct drafts. More mistakes were added to those caused by the troubled circumstances in which the text was written, and then typed by a garage employee. Gilson consoled me by telling me that similar mistakes had disfigured his first *Le Thomisme.* The treatise on Jean de Paris was later re-edited. Yet even in that state it transmitted a doctrine that became current. One day, during Vatican Council II, Msgr. Carlo Colombo, a theologian for Cardinal Montini, the archbishop of Milan and soon to be pope with the name of Paul VI, told me in St. Peter's during one of the sessions: "Montini urgently needs the treatise of Jean de Paris for his ideas on collegiality. See about finding a copy for him as soon as possible." The more correct edition would then serve men of studies, and an imperfect one would serve men of the Church.

I continued to gather material on the ecclesiology of the Middle Ages, in particular on the controversies aroused by the Great Schism and on the crisis that followed it in the fourteenth and fifteenth centuries. The result was a card file of all the writings, published or unedited, that were referred to in it. I have never had occasion to use this documentation, but it was of service to others in Europe and America.

Fr. Charvin, of Ligugé, who was patiently working on his monumental edition of the general chapters of Cluny, made long visits to the Department of Manuscripts, as did Fr. Cyrille Lambot from the abbey of Maredsous, a specialist in the manuscript tradition of the sermons of St. Augustine. Fr. Lambot possessed an intensely human quality, and he would tell me about his long experience as a monk and an editor of texts. I saw him again afterwards more than once at Maredsous. He tried to interest me in patristics and also suggested a research theme to me: preaching in Africa at the time of St. Augustine. The numerous pseudo-Augustinian sermons already discovered by him and by Dom Morin were augmented by the one I found among the manuscripts. I published some of them in the *Revue bénédictine* and I created, for all of them, a card file that included the identification of authors, the classification of the anonymous ones, the dates, the biblical versions employed, the references to the liturgy. It did not remain unused: Fr. Louis Barré, in particular, took it into account in his studies on Mariology. Nonetheless, my interest spontaneously returned to the medieval texts, with a preference for those among them that spoke about the monastic life.

Since I was living it poorly, I felt the need to write about it, as a compensation. What I was uncovering in the texts was agreeing with what my convictions had always been. I again found myself faced with a dilemma. On the one hand, I had begun to work on scholastic theologians of the thirteenth and fourteenth centuries, with the plan of spending my life studying ecclesiology. On the other hand, the Benedictine writings of the eleventh and twelfth centuries concealed treasures that I regretted were not better known. I was thus hesitant, and it took a decisive conversation with Gilson to help me out of the dilemma, which I will speak of later.

From then on, thanks to him, my passage from one field of study to another was achieved. He accepted into his series of *Histoire de la spiritualité* the manuscript of a volume on Jean de Fécamp, a little-known author, whose importance in the history of love—religious and courtly—was underscored afterwards and newly brought to light on the occasion of an Italian translation of the edited text in that volume. When I told Gilson that I had transcribed an unedited text of Pierre de Celle, he asked me to make it the subject of a book, and encouraged me in every way.

At La Source, community life was tranquil. I was sometimes asked to conduct religious meditations on Sundays for some students. I also had occasion to go and help the chaplain of the jockeys at the Chantilly race course, a lively place where there were still some clandestine Englishmen. Jean Porcher had gained for me an invitation to hold some public conferences in a parish in Paris where a relative of his was a lay worker. Those texts, only available in copies, were the origin of what would become *La spiritualité du moyen âge*. For a year I was also chaplain to the senior women Guides of the Sorbonne. Other encounters were the occasion for numerous conversations centered on authors such as Baudelaire, Apollinaire, Proust, Oscar Wilde, George Bernard Shaw and the "aesthetes" of the previous generation. Many times, I heard recitations by very diverse interlocutors of the "doctrine" of *Cotydon* by Gide. The indoctrination took various forms. Soon the time of Sartre would be coming.

Thus did very different activities alternate with each other. It was also necessary to give some course or public conference at the Institut Catholique. Many people came to ask my advice, whether at La Source or in some other place — especially at the B.N., during the main meal in some small restaurant. Should a young man get married despite the prospect of separation because of the war? Above all, was it moral to allow oneself to be led off to the Service de Travail Obligatoire (STO) [compulsory labor service] in Germany and be subject to it? Or should one cross through Spain and reach the Free French Forces in North Africa? Very often I had occasion to pace up and down the galleries of the Palais Royal in early afternoon while discussing these problems that were not speculative but vital. One risked one's life every time by taking a stand on such alternatives.

This also happened whenever we would move around, whether to go into the unoccupied zone of France or to go to Belgium, where my community, driven out of Clervaux, had taken refuge. We had to secretly cross over a demarcation line and then a border, which brought about situations at times comical but that could have become tragic. Adventures of this sort obviously leave very clear memories. I went to Lyons to visit the Jesuits of Fourvière, Fr. Fontoynont, Fr. Chaillet and especially Fr. de Lubac. I happened to meet some Dominicans at *"Économie et humanisme,"* such as Fr. Loew. Fr. Chenu, whose work I had admired for many years, jokingly classified me among the representatives of feudalism, while he ranked himself within the communal movement. From Chanly in Belgium, where the Clervaux community was staying, I went to Maredsous, to Chevetogne, to Mont-César, all monasteries full of vitality. At Louvain I met Albert de Meyer and others. We traded many ideas. With regard to Dom Capelle, he has never failed to stimulate me in research from the time that I first saw him in Liège in 1931. Dom Lottin also became a fine friend.

The monastery of Chevetogne would organize sessions and "theological weeks." While participating in one of these, I grasped that many ideas that seemed attributable only to patristics, especially of the East, were found in medieval monasticism. I then improvised, along those lines, a contribution that was published in *Irénikon* under the title *"Médievisme et unionisme."* The study of monastic culture by itself took on an ecumenical significance. Fr. Hamer, a Dominican who would become the number two man at the Holy Office, invited me to develop this insight in the form of a session to be conducted at the Dominican Studium of La Sarte in Belgium. Frs. Clément Lialine and Olivier Rousseau, of Chevetogne, gave me much advice about it.

Material penury brought on spiritual hunger, to which various initiatives responded. A word that became much used was "eschatology." I had learned from Fr. Stolz that the eschatological time, that of the "last days," had begun at Pentecost. But a shift in significance had become evident: the hope in the risen Christ's victory led to defining as "eschatological" everything that this evoked. One also had to react against the idea that it was a matter of the "last things." A layman involved in liturgical renewal expressed his annoyance: "We already have enough problems with our food tickets! And now we have to think about the end of the world!"

In the midst of all this ferment of religious aspirations, some of which could lead to simplifications, could medievalism somehow be useful? The casual meeting with a friend who was going there allowed me to be present at the very first preparatory meeting for establishing the CPL, the Centre de Pastorale Liturgique. Its origins were reviewed by one of those who most steadily worked there, Msgr. Martimort. At the monastery of the Benedictine nuns of Vanves, at Ligugé and elsewhere, this group brought together people full of ideas and zest, beginning with Dom Lambert Baudouin. Early in 1943, a first congress was finally held at Vanves, in the course of which many improvements were requested that were ratified by Vatican Council II.

The privations that we suffered were compensated by artistic and cultural activities. One evening I was able to attend, seated beside Arthur Honegger, a performance of his *Roi David*; I sought to interest him in the creation of a liturgical chant, sacred and popular, like the one with which he had enriched Claudel's *Jeanne au bûcher*. Another time, the premiere of a work by Olivier Messiaen had set off a row between detractors and admirers; I defended my right to stand with the latter. The Comédie Française had put on a production of *Le soulier de satin*. Access to theaters was still prohibited to clergy, but it was known that the rules were changing. Dom Basset had asked me to reserve some seats down in a box. Now, in the first row of the house, sitting there in his cassock, was no less a personage than Fr. Doncoeur, a then well-known Jesuit. We also had the privilege of seeing the first scene twice, played by Jean-Louis Barrault, because an electrical power outage had made them halt the performance. The play was long, yet we were not among those who were saying about *Le soulier*: "Luckily there was only one shoe!"

What became the series *Sources chrétiennes* originally was supposed to be called *Sources*. The Bibliothèque Nationale was preparing the publication of a journal bearing that title, of which only one issue appeared. I informed the committee for the new patristic series about this during its first meeting, so the title *Sources chrétiennes* was adopted. The series was inaugurated with the *Life of Moses* by Gregory of Nyssa; a few days after its publication, I saw somebody reading it on the subway.

I went many times to the new Saulchoir, located in the suburbs of Paris. Sometimes in the evening I also went to attend Mass celebrated by one of the first worker-priests. The book by Abbé Godin, *France, pays de mission?* [*France, A Mission Country?*], opened all sorts of perspectives: Cardinal Suhard was informed about it all. He would say, "I know, I know," without being able to say more. At least the bond with authority was always guaranteed. Concerning more remote authorities, Fr. Godin would say, "They are the brake, while I am at the motor." And one of my confreres, when we were marveling over some of his innovations, responded, "Don't worry, the Church will come along behind." The facts confirmed this. In short, those hard years had great intensity. Life was too enthralling to be taken up by manuscripts alone, something that some scholars did not manage to grasp.

2. THE POST-WAR PERIOD

At the end of June 1945, after having finished my work on the theology manuscripts of the ancient sources, I decided to leave the B.N. I tried to rejoin my community at Chanly, but I was stopped at Avesnes, since it was not possible to cross the Belgian border. There I saw the American liberation army deploying. Such organization, such use of technology and, at the same time, such casualness and such human generosity allowed me to believe that the United States might be the bearer of a true civilization. Yet not everything was without alarm and peril. In that atmosphere of hope and seriousness I wrote, having nothing else to do, the *Spiritualité de Pierre de Celle* that Gilson had asked me to do. Regarding this "Claudel of the twelfth century," with his exuberant fantasy and his pure contemplative doctrine, all my preceding convictions came to be expressed spontaneously, and I have never changed them.

Clervaux was still uninhabitable and without a library. My new superior, Fr. Fohl, therefore sent me to Paris for the winter. I lived at La Source; there I was able to pursue some personal projects, and I continued to find many friends, some of whom were returning from imprisonment. During that time I was introduced into Freudian circles, so that I was able to converse with the president of the Société Française de Psychanalyse; another friend, a follower of Jung, had me read for the first time some of that psychologist's writings; I would come across his thought again in the United States and in Zurich, in the institute bearing his name.

A new apostolic nuncio, Roncalli by name, had just been appointed to Paris. As soon as he arrived, he asked the archbishop to acquaint him with someone who could help him in his historical research. The chancery turned to the Benedictine monastery of Paris, whose abbot asked me to visit the nuncio. This was the first time that I ever approached a person of this caliber! But I soon felt at ease. This rather loquacious peasant's son liked to speak with an open heart, something that did not help diplomatic relations in which there is always the need to pay great attention to what one is saying. Thus he was content to express himself freely with someone who was nobody. From the first day he told me that he had always been interested in historical studies, and that had led him to meet the prefect of the Biblioteca Ambrosiana in Milan, Msgr. Ratti, the future Pius XI. That pope later needed him for a delicate position, that of apostolic delegate to Sofia. Msgr. Roncalli resisted, saying that it would take him away from his studies. However, the pope responded that it was a matter of a service to the Church, and the young scholar obeyed. When he arrived in Paris, he had begun to publish the Decrees for applying the Council of Trent in the Diocese of Bergamo. This was the edition he wanted to bring to a finish and for which he hoped that someone would do the research for him at the Bibliothèque Nationale.

He never lost the awareness of his origins and would speak enthusiastically about the province and the city of Bergamo. He told me, "Bergamo is to Milan as Versailles is to Paris." And he was proud that the decrees of Trent had been applied there before St. Charles Borromeo did so in Milan. He continued to be interested in the monastery of Pontida. At times he used to walk along the embankment of the Seine, browsing in the stalls of the antiquarians' old books; when he would find some copy that came from his native province, he would be as happy as a child...until the day on which he was informed by the Secretariat of State that it is not suitable for a nuncio to walk on foot through the streets of Paris.

During that time of the cold war, a confrere who had launched what he called "the Crusade of Peace" asked me to use one of my visits to the nuncio in order to obtain from him a blessing for this project. Archbishop Roncalli interrupted me as soon as he heard the word "crusade." "Never again utter that word around me! I have come from Constantinople, and I know that the mere memory of the crusades is enough to divide Christians." Therefore I understood, when he became John XXIII, why he changed the name of the "Eucharistic Crusade" to "Eucharistic Movement."

On the day of his election as pontiff, I found a way to be present in St. Peter's Square, and to be present for the audience that some days later he granted to a few bishops, among them Bishop Suhr, the monk from Clervaux who became the bishop of Copenhagen, and whom I accompanied in the guise of secretary. It was on that very day that John XXIII put an end forever to the strange custom of having the pope change his white skullcap twenty times, as if to make that many relics of them. He refused to submit to any such practice with so much humor and energy that no one dared to present him with a skullcap. Then he came into the room where the secretaries were and said, "At one time I too accompanied my bishop as secretary, and on that account I love to be with them." And as if to demythologize the part of the Sacred Palace where he was now living, he added, "And I still recall the moment when Pope St. Pius X came out through this hole," pointing to the door to the papal apartment. Thus he did not miss a chance to poke fun at everything that was pompous and uselessly solemn, in order to start introducing greater simplicity. This is why today simple and little people regard him as having been great.

In 1976, on the occasion of the ninth centenary of the founding, in Lombardy, of the Priory of Pontida (by Cluny in 1076 and still occupied by Benedictines), a congress on monastic history was held in that monastery. A friend took advantage of the opportunity to take me on pilgrimage to Sotto il Monte, the native village of John XXIII, a few kilometers away. At Rome, I had always heard negative judgments on the part of people who worked in the Vatican offices: according to them, there was no possibility of ever canonizing Pope Roncalli. And I had just read—in an Italian religious magazine—an article by an author who was accusing him of all the evils that society and the Church had suffered in the past fifteen years. By convoking the Second Vatican Council, he had committed a mortal sin of imprudence, for which he could not be forgiven. How surprised I was, on that morning of April 25, 1977, to find Sotto il Monte filled with pilgrims, some of whom had traveled quite a distance. Many of them could be recognized by their Venetian dialect, where he had been patriarch between the end of his nunciature at Paris and his election as supreme pontiff. All those people crowded the simple country house where he was born, in the little summer residence where he would spend his vacations, in the chapel where he prayed, in the rooms in which were displayed his letters, objects that had belonged to him, gifts that he had received in his successive posts, including those from his visits to prisons in France and Rome. In Milan, in some taxis, I had already seen medals with his image, and a driver told me one day, "Imagine, once I saw him seated at table with some workers outside of a tavern!" Without doubt, he was a legendary person. But legends are born only of great men. John XXIII became the model of the priest and the prelate who can stay close to the common people. And that whole throng at Sotto il Monte venerated him as a saint of this kind. I was told that the pilgrims are just as numerous every day, and even more on the anniversaries of his death and of the important dates of his life.

The immediate postwar period held its surprises. My old teacher Louis Halphen had been threatened with deportation; the same befell Marc Bloch, who later was shot to death. Some friends had forcibly carried Halphen away from his apartment and hidden him in a Jesuit novitiate in central France. There he had read everything he could find in the library, including the medieval monastic authors. When he returned to Paris, people tried in every way to reconstitute a library for him. I often went to meet him. He was troubled by religious problems. One day I happened to say the name of Yves of Chartres in connection with some manuscript. He had resumed the editorship of the series *Classiques de l'histoire de France,* and he immediately asked me to prepare for the series an edition of the letters of that bishop of Chartres. I had no wish to do so; my interest tended toward monastic texts. But he insisted so much and his situation was so painful that I thought I could not refuse him for long. I undertook the task without passion and with minimum effort. He reviewed the whole manuscript, pen in hand. His handwriting was always difficult to read, but now that his sight was very weakened, it had not improved in clarity. Indeed, he gave typists a lot of problems. This edition was accepted into the set, with reservations but without spite. One of the reviews was nonetheless so extremely fierce that it drew signs of sympathy for me. Undoubtedly I was not made for publishing critical editions.

During the summer of 1945 I stopped at Ligugé in order to write *Pierre le Vénérable*, requested by the Éditions de Fontenelle. In the company of this abbot of Cluny, I began again to breathe freely. And this diversion would have, indirectly, unforeseeable consequences. Before recalling this new period, it is doubtless the moment for rendering homage to two teachers who, over a long period but especially in those years, left a profound impression on me.

3. MARITAIN AND GILSON

The first memory that I have of Maritain is a quote by Rimbaud in *Art et scolastique*; I can still recite it from memory:

> Delicate, but not exclusive
> His heart, rather contemplative
> Nonetheless will know the work of men.

Contemplation and humanism—this was also the theme of Maritain's little book *Religion et culture*, which intrigued our youth as Benedictine novices of the first third of the twentieth century. When we began the study of philosophy, we used his early basic teaching works such as his *Sept leçons sur l'être*. But what helped us make the synthesis between humanistic culture and the desire for God were the beautiful little books of Maritain the poet, artist and mystic. In the background there always stood Raïssa, who in those years was translating and commenting on the treatise by John of St. Thomas on *The Gifts of the Holy Spirit*. She rarely appeared in public, and this fact inspired one day an untranslatable joke: "Aujourd'hui Monsieur Maritain est venu sans sa Maritaine."

From the mid-twenties Maritain the philosopher had to take a stand in the political arena in defense of the Holy See, after the condemnation of Action Française. His book, *Pourquoi Rome a parlé*, and his other writings on this issue helped many of our generation in this time of confusion. In the thirties, while I was a student in Rome, I had the chance to meet and listen to Maritain and Gilson; they were the first two to receive (at a time when this was exceptional) a doctorate *honoris causa* from the Angelicum, renewed under Pius XI by Fr. Stanislas Gillet, the master general of the Dominicans and a quick-witted man, often seen at San Gerolamo's. In the meantime, Maritain's monumental synthesis of philosophy, theology and mysticism was published, which he entitled *Les degrés du savoir*. It was the time in which Fr. Garrigou-Lagrange had reached the peak of his prestige in the field of spirituality; he regularly came to give talks to the community at Sant'Anselmo's. To his Thomistic and Carmelite competence, Maritain also brought a literary ability that rendered his every explanation "a beautiful thing," in the sense in which Valéry referred to "the beautiful things that are in the world," and "things of beauty," as Shakespeare had written.

Then, when I was sent to study in Paris, I took some of Gilson's courses at the Collège de France. Yet I missed nothing of what Maritain had to say, before the most varied audiences, on the problems of the Church and of the world. He was *engagé* (committed), after the expression then in vogue that Mounier had launched. Still, he always remained a contemplative. One day, on the invitation card for one of the philosophical "teas" to which Raïssa and her husband regularly invited some friends at their home in Meudon, the theme of the conversation was announced in these terms: "We will talk about Angels." I was reminded of what a learned Dominican had said: "Let us take a concrete example: the Angel." Yet this did not make us forget that during those very years Jews were persecuted in Nazi Germany and then in Fascist Italy. Maritain, Peterson and my teacher and friend Anselm Stolz recalled the mystery of the Jewish people as a witness to God. Maritain never failed to be a contemplative attentive to all religious and human causes.

The Second World War came. Maritain was in the United States. After his return, his delicious little book *Réflexion sur l'Amérique* helped many of us overcome the superiority complex that many Europeans cherished toward "the American way of life." He showed us that behind that superficial appearance there were a culture and a sense of humanity that could not but develop in later decades.

I met the Maritains again in Rome when Jacques was appointed there as ambassador of France to the Holy See. In the meantime, collections of essays that he had written in America during the war were appearing. These gave him the image of a "liberal," something not pleasing to everyone in Roman circles, notorious for their ready irony. Maritain did not keep his mandate for long. Toward the end of the fifties I was nominated, along with Christine Mohrmann and a few others, to receive a doctorate *honoris causa* from the Catholic University of Milan. Maritain was on the list of proposed candidates, but his name was removed by the Sacred Congregation for studies and seminaries. When this fact was announced to a group of friends, during a dinner at the French Embassy to the Holy See, the protest was unanimous: "We must all write to Jacques to tell him of our solidarity, and to congratulate him on his missed doctorate." On the day that we received our diplomas, Archbishop Montini, just named cardinal by John XXIII, came to attend the ceremony. It was he who boldly moved to restore Maritain.

Those years of suffering and of withdrawal in solitude led him to write his last articles in *Nova et Vetera* and his last book *Sur la grâce et l'humanité de Jésus-Christ*: there he poured out the overflow of his contemplation. To his knowledge of traditional metaphysics, of Thomism and of Carmelite spirituality, he courageously added new insights, inspired by the modern psychology that he employed in a very personal way. Thus over the course of eighty years this man of God had evolved, faithful to his original convictions, enriching himself and his readers with all the resources of contemporary knowledge.

On the philosophical and political levels, he succeeded in remaining free from any pressure, regardless of where it came from, and free both in his faith and in his thought. He was even too free to receive certain forms of official recognition. I can still hear Gilson saying, "I will not enter the French Academy until Maritain has entered it." Realist that he was, Gilson grasped that he never would be admitted. His greatness was of another kind. The message that he had transmitted to us so steadily was of reconciliation between obedience of faith and freedom of thought, between contemplative attitude and disinterested service to justice and to peace among all peoples.

It has been necessary to cite Gilson with respect to Maritain because, as different as they were, these two masters were two models of the same simple faith and of the same intensity of intelligence.

With regard to St. Augustine, St. Bonaventure and all the authors whom he approached, Étienne Gilson went directly to the essential problems and mastered an immense amount of information with order and taste. After becoming a professor at the Collège de France, each year he would choose as the subject for the courses some author or new theme; this provided us, during the summers following the courses, a regular and uninterrupted series of studies on St. Anselm, St. Bernard, Abelard, Dante, Petrarch, Duns Scotus, or on the history of the idea of the City of God. He excused himself one day to state a truism: "The thirteenth century would not have existed if the twelfth had not." His need for an integral understanding of Scholasticism drove him to discover— this is the term that is used—the doctrinal density of previous authors.

The clarity, the simplicity with which he faced the most abstract problems were disconcerting, to the point of offending certain intellectuals. I was a student in Rome when he and Maritain received the first doctorates *honoris causa* from the Angelicum, restored and expanded, in the new main hall that was jammed for the occasion. The next day Gilson held a conference on "Being and Essence" before a standing room only audience in the great hall of the Palazzo della Cancelleria. One of our professors, who labored in talking about the same subject and used more complicated language, soon got up and left as a protest against such facileness in introducing a bit of clarity in a field that seemed reserved to professionals of difficult abstraction. Earlier I set down my memories of Maritain, so this is perhaps the right place to point out that these two masters, friends of one another, had the same gift of shedding light on obscure questions. Gilson had the greatest esteem for "Jacques."

During the thirties, some scholars such as Fr. Mandonnet and Dom Wilmart dedicated themselves to the inventory, the editing, and the critical study of texts of St. Thomas and of many other authors. Gilson was the thinker who, beginning with this documentary material, brought the men to life. One recalls the command in Ezekiel: "Prophesy! Make these dry bones live again!" Already a whole group of disciples and admirers—M. D. Chenu, M. M. Davy, M. T. d'Alverny and still others— were inspired by him and, when needed, reviewed by him as well. I will never forget the first course of what became his *Dante et la philosophie* in which, with the frankness that comes with friendship, he literally reduced to pieces a magnificent construction by Mandonnet on *Dante le théologien*. It was a construction based in part on the symbolism of numbers. "Now," explained Gilson, "I have revised all the calculations: the operations were mistaken." He expressed himself with a prudence matching his vigor, and his critique was accepted.

After each of his courses at the Collège de France, people would follow him to what they called the *boutique* of the Librairie Philosophique Joseph Vrin, located not far from the Place de la Sorbonne. There we were among friends and could chat. In Rome, at the College of Sant Anselmo, I had taken a course from Fr. Stolz that in part was directed against the interpretation that Gilson gave on what was called the ontological argument of St. Anselm. While some saw in it a pure exercise of dialectic with the aim of "proving" the existence of God, my old professor had maintained that the thought moved solely on the plane of spiritual experience. Gilson rightly taught that both could be a new and original form of "gnosis"—in the best sense of the word—that did not fit into clear and previously known categories. Needless to say, while allowing myself to be convinced by Gilson, I lost nothing of my admiration and thankfulness for my old teacher. Whether it were a matter of Averroism or of the notion of Christian philosophy—problems much debated at that time—an amazing combination of genius and common sense often enabled Gilson to distance himself from scholars who had surely dealt with more variations that he had. Had he not once written that one must not have a manuscript in place of a heart?

A short time later, toward the end of the forties, a discussion arose about the formula *regio dissimilitudinis*, on its possible Plotinian, Augustinian or other origins. Gilson was the one who, after participating with some Augustinians in the choral office on the feast of their patron, observed that one of the responsories contained those two words that had been recited every year without interruption during and after the Middle Ages; was there then any need to look elsewhere?

What was fascinating in Gilson, along with his sharpness, was his spirit of synthesis. He did not feel bound always to prefer one author or one system of thought over another; he selected from them all. He had equal admiration for Descartes and Scholasticism, for St. Bonaventure and St. Thomas, for St. Bernard and Abelard. He confided to me one day that, in symbolic witness to this attitude, "I gave my son three names of medieval saints: Bernard, François and Dominique." In the series that he had instituted and in his *Archives d'histoire doctrinale et littéraire du moyen âge*, he accepted volumes and articles dealing with these very diverse works and periods. He had the skill to encourage and to stimulate. So many times during our conversations he suggested that I edit some text or write some article that he would publish!

The human refinement that he maintained in the midst of all his historical research appeared in the essays that he wrote on music or on the plastic arts, on problems of psychology or on social and political current events. All were soon compiled in volumes of *Études d'art et de philosophie*, which have not lost their flavor. With widely sold books, he was happy to help his friend Vrin to finance the scholarly works, sometimes large in size, that he got him to accept into his philosophical series. And, as a sign of his gratitude, he dedicated his *Théologie mystique de saint Bernard* to Vrin. Gilson also had had difficult beginnings. After convincing Vrin to publish my thesis on *Jean de Paris et l'ecclésiologie du XIIIe siècle*, the printing of which was hampered by the war, he consoled me—as I mentioned earlier—over the fact that typographical errors remained because of poorly corrected galley proofs. Indeed, he told me, when he wrote his first *Thomisme*, all he could find for printing it was a small workshop that was poorly equipped and unaccustomed to that kind of publication. But the printing errors had not prevented the book from being read.

Allow me to recall here an encounter that had a decisive influence over all my activities after the forties. While working at the Department of Manuscripts of the Bibliothèque Nationale in Paris and finding so many unedited documents from all eras, I was uncertain about the direction I should take in my studies. Scholasticism of the thirteenth and fourteenth centuries and the ecclesiology of the fifteenth fascinated me as much as did the monasticism of the eleventh and twelfth centuries. On a day full of anxiety, I telephoned Gilson. "Come over and see me," he said. And for the whole afternoon he did not stop discussing with me some problems dealing with monastic culture. In the end, his advice was very explicit: there were already enough researchers engaged in Scholasticism. There was more need for someone to specialize in the study of the monks of antiquity. Soon, I set to work on *Jean de Fécamp* and then *Pierre de Celle*, which he put into his series of *Études d'histoire de la spiritualité*. Later, when I was able to forward to him *L'amour des lettres et le désir de Dieu*, I felt I had to assure him that without him that book would not have existed. R. W. Hunt told me one time at the Bodleian Library in Oxford, "We will never know how much we owe to Gilson." Thus it is right that those of his disciples who survive him should pay this debt of thanks to him.

In the eyes of some people he could seem, at certain times, to be difficult in character, although he never appeared so to me. I always knew him as an amiable man, capable of appreciating all good things. He honorably kept his post among the Wine-tasting Knights who met in the Cellars of Cîteaux in Dijon. In his installation speech to the French Academy, he joked a bit about the difficulty of governing people—his own—among whom every wine was matched by a suitable cheese. During the war, when there were food shortages in Paris, I happened to be able to bring to him some of the cheeses coming from my native province; tradition has traced their discovery back to the monks of the abbey of Marolles. This very human person was also a great Christian. The earliest remembrance that I have kept of him came to me from a priest who had spent summer vacation in the village of Vermenton. Every morning at Mass there was just one parishioner, who would leave the church immediately after his thanksgiving. The priest inquired about him in the village, and they told him that he was Monsieur Gilson.

Later he himself would tell me more than once about the emotion that he felt when, during the Great War, one of his comrades, who fell near him on the battlefield, asked him to hear his confession. He did not want to, but the dying man began right away, and Sergeant Gilson could do nothing but pray over him. When in the sixties I happened to stop at the Pontifical Institute of Mediaeval Studies in Toronto, where he still came regularly, I learned that everyone there who saw him had genuine veneration for him. One of them told me, "We consider him a saint."

His faith and his sense as a man explain the interest that he showed, not just for knowledge, but also just as much for holiness. This was clearly evident when he inaugurated the chair of the history of spirituality at the Institut Catholique in Paris. This was the time when, stimulated by our mutual friend André Combes, he was enthusiastic about St. Thérèse of the Child Jesus. Indeed, this medievalist was prompt to grasp, from any era, any testimony issuing from an intense participation in the mystery of Christ. The discourse that he gave that day, and that opened a new series, was both a lesson in method and a plan of life.

4. IMAGES OF ST. THÉRÈSE OF LISIEUX

In 1943 the first national session of the Center of Pastoral Liturgy (CPL) was convened in Paris. It was held at the Benedictine monastery of Vanves, but was preceded by a guided tour to the Roman frescoes in the Musée des Monuments Français, in the Palais de Chaillot. This marvelous collection of church painting of the eleventh through thirteenth centuries had been entirely renovated. I was asked to introduce it with a presentation, which was later published in the journal L'art sacré, edited by Fr. Régamey.

Prior to the Second World War, the construction of the basilica in Lisieux was completed; Cardinal Pacelli had come to consecrate it, but it still was left without any interior decoration. The decision was made after the war to correct this, with reliance upon subsidies that were not long in coming. An artist was in charge of painting frescoes on all the walls and was given complete freedom. Since he did not know what to portray, he turned to Fr. Régamey, who sent him to me. I was given the task of preparing for him an iconographic plan. A huge responsibility, which I did not want to assume alone. I asked — and my request was granted — to be helped by Msgr. Aimé G. Martimort, professor of liturgy at the Institut Catholique in Toulouse, and he accepted. We were both friends of Msgr. André Combes, who was then the foremost expert on Thérèse of Lisieux.

From my childhood, like all Catholics in the twenties, I had heard about Thérèse when she was canonized. I knew nothing more of her than some affected imagery that was widespread. During a car trip through Normandy and Brittany with my family, I had visited Lisieux. I particularly remembered the good meals washed down with cider. Nonetheless, in my secondary school there was a priest who was a bit of a poet, or a mystic—perhaps both—named Fr. Paulin Giloteaux. He had written, among other things, at least one book on Thérèse but he was not taken very seriously by his colleagues. He was the one who would clandestinely lend me, volume by volume, the *Année liturgique* of Dom Guéranger for my furtive evening reading before lights-out in the dormitory. I gathered that this little saint with her hands full of flowers must have possessed some greatness.

The iconographic plan gave me occasion to return to Lisieux, with Aimé Martimort. We examined the building together with the decorator, without meeting anyone at Carmel. It had a role at that time in Church politics as well, and we did not want to be associated with it. But from January to the end of May 1946, for five months, there was an exchange of letters, which I kept, with the Pilgrimage Administration. It all came to an end, however, mainly for practical reasons: the promised funds never came through and others did not appear. The basilica was never decorated.

Nevertheless, intense labor was accomplished in those months, which I have never regretted. We had decided that there would be no portrayal of either St. Thérèse or of her relatives in earthly life, but that images would be culled from all her writings on the Christian mystery. Martimort and I devoted ourselves, although working separately, to a careful reading of all Thérèse's works. Combes had made long visits to the Carmel of Lisieux. He had some texts in their original version, some unedited, and some photos before they were retouched. At that time a campaign was in progress to have all of this published, and the request was accepted, though not without controversy. Combes' control was for us an invaluable guarantee. He thought, as did we, that the authentic writings were enough and that there was no need to resort to interpretations that were then widespread by some circles that considered themselves authorized. Thus we worked, and it was an exciting experience. After reading all her writings with pen in hand, I wrote a long report, full of references, that served as the basis for the plan that we presented, and that I still keep. I was advised to publish it, and it remains one of my projects for my old age.

The results of our research consisted of two parts: first of all, a synthesis of Thérèse's doctrine, that took especially into account anything in it that could be portrayed; second, some proposals aimed at its spatial and iconographic transposition to the basilica's wall surfaces. It was not a question of imposing a personal interpretation of Thérèse; I was not inclined to do such, all the more because I was never involved in any controversy of this kind. One of the first spiritual retreats in which I participated at Clervaux, early in the twenties, was conducted by an intelligent theologian, Fr. Petitot. This Dominican was among those who were then taking significant parts in those discussions. From that time at Clervaux, Thérèse was much venerated by many of us, while others showed a certain reserve, not to say a skepticism. After the war, devotion to her underwent a revival. Everything would be rekindled by Combes' discoveries.

From the perspective that was proposed to me, in my contacts with Chevetogne, with patrologists and medievalists, the interest in Thérèse derived not so much from her current reality in the life of the Church as from her traditional character: for example, the great scenes that she loved to imagine were those that I had admired a short time earlier in the mosaics of Ravenna and of the Roman basilicas of the best Roman-Byzantine period. What was the explanation? Thérèse was what might be called "visual." She spontaneously represented to herself beings, personages, and even ideas in the form of images. Thérèse sees. There is in this an element of spiritual psychology that grace uses and that at times attains extraordinary visions: Thérèse sees the statue of the Virgin bending toward her; she sees her father with his face veiled. At the beginning of the fourth chapter of *The Story of a Soul* she acknowledges that she has loved images since her childhood. Indeed, in her poems and her prose, what makes the text more precious is not so much the rhythm of the phrases—although Thérèse does not lack literary ability—but rather the sureness of her gaze. Moreover, from her journey to Italy and her visit to Rome, she kept a very vivid memory of many "things seen."

But what does she see? Nature and the biblical universe or, as she herself says with expressions that, doubtlessly without her knowing to what extent, form part of the ancient and medieval spiritual tradition, the "book of nature" and the "book of life." She was marked first by the strong "impressions" made on her in childhood by flowers, birds, clouds, and the shining sun. She always lived in the city, but only a short distance from the Norman countryside, verdant and flowering, under a harsh climate. Her family's home—which bore the distinct name of "Les Buissonnets" (the little bushes)—had a garden, and people could walk around the neighborhood. Her imagination was not that of a peasant, but of a town dweller, with eyes that remained simple and with an uncomplicated spirit. Before nature she was moved like a child, and found spontaneous symbols there: many of her comparisons are inspired, not without poetry, by the seasons, snow, lightning in the sky and especially flowers, generally appearing as "little," in keeping with the diminutive employed in her home's name.

Thérèse also sees nature through the Bible. She uses many phrases that indicate landscapes, plants, animals — especially birds — that she could never have seen. She knows them, with their symbolism, through the Gospel and the Old Testament texts contained in the missal, and especially through the Song of Songs, which the liturgy and St. John of the Cross made familiar to her. Among her sources she also cites L'année liturgique of Dom Guéranger. In her a landscape, a flower or a bird immediately evokes a reality. During her childhood she noticed simple images, and her sisters explained their meanings to her. At Carmel, thanks to her readings, this imagery is broadly developed and its symbolism enriched. She sees biblical personages against their background, in the midst of active scenes in which every element speaks to her.

Thérèse spontaneously projects this evocative and creative imagination on the ideas that she has formed of the Christian mystery. She puts everything in a scene in its turn. The dominant background, in which everything begins and everything will end, is heaven. She describes very often the setting, the personages, their occupations, and above all their joy. The central personage is Christ, who is the image of the Father and who sends the Spirit. She almost always sees him as King. Around him is his court: all the choirs of angels, then all the classes of saints — the Virgin, St. Joseph, and a whole litany of others. There are some to whom she likes to go back: ancients, such as the Holy Innocents and St. Cecilia, and more recent ones, such as Joan of Arc, and the men and women saints of Carmel. An entire glorious and lovable group of people who constitute her customary company.

How does she reach them? Through the Christian "path," that is, above all, the way of Christ. She knows it and she remembers all its details, according to the Gospels; she emphasizes especially the scenes of forgiveness and certain parables. All of it indicates the road on which the Church goes to meet its King. She has a profound sense of the universality of the Church in her time: in mission lands, in priests, in the papacy. She also thinks about the unity of the Churches. The bride of Christ is queen, and she is called to share Jesus' triumph. But, like him, in some of her members she must first pass through martyrdom.

It is this global vision — truly "Catholic" — faithful to the Christian mystery that we had to try to project onto the walls, so that it might be communicated to the multitudes that would contemplate it there. In portraying the Christian message in relation to St. Thérèse, it was important to show, as far as possible, the message of St. Thérèse and, as much as we could, by following her school and through her influence, to portray it to ourselves in order to live it as she did.

The central idea, which appeared in the prologue of *The Story of a Soul*, is expressed in a psalm verse: "I will sing forever the graces of the Lord." This theme, implicit in her poems as well, illumines the vision of the Apocalypse (chaps. 5 and 7): "You have redeemed us by your blood, men of every tribe, tongue, people and nation." Hence the choice, for the vault of the apse, of a heavenly vision in which there would be, before the Lord, Mary, "the saints who have passed through the time of great tribulation," those who have merited heaven, the Holy Innocents. The triumphal arch would have formed part of the same ensemble, this time to display God's grace over the earth. On high, in the center, the redemptive cross with the "sacred wounds of mercy." On the sides, after the model of St. Mary Major, some gospel scenes among those most frequently meditated on by St. Thérèse: the prodigal son, the adulterous woman, Zacchaeus, and others. These subjects could have been done according to the simplified style of Sant'Apollinare Nuovo in Ravenna, where many of these are represented.

A second great complex consists of the cupola and the transepts. Throughout her life, St. Thérèse longed for martyrdom and for the most universal missionary apostolate. These themes were too fundamental not to occupy an important place in the iconography. Yet at the same time St. Thérèse realizes that her desires are too great: she would want every kind of death; she would want to preach through all the earth from the beginning to the end of the world...; she finds her peace only in chapters 12 and 13 of the First Letter to the Corinthians: "Aspire to the greater charisms.... If I do not have charity, I am nothing...." Charity is thus the synthesis of all her longings; it is seen by her as a fire that spreads out everywhere from the heart of the Church, that inspires the martyrs, the apostles, the doctors, and at the same time as a heavenly vision: the King and the Queen (who is the Church) have at their side the child who "loves those in combat," who "dares to gaze at the divine sun."

The view of the ceiling would then have illustrated, in a kind of symphony dominated by red, the color of flame, the scene in which as a "little child, I stand next to the royal Throne," with everything — windows, pendentives, tambours — surrounded by angels and saints, apostles and martyrs, warriors and doctors. On the transepts, the Sermon on the Mount and the Discourse after the Last Supper and, in the windows, yet more saints. On the reverse of the façade the "return from the wedding," the day on which Jesus will come in the splendor of his glory, when "everything will be revealed, the secret sacrifices," all the acts of mercy. On panels along the length of the nave would be evoked the main themes of Theresian doctrine: infancy, trust, interior trial, suffering and spiritual effort in all their forms — Jesus before Herod, with his veiled holy face, hidden but radiant. On the cornerstones, scenes of the life of Christ. In the windows of the nave, stylized symbols chosen from among the images most often mentioned by St. Thérèse: for example, lilies of the valley, roses, ears of grain, bunches of grapes, the lyre, the palm of martyrdom, the dove, the eagle, the sun. Many of these subjects would have been sculpted. For each of these there would have been set on the exergue, as far as possible, a text of the saint referring to it.

A broad theological, cosmic and evangelical vision! To have discovered it, to grasp its doctrinal consistency and poetic richness, to imagine making it perceptible to believers and perhaps to others: all this remains a lovely and inspiring memory that compensates for all the miseries that cannot help but be perceived. The message of Thérèse was resumed in that phrase from Claudel's *Jeanne au bûcher* [Joan at the Stake], with the ascendant melody with which Honegger accompanied it: "There is love, which is the strongest."

Vichy, June 24, 1984

5

The Discovery of St. Bernard

It all began with a ski trip. Up until now, not much has been said about St. Bernard because I knew nothing about him until I was thirty-five. My studies were never determined by purely historical, intellectual, or academic concerns, but by life and by problems that it brought on. At the time that I entered the novitiate, a jovial old monk taught us monastic history; he came to the dispute between the Cluniacs and St. Bernard. His classes were lively; he quoted us the most entertaining passages and caricatures in the satire that Bernard had written against Cluny. Their tone had annoyed me. I decided to read only strictly Benedictine sources. That was doubtlessly absurd, but I kept to that plan and when I discovered Jean de Fécamp, Pierre de Celle and many other representatives of traditional monasticism, I found all the elements of an authentic Benedictine spirituality.

At the beginning of 1945, the monk from Saint-Wandrille who was in charge of the *Éditions de Fontenelle* asked me to write something on Peter the Venerable for a series on "monastic figures." I went to stay for several weeks at Ligugé to read the life and works of that abbot of Cluny and the publications about him, and finally to write that volume. Once again I was satisfied by this classic, humble and complete documentation that contained a lesson within itself. A Dominican who had come to Ligugé, with whom I spoke, exclaimed, "So there is a monastic theology!" This formula went into the book and thus I closed that parenthesis.

A short time later, Fr. Cayré asked me to write on St. Bernard for a series that he was starting, entitled "The Great Mystics." While I was studying Peter the Venerable, I had discovered — or thought I had — that a sincere and profound friendship existed between him and Bernard. Moreover, I happened to read some letters that the latter had sent to Peter, and I was told that if Peter was so likable, then undoubtedly so was his friend. I then returned to Ligugé, in 1946, and once again I spent some weeks reading the *Vita* and the works of St. Bernard and the publications about him. The result was a volume about which a Benedictine friend said to me, "You have made St. Bernard more attractive. You have transformed him into a stained-glass saint." I answered him with some insolence: "I have remade St. Bernard as God would have if his work had been finished. After all," I added, "whatever is truest in human beings is what is best in them."

The following autumn, since the library at Clervaux was still not always accessible, my superior proposed that I take a sabbatical year in Switzerland during the winter, then at San Gerolamo's in Rome for the spring. The letters left there by Dom Wilmart had to be classified, and I was given the job of doing it. I then spent three months in Obwalden, at the abbey of Engelberg, founded in the twelfth century by an abbot named Frowin; he was such a great admirer of St. Bernard that he procured his writings even before they were edited. In the meantime, I learned to ski; I also took walks with a Spanish priest who was lodged in the guest wing. We became friends. One day he said to me: "You ought to visit the libraries of Spain. I will get you an invitation from Fr. Pérez de Urbel, a Benedictine who is very influential at the National Council for Scientific Research."

One day when the weather was bad, I went into the library and opened the cabinet for which the abbot had given me the key. In the first volume that I picked up, on the first page that I read, I got the impression that I was looking at authentic texts of St. Bernard, but which I absolutely had not seen in editions while I was preparing *Saint Bernard mystique*. Nonetheless, since I had not come there for that, I closed the volume, the bookcase and the library. Sometimes at night, or between snowfalls, I kept telling myself that if there were unedited texts of St. Bernard here, it would be a shame for them to remain there completely unknown. Some days before my departure, I copied them and in an article that appeared in the *Revue Mabillon* I pointed out the problems that any editor of St. Bernard would be faced with, given the fact that certain texts were still unedited, or else existed in redactions different from those that had been published. Then I again closed this parenthesis and forgot about it.

In Rome, where I wrote a book entitled *La vie parfaite* [The Perfect Life], Fr. Salmon introduced me to Fr. Matthieu Quatember, the procurator general of the Sacred Order of Cîteaux. We became friends. Originally from Sudetenland, this man—who had changed nationalities more than once—was cultured, religious, somewhat idealistic and had great plans. During the winter that followed my departure from Rome, in 1947, he wrote to ask me to undertake a critical edition of Bernard in view of the eighth centenary of the Saint's death in 1953. He had read my article on the *Inédits d'Engelberg*. I tried to dissuade him on the pretext of the difficulty of the task, of the time and resources needed to carry it out, and all the reasons that anyone would invoke in a similar situation. In the meantime, I had been invited to Paris to a UNESCO meeting on new possibilities in the field of information. An idea occurred to me: if the Church were to put to the service of its works the same means that the children of the world were putting to the service of theirs, then many things would become possible. Fr. Quatember was insistent in his letters. I brought all this to my abbot. The next day, when I went back to him, he told me that I should accept. I set conditions, most especially that of being allowed to make a journey, with a companion, of at least two years to all the libraries in Europe in order to track down all the manuscripts of St. Bernard and to microfilm those that seemed useful. This was no problem.

Since the Spanish project was taking shape, I went to spend six months in Spain. They were enchanting. I have many memories of it, nearly all pleasant. Beginning with the Benedictine priory in Madrid, I went to all the libraries of that still mysterious country, inaccessible then to foreign tourists. That gave me the chance to admire artistic and educational sites and monuments. The picturesque element was accompanied by a certain "chivalrous" flavor, the legacy of Spain's past grandeurs. My friend from Engelberg introduced me to researchers, to men of letters and of thought, in particular to Menéndez-Pidal — "Don Ramón," as he was called — with whom we met. At Barcelona Don José Vivès made us welcome. Besides the manuscripts of St. Bernard, we looked at many others.

The definitive decision that put me in charge of doing an edition of St. Bernard, came from the authority of the Order of Cîteaux. I met Fr. Quatember at a monastery in Belgium. The abbot of that house treated us kindly. One day I was asked to identify the wine that was being served to us. Although I was no connoisseur, by chance I succeeded. Immediately — we were conversing in German — Fr. Quatember exclaimed, "Das ist Quellenforschung!" ("Now that is research in sources!") And that confirmed his decision.

The time had come to undertake the journey for manuscript research. Thanks to the catalogue collections of the Bibliothèque Nationale in Paris and of the Vatican Library, thanks to the accounts of "literary journeys" and of other works of this kind, the research had been prepared. But my companion and I were also going to places where we could not tell if there would be any manuscripts. That made for an endlessly exciting hunt. We had decided to start in Italy in the springtime. Fr. Quatember had furnished us with a valise holding all the equipment for making microfilms: a high-precision cine camera, a photometer, rolls of film—a small fortune, given the postwar circumstances. The first evening, in Naples, after a work session and film shooting, we were waiting on the street for a tram in order to go and take a train to Sicily, when the valise was stolen from us. The job was done skillfully by professional thieves, and the police gave us no hope. The only result of our report was that the next day some newspapers in Naples gave fantastic versions of the episode. When we went back to the library, we were asked which of the versions was the true one. Were we really American filmmakers getting ready to make a movie about bandits in the South of Italy? Left speechless, we went up to Rome. I telephoned Fr. Quatember, who immediately replied, "I was expecting this." He decided that from then on we were to have the microfilms done by photographic services of each city or library. I wanted to thank the thief, because his incursion spared us much time and effort.

We took an airplane to Palermo and made our way back from southern Italy to Rome. Summer was coming in with its suffocating heat. We had planned an itinerary that was, so to speak, air-conditioned. Since I was invited to take part in July in a congress of Catholic university academics of the Scandinavian countries, I took advantage of it to visit the libraries of Denmark and Sweden; from there I went to England, where I rejoined my companion. During the summer months we traveled through the northern countries: Scotland, all of England, Ireland, the Netherlands, and Belgium. In the spring and the fall we went to Italy, Portugal and France. In the winter we went to countries where the heating was good: Austria, Germany, Switzerland. All this in fact took three years, which were exciting ones. Besides the surprises that the manuscripts held for us, there was also the wonder at viewing the cathedrals, palaces and monuments in which or near which the manuscripts were kept, as well as our meetings with specialists such as Professor Bischoff in Munich, Dr. Lowe in London, François Masai and the Bollandists in Brussels, and many others in many places.

Our sojourns in London, in Oxford—with R. Hunt, B. Smalley, N. Ker, R. Mynors—and in Cambridge were particularly long and enriching. There I began to develop with Dom David Knowles a friendship and an admiration that would never flag; when he retired, I went to visit him. Together we also wrote a small book. It was at Oxford that I had occasion to speak about St. Bernard for the first time in a university, before the students of Dr. Pantin. On every weekend and on all possible occasions, we naturally went to visit monasteries in every region, even to lodge in them.

All this traveling around was not very helpful to my digestive system. One day, gripped by a liver pain while on a bench in a Brussels station, I had to leave urgently to try a cure in Vichy. Since then I have remained faithful to that treatment. My sojourn in that city, where several missionaries had come to restore themselves, was the occasion for new encounters and new friendships. There I met regularly with Msgr. Baron, whom I had known as the rector of Saint-Louis des Français in Rome. Thanks to the friendship of my physician, himself a historian and bibliophile, I was able to learn about the history, literature and spirituality of thermal water cures, which led to producing an article that appeared in the *Bulletin de la Société historique et archéologique de Vichy*.

All the documentation on St. Bernard gathered during the course of our travels was classified at Clervaux, during one summer, with the collaboration of young members of our community. That allowed us to prepare a volume of *Vorstudien* (preparatory studies) that was able to be published under the title *Études sur saint Bernard et le texte de ses écrits* for the centenary celebrated in 1953. In the same year a congress was held at Dijon, the proceedings of which were entitled *Saint Bernard théologien*.

We had believed that the long series of eighty-six sermons of St. Bernard *On the Song of Songs* would be the part of his works that, because of its homogeneity, would present the least difficulty and could therefore be the first one prepared. In fact, we discovered that this work, written by Bernard over a span of eighteen years, had been the object—while he was still alive and then right after his death—of partial editions, revised and corrected many times. The manuscript tradition was quite complex. That is when I felt the anguish of the editor who hesitates in the face of different redactions of the same text. At Engelberg I had not foreseen that this task would be so toilsome. In order to examine closely some manuscripts, I had to go back to many countries: Switzerland, France and especially England. Finally, in 1957, the first volume was able to appear. Another seven would follow, up until 1977.

The work, then, went on for thirty years, and it never failed to be interesting. Given its purpose, it was based mainly on the manuscript tradition; yet even this attracted attention to all the literary aspects of Bernard's work, which were the subject of publications. Many of these were compiled in a *Recueil d'études*, of which five volumes appeared between 1962 and 1992. When Éditions de Seuil asked me for a little volume on St. Bernard for the series "Maîtres spirituels," my attention turned especially to the Saint's culture and the spiritual problems that it did not fail to pose for him. I was not prepared to work with his doctrine, nor much less with the extremely complex subject of his political role.

Nonetheless, I was in contact with all the specialists who dealt with these, among whom a high place is held by Msgr. Piero Zerbi of the Catholic University of Milan.

Ten years later, after having had occasion to work with some psychologists, I thought I was ready to attempt a first application to St. Bernard of the "psycho-historical" method. The work was reviewed by a professional psychologist with a view to an American edition. Many of the acquired or suggested results are now found in the first volume of the new translation of St. Bernard in the *Biblioteca de Autores Cristianos* (BAC), published in 1983.

As volumes of the edition were appearing, a concordance of all its words was being prepared in the Netherlands. Now it is finished. An index of biblical quotations and of terms was compiled from it, and many duplicated copies of it are circulating. It is far from being perfect, but it is widely used. It is easy to recognize the works that were used in its preparation, even on the part of those that note its limits. The bilingual editions—Latin/Italian, Latin/Spanish—which now have appeared correct the mistakes that the Latin critical edition inevitably contained, and which were compiled in a list.

Perhaps a mistake was made in placing me in charge of doing the critical edition of St. Bernard. But the mistake has been committed, and the edition is done. And it is not to be redone, even though it can be—and has been—improved by some corrections.

Just after writing the preceding, I happened to open a file folder, and there I found a letter from Gilson dated 1957, in which he says, with regard to some book or other that I had sent him: "The further I go, the less I believe in the judgment of people. Above all, I certainly do not believe in mine. A book is an act of which only the author knows the motives, the meaning and the scope and, in a word, the purpose. Moreover, once the book is printed, it is too late to talk about it. Then it is necessary to think about the next one."

Blessed is the man who has left only unimpeachable works! His reputation is assured for a quarter of a century, as A. de Meyer told me one time with respect to "those fine theses that set the state of knowledge for twenty-five years."

St. Bernard became one more friend. Once I was invited to Cambridge University to tell how the edition of St. Bernard had been "constructed." I concluded by saying that I fervently wished for the ultimate surprise, when I would meet him after death. An editor of John of Salisbury reacted to this with astonishment by saying, "I would be terrified," that is, at the very thought of meeting him.

While waiting for this, with patience and curiosity, I note gladly that many young researchers, thanks to translations done on the basis of the new edition, are progressing with research in "Bernardology." Bernard, who did not at all lack a sense of humor, must be smiling over this, and perhaps is saying those words of Scripture on which he had commented: "My secret belongs to me."

6

Vitality of Monasticism

1. ITINERARIES AND EXCHANGES

Parallel to the work on St. Bernard, I was repeatedly being asked to take up another task. Up until then, all the time I needed was available for me to read manuscripts that no one had ever read, to write books that hardly anyone would read. My gratitude could never be too great toward the institution to which I belong and to the superiors who keep watch over its functioning. Now I was being sent to share with others what I had had time to accumulate. It was the occasion for a new series of journeys to different parts of the world, beginning with Europe, about which we are talking here. The people that I encountered were never just listeners; I gained a great deal from them.

This activity started in the fifties, well before Vatican Council II, of which the texts are the result of several decades of studies, and sometimes of sufferings. The occasions varied: talks given in communities, retreats, series of meetings on St. Bernard or on monastic problems, congresses focused on religious life, assemblies of contemplatives, at the national or regional level in Belgium, France and elsewhere, general chapters; contacts with the Taizé Community, with the Anglican Benedictine Abbey of Nashdom, with the Conference of Religious of the Church of England. Also, participation in congresses of medievalists or courses to be given in some universities offered the possibility to visit different monasteries or to carry on diverse activities, as happened, for example, in the prisons of many countries, in Africa, in the United States, in Italy. Indeed, it was in an Italian prison that I met Cardinal Casaroli, who came there regularly despite all his duties, even after being named Secretary of State. The inmates of that juvenile prison could never have imagined that he was the number two man in the Catholic Church. One encounter held at the request of Fr. J. Nourissat with a group of pastoral workers in prisons gave rise to a little book, entitled *Libérez les prisonniers.*

Du Bon Larron à Jean XXIII [Free the Prisoners. From the Good Thief to John XXIII].

The activity addressed to religious took place in Italy, especially in Rome, in the Netherlands, in Portugal, in Ireland, in England, in Belgium. In France, the annual congresses on "Problems of today's woman religious" always left room in their programs for history. In Spain the Society for Monastic Studies would organize "monastic studies weeks" that dealt mainly with archaeology: it became necessary to emphasize, little by little, the permanent problems of spirituality and those of life today. Some feared that a congress of historians would turn into a spiritual retreat. In 1980, on the occasion of the fifteenth centenary of St. Benedict, meetings and conferences multiplied and culminated in a congress that closed at Montecassino. It seemed to me that the main lesson to be drawn from so many scholarly studies was that of freedom, and this was the theme of the concluding discourse that I was asked to give: St. Benedict, free with regard to everything that had preceded him, and the Benedictine tradition, free with regard to St. Benedict.

In the meantime, I did not neglect making numerous sojourns to Clervaux, where the abbot and the community helped me continually in every way possible. For two years, I was also director of the guest wing; I could do so only off and on, while still prolonging my sojourns especially during the summer. It was a very beneficial job, since it allowed me to meet wonderful people: pilgrims, participants in spiritual retreats, all kinds of seekers of God.

The public to which I was sent out was quite varied: Benedictine monks and nuns, surely, but also Trappists and Trappistines. I have never forgotten the friendship of their many monasteries — it was not understood by everyone, but this was no reason to put an end to it. Several meetings were regularly held among the Cistercians of Lérins. Moreover, there were some communities of nuns of other orders who wanted to hear talks about the contemplative life. Before writing a chapter on the Carthusians in *Histoire de la spiritualité*, I went to the Grande Chartreuse, where I learned the doctrine prevailing at that time. All this made me conclude that "monasticism" was not identified with this or that institution, but depended on a typology applicable to many of them.

A centenary — that of St. Liutger, celebrated at Essen, Germany — and a conference held at the Görresgesellschaft in Rome led me to verify the grounds for commonly held notions that had recently arisen regarding the so-called "missionary monks" of the Middle Ages. The results did not please everyone in Europe, and this did not fail to have practical consequences. Without taking sides in these small controversies, some American historians reserved their freedom of judgment.

Many of the reports that I gave were published under the form of journal articles, then compiled in volumes. They had a strong monastic stamp, and in them history strove to place itself at the service of current affairs. The two problems that were most often posed dealt on the one hand with the peculiar characteristics of monasticism as compared to other forms of religious life, and on the other with the future of monastic life or of religious life in general. This revealed a certain anxiety, in the face of which it was important to renew courage, without dissembling the effort for renewal that was being required. The events of May 1968, in France and elsewhere, stirred reflection on the role of young people in the whole evolution in progress.

All these problems of monastic affairs interested the Jesuits who edited journals such as *Études* of Paris, *Nouvelle revue théologique* of Louvain and that of the Gregorian University, and they were asking me for articles or conferences. In addition, I was teaching regularly, at first at Sant'Anselmo's, then at Lumen Vitae in Brussels, at the Gregorian and for some years at the Claretianum in Rome. During these encounters with so many young people, I often received healthy shocks from them. After one of these, my interest concentrated ever more on Christology and on its bearing on monastic problems. At an earlier time in the Gregorian, classes were taught in Latin; then they were given in Italian. There was no difference between these two modes of making oneself understood. At least, I told students, "it helps you to understand how people talked in the Middle Ages." Beginning in the sixties, these young people gave the impression of being the first ones to pose the real questions, which they were going to resolve definitively. History allowed them to become more modest, and to gain a sense of what is relative and temporary. In the eleventh or thirteenth centuries, similar questions were posed: many opinions were compared then, and the solutions given were never perfect or definitive! I did away with exams and asked each one to write "whatever he wanted about whatever he wanted." Thus each year I receive a pile of "essays," in many languages, that often fill me with admiration and sometimes with emotion because, with respect to the theme they are discussing, the students show openly and gladly the motives—personal or pastoral—for having chosen it.

During the Second Vatican Council, I had no difficulty in gaining entrance to St. Peter's. I went there every morning, at the time when the coffee bars opened, after having worked already for several hours. There I met with friends, bishops, and theologians deemed experts. It was the time in which jokes would circulate that conciliar humor had generated during conversations as evening fell. Very entertaining! It was also a way of following the movement of the "Church on its way." The atmosphere in the *aula*—the nave of St. Peter's—was one of a beautiful and intense experience of Church. In the side aisles, in corners, in the stands where observers, guests and experts were located, one could freely exchange edifying words. The final day of the last session, I walked to the end of the nave to take one last, unforgettable look at that majestic presence of Church. I do not say of "the" Church, for the Church is everywhere. But there it was represented in an action that at the same time is one of the aspects of its mystery, and is a wonderful sight. Then, as the basilica was emptying, I went to pray one last time before the Confession of St. Peter. I cherish a touching memory of the bit of assistance I was able to give at that time to Cardinal Spellman, a very powerful prelate who, especially after the rejection of his proposals on the doctrine of war, had lost any power and, at least on that occasion, any companions.

After the Council, I was part of the executive council for the application of the Constitution on the Liturgy. We were presented in an audience to Paul VI by Cardinal Lercaro. At that time the struggle was continuing between opposing tendencies that had enlivened and sometimes agitated the Council starting with its preparatory period. Yet there was no doubt about the direction in which the Church and its monasticism would advance.

2. MONASTIC IDENTITY

Two fundamental realities had to be affirmed as preliminary to the examination of particular problems: the specificity of monastic tradition and the precise content of the notion of tradition.

In the light of historical research, the identity of monasticism imposed itself in all fields of culture. First of all, obviously, in that of spirituality. Monastic life is a contemplative life: to what extent, and why? The answer necessarily implied the maintenance of a kind of pluralism—and also of a "multipluralism"—and at the same time the in-depth study of a theology of prayer, especially in its relation with the prayer of Christ "contemplating on the mountain," as Vatican Council II had defined it, echoing a long tradition. Forms of life had to be safeguarded in which the contemplative ideal had been strongly preserved over the course of centuries, especially at Cluny and in the wake of Rancé. Every stand taken in favor of some cause naturally provokes an opposition, with all its practical consequences.

This contemplative orientation of monasticism had yielded a particular way of doing theology. The phrase "monastic theology," as I have said, was suggested to me by a Dominican in 1945 and had passed into *Pierre le Vénérable*. It was used again in connection with Rupert of Deutz and others and, beginning in 1953, applied to St. Bernard and to the Cistercians. Some—few, frankly—believed that in it there lurked a prejudice toward other modes of doing theology, and they attacked it. There was no reason for prolonging a sterile debate, even at the risk that the formula be rejected by anyone wanting "to do good theology as it is done elsewhere." It was necessary simply to show the correct relation with traditional theology as a whole. This notion had been proposed for the first time in the twelfth century. Today it is broadly applied to a form of Christian knowledge that remained in favor up till the sixteenth century. Finally, it surpasses the field of history and has been resumed with regard to some orientations of contemporary theology.

This specificity of the spirituality and theology of monasticism appeared in the literature that it produced. For the purpose of making it known, and thanks to the kindness of my confrere Fr. Jean-Pierre Müller, a subseries of *Studia Anselmiana* was inaugurated with the title of *Analecta monastica*. I wrote its first two volumes, and then it was opened to other collaborators; another five volumes were published that illustrated, by means of texts and studies, the whole contribution of monasticism. Some conversations held at Sant'Anselmo's over the winter of 1955-1956, before an audience consisting of young Trappists, were the basis of the volume entitled *The Love of Learning and the Desire for God*. It seems that this too is ignored, or at least challenged, but the book has not ceased to be reprinted in various languages.

This sharing of monasticism in the Church's common culture is confirmed by the fact that Cardinal Garrone and the editors of the journal *Seminarium*, the organ of the Congregation for Catholic Education, have requested several articles on this theme for their periodical, which is destined to make its way into all the seminaries in the world.

To these approaches to monastic culture as a whole, there should be added the studies occasioned by the millennia of the foundations and the reforms of the tenth century—those of Mont-Saint-Michel, of San Pietro in Perugia, of Brogne, to say nothing of that of Mount Athos, celebrated in Venice; by eighth centenaries such as that of the abbey of Orval or of the canonization of St. Bernard; by first centenaries such as those of Maredsous, Solesmes and Belloc. Every specific study confirmed the homogeneity of a culture that was not the only valid one in the Church, but that must be acknowledged for what it has been and, if possible, kept alive. And this did not fail to be realized.

3. Tradition and Discernment

Another fundamental given, whose correct notion had to be explained, was tradition: this word is sometimes invoked to cover everything that is opposed to renewal. I do not know by what confluence of circumstances I was invited to speak on an island in the Mediterranean to some students whose fathers worked in NATO; in that organization there were representatives from all the countries. The theme that I was to examine was "tradition." With the help of an anthropologist, I did readings and studies on this subject so as to be able to show what tradition was and what it was not. The commentary on each of the terms of the definition that I offered—the past that lives in the present—was the subject of a publication on "openness to the present." The title given in the English translation was: "Tradition, an open door to the present."

If tradition is not a prolongation or imitation of the past, then it implies a discernment of what in the inheritance received from the past should be preserved and what should not. This point gave rise to a series of reports—at times given in the form of lessons before a large audience, particularly at the University of San Francisco—on the relations between "Gospel and Culture." A theme of this kind should be examined first as a whole, then in its applications in different fields and also in the forms assumed, in the course of successive ages, by the exercise of authority and obedience, or in those of commitment in the monastic life. I was glad to quote, in the introduction to a compilation of *Discours de Paul VI aux moines* [Discourses of Paul VI to Monks], a passage in which the Pope stated, at Subiaco: "Being attached to tradition does not mean being attached to the past; it means keeping an open mind toward the life and the time to come. Long for the future!... Tradition is not a museum, a cemetery, an archaeology. It is a plant that flowers again every springtime, a wellspring that continually revives."

4. Mystery and Problems

For monasticism to remain faithful to itself in a changing society, it could not avoid coming to terms with many questions and finding answers to them. Gabriel Marcel's terminology should perhaps be applied to this, when he said that "mystery" tends to "be reduced to being a problem." This was more a matter of a requirement of life itself, and vitality consisted in confronting these new necessities in order to overcome them. With regard to every question, it was important to refer to the mystery and it was necessary to have enough faith in the mystery in order to relativize the problems and not to exaggerate their importance.

They were posed with regard to observances and to major orientations, and also to secondary practices that still dealt with existence. On each one of these aspects we could write a chapter with dates, facts, names, texts, and many anecdotes. It will suffice to recall, as an example, how progress was made on one problem, and then to indicate another.

The first point on which I came to observe the necessity for a change in the continuity was that of eremitism. This was not my personal problem; I had come into the monastery to flee solitude and silence, and I have never been disappointed by community life and by the communications that it involves. But I realized that some of my confreres aspired to live as hermits. In 1937, during my year of studies in Paris, one of them asked me to help him seek advice on his vocation from a Benedictine whose books on spirituality were then considered to be the most authoritative. His response was immediately and absolutely negative: the vocation to solitude could only be an illusion, a temptation, a proof of unsociability. This is what all reasonable people were saying and writing. I could never have been able to live more than a few days in a hermitage without getting sick, as an experience of mine one day would show. Yet it is enough to observe one fact—the action of the Spirit—for apparently solid theories to crumble. Community life had been made into an absolute, the only valid form. Was that right?

In the meantime, during the war and then afterwards, vocations to eremitism had become a reality. There were indeed some hermits. It came to be known that one or another of them was living in hiding, concealed under a pseudonym, without a known address, as a dishonorable member of the great cenobitic institution. I have kept a collection of correspondence, of reports, and of plans that date back especially to the years between 1946 and 1955. Fr. Doyère, a Benedictine of Wisques, was writing in favor of the hermits. Fr. de Saint-Avit, of Solesmes, was consulted. Fr. Winandy was publishing. Dom Jean Sainsaulien opened a broad historical inquiry, sponsored by Marrou at the Sorbonne, on the history of eremitism. The first positive sign was found, after ten years of discussions and exchanges of opinion, in a brief anonymous article in *Osservatore Romano* of April 11, 1957. It provided a synthesis of all the possibilities and difficulties, with a balanced and rather favorable judgment.

The task of history was to furnish elements for discernment. Once the facts were known and acknowledged, it was necessary to elaborate a doctrine and then set a juridical statute. One of my confreres, who had transferred to the eremitical life among the Camaldolese of Monte-corona, asked me to go to the hermitage in Frascati, near Rome, to write a book on Blessed Paul Giustiniani, the founder of that Institute. I went there, but the solitude weighed so heavily upon me that I could not stay there for long; once a week, every Thursday, I went down to Rome to see my confreres at San Gerolamo's. And despite that, I was sick. In about three weeks I wrote a life of Blessed Paul that was published in 1951 under the title *Un humaniste ermite*. The following year I made another short stay in Frascati and penned a work that appeared with the title *Seul avec Dieu* [Alone with God]. Thomas Merton, by then working with the eremitical problem, came to know about it — and that was decisive for him — and wrote a preface for the American edition. The Prior General of the Camaldolese asked me to write a volume that was entitled *S. Pierre Damien ermite et homme d'Église*. Several congresses followed on the theme of eremitism. Some canonists drew up institutional plans. My con-frere and former abbot, Fr. Jacques Winandy, gathered around himself a colony of hermits in British Columbia on the Canadian Pacific coast; I went there twice. Then, little by little, the eremitical reality was accepted. This "Hermit Colony of St. John the Baptist" no longer had a reason to exist: by then — and still today — at most monasteries there was at least one hermit. Some thirty years of research, suffering and, at times, strug-gle were required to achieve a peaceful and tranquil eremitism in con-formity with tradition.

I had not wanted to become a priest. In 1927, then in 1928, when I expressed the desire to be just a monk, I was urged to drop that strange idea. I then accepted without fuss studying for the priesthood and then being ordained. But later on as, little by little, reflection by many people was deepening on what being a monk meant, the idea was advanced that this vocation sufficed by itself, just like the priestly vocation, and that therefore they could be disassociated. Since requests of this kind were becoming more frequent, Rome decreed that, before one made solemn profession, he would commit himself in writing to receive Holy Orders. Yet the idea could not be halted. I was asked by various parties to study the history of the problem and to talk about it at some conferences of theologians. Moreover it was of interest not just for monks but also for those dealing with priestly vocations, formation and function. Whether one was favorable or not to the priesthood for all monks, doctrinal or moral justifications could be found for both positions. If one was opposed, then legislation had to be modified, and that was up to the canonists.

History uncovered a variety of realizations of, and motivations for this that had been legitimate, and to explain how they came about, slowly and tardily, to recent practice and codification. The monastic vocations that dared to assert themselves as non-priestly became ever more numerous. The idea was progressing. There was resistance, skirmishes, authoritarian stands, rethinking on the part of certain circles. Nowadays in many monasteries there are monks who are not priests.

Since the beginning of the forties, the situation created by the war and the forecasts that were being advanced about the postwar period led many of us to consider the possibility of living monastic life in a less costly way than in the abbeys—often admirably—that had been built in Romanesque or Gothic style during the Romantic period, or in Baroque style where it existed. People dreamed of "monasteries of simple life": brotherhoods of lower numbers, whose forms of community life, of governance, of economy, of work, and of hospitality would better agree with the new conditions of society and of life. Some plans circulated, different publications talked about them, and the earliest attempts began to take shape. Various "rules of life" were successfully published. Forty years later, many of these groups have grown old or have disappeared; others live on or have opened the way to even newer institutes, in which this simplicity of life is joined to a solid structure. The old monasteries, for their part, are surviving honorably. This recent chapter of monastic history nourishes faith in those institutions that have "foundations" in past experience, who avail themselves of the juridical structure for mutual assistance within an order. What remains undeniable is the more lively perception of what is essential in monasticism, in relation to which the sometimes artificial, solemn and even complicated forms might develop that a recent epoch had imposed on it.

Likewise, where the dormitory had been in use only since the seventeenth century, should there be a return to the cell, more in conformity with tradition, with the requirements of recollection, with the sensitivity of our times? Moreover, could contemplative life be conducted only in the country, with a rural type of economic infrastructure? Or was monasticism in a city also justified? Everything could be said and written—and it was—for or against each of these hypotheses. History helped to determine if there was a spirituality of the cell and of urban monasticism. Both now have won the right of citizenship.

Many analogous problems continued to be posed before, during and after Vatican Council II: the exercise of authority; the practice, motivation, and role of obedience; the definitive character of profession; the consequences for prayer in the evolution of the liturgy; the new experience of time favored by today's civilization; the nature of contemporary aesthetics; the relationship between the permanent values of ascesis and the current needs of psychological development; between the "chapter of faults" and the review of one's life. In the sphere of prayer, the open horizons of modern psychology contributed to the evaluation of elements such as distraction, sleep, boredom, and this in reality was linked to ideas of monks of both Antiquity and the Middle Ages. On all these points, it was necessary to be informed about the past, attentive to the present and open to the future, all at the same time. Around 1975, in Italy, when the editors of an *Encyclopedia of the Twentieth Century* asked me to write the article "Liturgy," I specified that it should deal only with problems relating to the years 1950-2000.

Moreover, it was necessary not to deceive oneself about what was being thought, done, said and written. On the occasion of the Brussels Universal Exposition in 1958, and then during a talk held at Saint-Louis des Français in Rome, I dealt with the history of humor. It was simply a matter of showing its permanent relevance. The article in which I attempted to do this also furnished a liturgical contribution to a monastic dictionary, and that shows that the need was felt for this detachment that allows us to smile despite everything. For a *Dictionary of Spirituality* that appeared in English, one of the entries that I was asked to do was "Humor." More and more in recent years, some took delight in writing on the history of death or of fear, and this sometimes became a mode of showing that the Church, by means of fear, had sought to exercise "repression" and "control" of consciences. During a congress on death that was held in England, it was inevitable to talk about corpses, skeletons, tombs, epitaphs, the *dance macabre*, everything that was lugubrious and depressing. Books were published on the same topics. I chose to examine *La joie de mourir selon saint Bernard* [The Joy of Dying According to St. Bernard] and at the end I asked, "When will there be a symposium on the history of joy?" To my great amazement, the suggestion was well-received and a program on this theme was arranged.

Finally, one of the fields in which it became more interesting to follow the renewal is that of female monasticism. God knows how much — starting with fundamental convictions that remained sound — a discernment was needed on points that were at times important: the right of nuns to govern themselves, reasons for and forms of cloister. One day, to my great surprise, I received an invitation to the first meeting of a commission charged with preparing a document of the Holy See on the cloister of nuns. I checked to make sure that it was not a mistake, and then went to it. I was asked to prepare the plan for the doctrinal part of this decree, which I did. This text was published elsewhere, but its substance was contained in the first pages of *Venite seorsum*. This was the first time that I took part in a commission of this type; it was expected to be the last time and what followed would have confirmed this supposition. I was then totally free. It had not been foreseen that I would also be interested in the "practical norms." I did not want to miss a chance to foster a renewal, which moreover was stirring up much resistance. During a session for nuns at Ligugé, I managed to make a round trip to Rome within one day so as not to miss a meeting of that commission. I have kept an entire file on it. It was very edifying to see how they were working there. Fifteen years later, the prevailing laws were changed: nothing was able to hinder sound evolution.

Soon I was to discover in Poland new proofs of the vitality of female monasticism. It was necessary to make evident a spirituality more than rigid legislation. A large contribution was made to this by the discovery of the writings, until then unedited, of Catherine de Bar, Mother Mechtilde of the Blessed Sacrament, the foundress of the Benedictines of the same name. In them was to be found the best of the Maurist tradition, prior to the romantic parenthesis of the nineteenth century. The other Polish nuns also had a very rich past. It was important to give all of them confidence in themselves: they were no less "Benedictine" than those who had appeared two centuries later. The study of the works of the great spiritual writer, Catherine de Bar, has been for several years a source of joy for me.

Years ago, on the occasion of a congress of medievalists in Seville, I understood again how much Andalusia, along with all of Spain, had been marked by Islam. Now, it was from that same country that many of the practices and notions came that subsequently were imposed on all contemplatives. There is a discernment to be conducted on this. One session of the Spanish Society for Monastic Studies had the theme of "Female Monasticism."

With regard to the renewal in each one of these areas, the following process appeared: longings "at the base," in the men and women who are the subjects and the agents of history; resistance; a medieval research that contributed to liberating the present from certain dead weight inherited from the past, generally recent, and to elaborating a doctrine; progressive pacification; the appearance of islands of immobility; and finally, always, life would win.

In 1946 at Chevetogne, in his difficult years, Fr. Congar had told me: "We continue to work; the results, nonetheless, will be acquired." Along with his research on the manuscripts, but without doubt occasioned by and thanks to them, it was necessary to practice a "committed" medievalism: there were causes to be served, and that was not without risk from a strictly academic point of view. Besides, pure historical objectivity had been put into question by various thinkers. If one was concerned about existence, about those "existing," one would study medieval history in order to have the right to do something else. In the immense movement of ideas that has made these recent decades so fruitful, a labor of this kind on the Middle Ages was surely not important. It is difficult to judge whether it was useless. At any rate, it was exciting.

St. Paul Outside the Walls,
January 21, 1984

7

Polish Interludes

I was asked to make three sojourns to Poland, in 1975, 1979 and 1982. I would have gone back there the following year, if I had been able, and I have never ceased to be invited. Will I still have the physical strength and the courage needed to do it? These are indeed necessary (unless one is there as a tourist) if one is supposed to work there to help, and especially to encourage, the nuns and the monks. This country, more than others, does not leave people indifferent. More than elsewhere, there are causes to defend. There one is unable not to feel everywhere the flourishing of the intense and intimate life of an entire people, and not partake of it. Those three sojourns left many deep impressions in me, strong and beneficial memories. With the help of a Benedictine nun who had learned English and French perfectly during the war in a clandestine university, I was able to spend some days in thirteen monastic communities of different Orders. I went to some of them two or three times. They are scattered from north to south, from the Baltic coast to the country's southern borders, along the eastern borders and in the center; it was planned that I would visit the west on a later journey, which is yet to be taken. I also happened to visit some families, as well as the University of Lublin, where I met some historians whom I had previously known and had seen again at various congresses in Europe and in the United States. At a meeting held in Oxford, I even had to present a paper written in German by one who was refused an exit visa. From Poland I brought back photos and slides—those whose sale was authorized—and others that I got more or less clandestinely. Indeed, beyond the official Poland, which one is encouraged to admire, lies the real and profound country. This latter has also developed in these last ten years. Thus it is fitting to recall in successive order what I was able to observe in three periods of its human, political and spiritual evolution.

1. UNDER GIEREK

In this type of scattered chronicle, it is possible only to note, without great order, some general impressions and some small revealing details. Nonetheless, in these particulars, when one has not witnessed them but has heard them recounted, it is necessary to distinguish what has really happened from what the collective imagination has added to it. Indeed, a legend is already apparent: just as a clandestine press exists, so also are there anecdotes that are told to us secretly and that are modified or expanded as they make the rounds. Everyone adds something to it, more or less.

The first impression, on the whole, is that of finding oneself on an island of medieval Christianity or, at least, one different from the post-Christian societies of the West. This is the only country in the world where I see soldiers in the streets—all belonging to the people's army—lifting their caps to salute a priest. It was recommended to me to come in my habit or at least in easily recognizable clerical clothing. This secured for me, starting with the customs check at the airport, signs of respect that here do not constitute clerical privilege, but rather are a display of attachment to the Church and of protest against the imposed regime. One still sees children going into a church as they are heading to school—the atheistic school—to say a prayer. Many people, and all the children, when they come across a priest, greet him and say aloud in Polish, "Praised be Jesus Christ!"

Everywhere one immediately perceives in many conversations a certain sadness as well at the memory of the past and an irony with regard to the present situation. There is no family that did not have to suffer, that did not lose at least one of its own members during the Second World War. Many adults of today witnessed, as children, horrible scenes that marked them for the rest of their lives. "Forgiving is easy," a nun told me in alluding to letters of reconciliation exchanged by the Polish and German bishops, "forgiving is easy, but it is impossible to forget." In the cities, all sorts of monuments or commemorative plaques recall the places where atrocities occurred. On Sunday mornings people are found who were present at these scenes of cruelty and who return, on a kind of pilgrimage to the victims, to where they took place. A certain heroic atmosphere derived from this past instills courage for facing the present.

On the occasion of the centenary of Dom Guéranger, a liturgical congress was held at Krakow, in the archbishop's palace. Cardinal Wojtyla is absent, as often happens; this time he is in Rome for the meeting of the presidents of the Episcopal Conferences. The discussions take place partly in Latin. We are undoubtedly in the last country where this is possible. One of the German liturgists speaks publicly in his language for the first time, it seems, after the war. He thanks the organizers and the audience for having allowed him to do so. Yet the foreign language that the young clergy now study is English.

One unceasingly hears outbursts of discontent in the innumerable jokes mocking the enemies, past or present, of Poland. The same phenomenon occurred in Nazi Germany. Or else, again, they joke about the systems used to deceive the Communists or to get around the laws used to impose obligations that are not accepted. One hears so many witty remarks that one can neither remember all of them nor write them down. And this joy, which is profound, which is a form of hope, mitigates the sadness.

In this difficult atmosphere, a reality survives that, according to the regime's ideology, ought not to exist: monasticism. A vast congregation of Benedictine nuns has developed, beginning with one monastery, restored in the east of the country after the Lutheran reform. They maintain the same type of cloister as do the monks. The circumstances of the era of their foundation did not allow them to apply the decrees of the Council of Trent on this point; the bishops and the pontifical legates of that time acknowledged this. And since they believe in their vocation, they preserve it without the juridical and material protections that were imposed elsewhere. For example, during the apple harvest—which constitutes one of their means of surviving and of practicing charity— they go to work in their fields, located five kilometers away; they recite the office out there and eat there, and the farm people are edified at seeing the nuns work like they do. Not many are seen, as in America, driving tractors, since there are few of those. But they lead their work horses very well.

As often happened in the Middle Ages, and as still happens in certain African regions or in the Philippines, the monastery, which lies at the origin of a town, remains its center, or more exactly its heart. People go there to seek food, medical aid—although now there is a physician to provide prescriptions—help in writing a letter in Polish or in a foreign language, and above all counsel and prayers. The community inspires the whole settlement and even the region.

Elsewhere a group of women oblates—in agreement with the local pastor—dedicate themselves to the spiritual and pastoral care of a village and of the ones surrounding it. Among the other services offered by them, they embroider banners that always render great honor to those confraternities, guilds and associations which are now called trade unions. When postal employees, officially Communists, asked them to make a banner for their own category, they hid a medal of St. Benedict in a fold of the cloth. Moreover, the town clerk carries the canopy during the procession of the Blessed Sacrament. One smiles, yet there are so many circumstances that call to mind a sad past! In one community where I am lodging, they have me sing all the offices because the chaplain, a former deportee of Dachau, lost his voice there forever. In that same place a religious brother — whom the bishop has assigned to preach — reads from the pulpit a discourse by the pope. This is the only chance for the faithful to be made aware of it; the nun who has translated it is the only one to have seen its text.

The history of the monastery of the Benedictine nuns of the Blessed Sacrament in Warsaw is especially moving. In the very center of the old city there is a magnificent building in the classic French style of the seventeenth century, extremely pure, of perfect proportions, with a harmonious façade looking out on a vast square which is full of flowers in the summertime. It is all white, like new, because it has been rebuilt. It seems that the interior is not as pleasant to see or to inhabit. Indeed, except for the official buildings which are open to the public, although many façades have been rebuilt, what lies behind them has not. At the entrance to the church, as in many others, some photographs show the state of ruin to which it had been reduced by wartime bombing. The whole community of thirty-five nuns lived then in refuge in the crypt. They had brought in and taken care of a thousand wounded people, with the help of some doctors and of four priests. One day the news came that a new wave of bombers was heading toward that part of the city that looked over the Vistula River, but that there was still time, for the men and women who could or wanted to, to go and find safety elsewhere. The prioress gathered the community and explained that any of the nuns who did not feel ready to die that day were free to go. Almost all of them made the offering of their own lives, remained and were killed with all those who could not be transported. Some did not have this grace and found shelter elsewhere, while still others were buried under the rubble; some were able to be saved, pulled out through an open hole in the ruins. One of the survivors is still there, as a marvelous example of humility. After the war, the influx of vocations was such that a new foundation could be made.

There, as elsewhere, the great number of new entries brought on various problems, because the discernment of one's contemplative vocation had not been achieved with the necessary tranquillity. For the most part this world had been traumatized by what it had seen and experienced. With enduring courage distinguished by daily heroism, all these young religious dedicated themselves for thirty years to its reconstruction, in the midst of difficulties, privations and obstacles of every kind. Today many of these nuns, now adults, are physically worn out. They say that they wanted to sustain all this effort so that the following generation might avoid going through the same sufferings. Moreover, in order to earn their living and to help others poorer than themselves, they work in very harsh conditions: gardening; the making of hosts in a country where Communion is received often; starting in the fall, with a view to Christmas and New Year, the preparation of those "wafers" covered with Christian images that are exchanged among families: folklore, without doubt, but it constitutes one of the ways of preserving a Christian culture.

Despite everything, the nuns have maintained—and intend to maintain—the perpetual adoration of the Blessed Sacrament, day and night. And yet, recently, they have been told that they are not "pure Benedictines," because their tradition goes back only to the seventeenth century and they do not imitate the ones that arose in other countries at the end of the nineteenth. The first thing to do was to restore their confidence in themselves, in their own identity, in the worth of their tradition—which is that of the Maurists. The only thing that survived the bombings was a solid and marvelous double-grate of wrought iron that dates back to the seventeenth century. The whole monastery was rebuilt around it. Now the religious would prefer to do without it, but the government demands that they preserve it because of its artistic value. Anything that is religious is hindered, but there is pride in the culture inherited from that past.

A living tradition. In a monastery that now lies in the zone annexed by the Soviet Union, even today there are still Benedictine nuns. They accept novices, who from time to time gather in small groups. The Russians are unaware that they have novices. Regarding the others, they are amazed that there are still nuns when there is no longer a convent. Other examples of innovation or of courageous adaptation to completely new situations could be cited. One symbol, in the church of the Benedictines of the Blessed Sacrament, is a monument situated at the foot of a mausoleum that commemorates the thousands of victims of the bombardments. It was surely inspired by a Baroque theme and shows an angel weeping and drying his eyes with a handkerchief; above, another angel smiles and points to heaven. There was suffering. There is hope.

In what spiritual and cultural climate, if it can be so expressed, does this monasticism live and survive? The answer is complex. In the first taxi I took, upon leaving the airport, the driver explained that he had to go to Mass as far as possible from his home so as not to be noticed and risk losing his job. Gierek was then on a visit to Paris. I spoke of him as a sign of détente. "Well," he told me, "he is a French Communist going to see the others. The Soviet Communists, the ones dominating our country, are much harder, and sooner or later he will have to yield to them." Indeed, an atmosphere of non-freedom is imposing itself little by little. The only foreign newspaper that can be read is *L'Humanité* (the French Communist newspaper), sold only at the airport. Interesting, but its information is limited. Moreover, the issues are always several days out of date. One cannot buy either picture postcards or slides of any church interior, but there are some available of the Palace of Culture, located near the Russian embassy, the base from which the country is governed. The same happened — we are assured — even during the time of czarist domination.

No one believes the propaganda any longer; upon hearing grand words, everyone smiles, either covertly or overtly, depending upon whether they feel they are being watched. Still, some have to recite their "lesson." A religious, while showing a historic church, had used the word "soul." Suddenly the visitor, a ranking Soviet Army officer, tells him that the soul does not exist. On a battlefield where corpses are left for several days, everybody sees some phosphorus rising; that is the soul. And so on.

Humor is the revenge of liberty; jokes are a defensive power. Three friends are discussing where to find the earthly paradise. In France, says one: it is the only country where there are apples fine enough to provoke original sin. In England, another replies, because only there has a surgeon succeeded in removing a rib from a man. No, they conclude: it is in Russia, because they have no clothing there and believe that is paradise.

This bargaining scene is recounted: in a village, the secretary of the Communist Party asked his pastor to write him a speech for delivery at the next party meeting. "Very well," the priest answers, "provided that you carry the canopy during the procession of the Blessed Sacrament." "I will, but in that case you have to lend me the flowers for the May Day holiday."

In Gdansk, someone set fire to party headquarters, next to a church. The firefighters arrived, saved the church and let the headquarters burn.

In the same city, the monumental church of St. Bridget had been totally destroyed during the war. "Churches cannot be built in the new neighborhoods until St. Bridget's has been rebuilt," the government proclaimed, calculating that it would take about forty years. But everything was finished in four years with everyone's help.

A Polish Communist is like a radish: red on the outside, white inside. And so forth. People laugh and forget things for the moment.

Official atheism is running aground, but this is not at all halting the process of secularization coming from the West. The growing urbanization uproots country people from the soil, from their traditional roots. The desire to live "in comfort" is all the more felt the more it is denied. A bishop, speaking to me in German, remarked on the progress made by what he called "sexualism." Many look with envy on the West and adopt its fashions. For everyone in school, learning Russian is mandatory, but no one wants to learn it or speak it. Instead, English — actually, American — is always more studied. In the country, especially in the suburbs, many boys wear long hair, like the hippies of the times. However, unlike some of them who make their hair grow artificially, they simply no longer cut it.

Already some young priests have a well-groomed head of hair, "styled" as in the United States. One of the justifications that they make is that Jesus is usually represented with long hair. On the occasion of a dinner in the archbishop's palace in Krakow, for which the food was poor and meager, yet served on silver tableware bearing the coat of arms of a past archbishop, it was pointed out to me that, in their portraits, the prelates of the seventeenth and eighteenth centuries had locks of hair dangling down along their cheeks. So, always, seriousness is mingled with humor.

The whole framework — church, palace — shows that the Church has been at times proud, in all senses of the word: arrogant and perhaps haughty. Now, through humiliation, it has become humble. It has shared in the culture of times past. In the monastery of Kreskow, the sarcophagus of Bolkos II, who died in 1367, was sculpted in 1738. Perfectly represented there are the three "orders" of bygone societies: a peasant with his work tools, a knight with his shield and arms and, in the middle, a monk in prayer.

All of this past has also been a school of courage. For more than a thousand years (the millennium was celebrated in 1966), this people has struggled for national and religious independence. The Church has at times benefited and at times suffered from these vicissitudes. Catholic Austria, Orthodox Russia and Protestant Prussia quarreled over the country. One often hears talk about the triple partition of Poland, before that of Yalta. So many wars among these parts! One cannot forget that the country has at times been betrayed by Catholic powers, including that of the popes, nor can the remark by one of them in the nineteenth century that "Order rules in Warsaw" be overlooked. Nevertheless Poles, on the whole, have remained Catholic or have returned to being such, in part thanks to the Jesuits of the sixteenth and seventeenth centuries. In this work, the Benedictine nuns had an important role, through the education that they gave to the daughters of old families.

These past experiences enable many Catholics to maintain a fine freedom of judgment concerning the Vatican's religious policies. Pope Paul VI, it is said, protests against the oppression of Franco (at least that is what the mass media proclaim), but he says nothing about this or that Russian priest imprisoned for eight years for having clandestinely given the anointing of the sick to a dying woman. At Helsinki, Casaroli signs a declaration that will be used against the Church in the Eastern countries; he could have—and should have—gone there and spoken his piece without signing anything. It is quite difficult for a foreigner in transit to take into account all the facts. But if there exists at least some freedom of speech, it is among the Catholics and not the others.

The relatively high number of vocations to the priestly or monastic life poses some problems. Especially for the men, there is an element of material and social advancement, of access to activities not lacking in self-interest. Yet this is also the only way to give meaning to existence, to react against the disappointment caused by the ideology such as it is practiced. In the beginning some believed in it. Now, no. The same occurs among party members: many, it is said, are practicing but not believing Marxists; and some Christians are non-practicing believers so as to keep their jobs.

Invited to give conferences at the Catholic University of Lublin, I admired the enthusiasm there of the professors and students. This is one of the few places in the country where lay people can work on something other than "material civilization," and in groups besides. There are almost more professors than students, at least in certain faculties; their number is limited by the government to twenty for history and to four for the history of art; no one can attend classes in law. All told, there are two thousand students, compared with fifteen thousand in the state university. The group of historians is fervent and courageous. Despite the obstacles of an economic kind and despite censoring, they are extraordinarily active: they produce numerous publications, and excellent ones at that, although paper and printing authorization are obtained only for a few copies. The conviction of the teachers is matched by that of the students, even though their diplomas will not be recognized and they will find no employment. I take advantage of my status as a foreigner to put my contributions and my reports on the level of spiritual psychology. But they tell me, "So many Catholics, at times even priests, when they are in Poland, feel obliged to place themselves on the level imposed on us! Speak to us as Christians, as people of the Church! As for us, there is no question of attempting a rebellion: the Red Army would immediately come into the streets—it is already there, but hidden—like in Budapest and Prague."

A hard life! A Pole meets another one abroad, who asks him, "How is it going in Poland?" "Wonderfully well!" "How do you know that?" "By the newspapers, naturally!" In reality, one sees people lining up in front of stores, at tram stops, at taxi stations. The trains, jammed, are inadequate, although there are some first-class compartments for the privileged of the regime. At the hotel of the official tourist agency, one runs across Russians; they behave as dominators, as colonizers, and do not seek contacts. Among those who unload the tourist buses, a contrast can be observed between the generation of parents, of middle-aged adults, solid, robust and a bit uncouth, and the younger generation, frail and refined, and who imitate the West. The official guides are girls in miniskirts; the boys wear loose pants, after the Western style. In the lobby, the only two international newspapers are *Pravda* and *L'Humanité*. The room is dominated by a bar surrounded by glass walls. One customer remains seated permanently with a drink, and is looking at the public. People are being watched.

2. UNDER WOJTYLA

In 1978, the Archbishop of Krakow became Pope with the name of John Paul II. Everyone is still filled with the joyful memories that his election produced. At Rome they had told me, "The great temptation for the Poles is now pride, because one of them is pope." And I had answered, "I strongly fear that this is just your reaction as a member of the Curia." Many there are openly unhappy, disappointed and sometimes jealous. In reality, the Catholics in Poland were showing great modesty. Besides, what shouts of triumph would have been heard if the conclave had elected someone from Canada or the United States, or from any other country than Italy?

Then the new pope returned to his country on a visit. A witness told me of having seen on television—which was broadcasting the scene live—Gierek wiping away a tear with a quick move of his hand in the emotion felt at greeting the pope on his arrival. In the evening edition, prerecorded, that sequence had been removed. Nonetheless it was said that even Brezhnev had reproached him for not appearing cordial enough toward the visitor. The new pope is already a legend. People recall funny stories about his ski outings and his maneuvers around the police. One day, while he was on an excursion in hiker's clothing, he got lost in the mountains of Czechoslovakia, a little beyond the Polish border. They stopped him. "Who are you?" "The archbishop of Krakow." "And I'm the pope!" answered the guard, thinking it was a joke. "Where are your documents?" "I left them back in Krakow." They telephoned the chancery. "Where is your cardinal?" "We don't know; he has disappeared. He went on a trip to the mountains." He was identified by voice over the telephone and sent back into his country.

He often went to the Benedictine abbey of Tyniec, near Krakow. In the diocese he was called "our cardinal" or "our Uncle Karol." Now he is "our pope." On taxis there are portraits of him or small images or medals, as occurs in Italy with John XXIII. A talisman? And why not an act of faith, of trust? And the struggle continues. Yet his visit has shown to Christians the power that they constitute, and the government is compelled to take it into account. Officially nothing has changed. Concretely, many forms of resistance are reinforced. For example, clandestine publishing houses are now so numerous that it is impossible to control them.

In the churches there are signs that depict a radio station on which are shown the frequencies and the broadcast hours of the Vatican in Polish. They get interference, and a huge building is pointed out in Wroclaw in which whole teams of technicians are working on jamming Radio Vatican and Radio Free Europe. In a religious community, during the visit of the pope to the U.N., we tried to listen to his speech both in English, from different stations, and in Polish translation, from Vatican Radio. It was very toilsome. Indeed, the more we would raise the volume to hear the speaker's voice, the more the jamming would increase. Yet in the cloisters the effort is made because it is the only way to find out what the pope has said. During his speech to the U.N., on Vatican Radio every sentence uttered in English was immediately translated into Polish; at that point the jamming would become more intense. All this brought to mind the worst moments of Nazi occupation during the Second World War.

Propaganda follows its course, exploiting patriotism. I have never seen elsewhere so many war films on television or on cinema signboards. Naturally they always show the misdeeds of the Nazis and never those of the others. In the church of Kreskow a bas-relief portrays the story — or the legend — according to which sixty monks were crucified by the Hussites. The official guide explains that the abbot had them massacred because they had revolted against him. The next item is a miraculous icon. The guide says, "The monks gained a lot of money from this." Doubtlessly this is not completely wrong, but this does not prevent some tourists from making the Sign of the Cross and genuflecting. Under Nazism, a monk who was showing these works of art suggested to the SS, "It is better for you to take off your caps if you do not want to be taken for Jews; they leave their heads covered." It was here in the tenth century that the duke Wenceslaus was killed by his brother, a pagan, at his mother's instigation: before his tomb a lesson is being given on the society of the *ancien régime*.

The walls are covered with beautiful works of art. In a double series of lateral frescoes, the scenes from the life of St. Bernard correspond to those in the apse that illustrate salvation history. In the rear of the apse, a large painting was done by a drunken artist. His wife asked the abbot to give her half her husband's pay so that he would not drink it away. In revenge, the painter redid one of the figures who ever since then displays his rear end in the direction of the abbot's chair. This Baroque art is truly Catholic: the whole Church, all of history, all the saints are there, together with the elements of the cosmos. Numerous angels are flying and dancing everywhere, suspended by invisible wires. This evocation of the heavenly paradise instills joy and hope. Even in the cemetery, some angels seeking to assume a sad air fail to do so. Space, breathing room, harmonious and non-oppressive grandeur.

In this new Polish sojourn I notice that the standard of living has gone up, although without being on the level of the West; people are well clothed, especially children; red dominates, but it is Poland's national color. If it were a symbol of Communism, it would not be worn. The number of automobiles is growing. Certain foods are still lacking, such as meat and fish; much processed meat is eaten without people knowing what is in it. A taxi driver, showing me the gardens of those who can afford one near the city, tells me, "Anyone with a garden is practically a minister." A youth confides to me, "We have any pleasure we want, but the result is that we are bored." Abundance increases, and with it permissiveness and delinquency. Everyone, like elsewhere, is barricaded and guarded by watchdogs. This is the only country where I have heard it publicly acknowledged, by government employees, that there are thieves. In an airport — although one for domestic flights and not international ones, and thus not frequented by foreigners — a loudspeaker advises passengers to see to it that their baggage is locked tight before checking it in.

The two weapons of the regime, one hears repeatedly, are fear and lies. The worst thing is the lack of freedom: there is nothing else except the official ideology. Now, it is perhaps this form of persecution, that is, constraint, that stimulates Christian life. Certain officials send their children away to a distant corner of the country with a grandmother or an aunt to be baptized or to receive First Communion. This statement is passed around as coming from someone who had visited a church converted into a museum of atheism: "I went in as an atheist and I came out as a Catholic." In other places, as is known, it is worse: in East Germany, in order to become career officials, people must sign a statement committing themselves to leave the Church. Thus there are entire districts of unbaptized but believing Christians.

Someone has lent me the work by Fr. Ernest Marie de Beaulieu, OMC, entitled *Un héros de la Pologne moderne. Le père Honorat de Biala, Capucin* [A Hero of Modern Poland. Father Honorat de Biala, Capuchin] (Toulouse, 1932). The biography of this religious, who lived from 1829 to 1916, provides a remembrance of the history of Poland during the nineteenth century: the oppression of Catholics by the czars, in the name of Orthodoxy, was stronger than that by Communists today in Poland, equal to that of Christians of every confession in the Russia of our age. The systems were the same: informing, spying, deportation; Siberia was everyone's obsession. In 1892 all the religious still living were gathered into two convents so that religious life could spread from there. There was no intervention by Rome. Clandestine organizations and ordinations could not be stopped. It is incredible how Catholicism resisted for some generations the czars who wanted to unify their empire through Orthodoxy. Now the attempt is to unify it through atheism. Yet a religious told me that a Russian soldier, while visiting a church, stayed in the back of a group and before exiting, seeing that he was alone, took out from under his jacket a small medal, carefully hidden, of the Blessed Virgin that had been given to him by his grandmother.

In the immense square of Warsaw where the pope celebrated Mass, someone said to me, "Who would have thought that a cross this monumental could be lifted up here!" In Gdansk I was brought to visit a place, marked by a cross, where some workers were massacred in recent years. It is a place of ceaseless pilgrimage. Souvenirs are sold, but not the photos of this cross and the emblems of *Solidarnosc* that people distribute to each other. I show a friend two articles in *Le Monde* — which I found by chance in the airport — about a recent journey of John Paul II in Ireland.

He immediately tells me: "Oh, we know this method! If they want people to think that someone is an oppressor, they don't have to say it openly to get a reaction. They have to insinuate it. Here in one article they say that the pope's journeys are an expensive luxury. In another they denounce the fact that he pays his employees badly. So...."

One Sunday, a solemn Mass that I attend is like the ones I heard in my youth. The pews are emptier the closer they are to the altar. The men are standing in the back, even during a long sermon, even in the corridors of the entrance portico, which is Baroque, and where they neither see nor hear anything. But they are present. There is little "active participation." Nonetheless in the nave, when the Our Father is intoned through a microphone, almost everybody sings it. There is no reaction, not even a head movement when the celebrant invites them to exchange the sign of peace. A boy with a surplice stretches a cloth over the communion rail. Few come forward to receive the host—one out of ten—and they are mostly women and children. The Eucharist is accompanied by a long series of hymns, intermingled with the reading of some text. The people themselves have learned, albeit out of habit, to come and stay. The Poles have been able to keep this religious practice despite thirty-five years of atheistic propaganda. Nonetheless, there has been some renewal after the Council: the Mass is in Polish, the altar has been placed nearer the nave, the celebrant stands facing the people. It is not a liturgy after Lefebvre, but it is still that of a very clerical church, accepted by the faithful and by their pastors. The young priests are introducing change. The Lefebvre case, however, has been exploited by the mass media in order to divide Catholics and because it implies an opposition to the pope. A bishop, upon learning that I am French, is moved: "Your poor country, where all the Catholics are fighting with each other!"

Since it is still in the majority here, the Church considers it almost as a right that seminarians be dispensed from military service. They cannot believe that we have been soldiers. "The gate of paradise has to be well guarded," it is said with regard to the Russian border, very close to a city where the seminary has two hundred students. This year eighty have entered, despite the total absence of any religious teaching in the schools through which all these aspirants to the priesthood have passed. The seminaries are too small. A bishop explains to me in detail all the obstacles that must be overcome to obtain the permit for building a new one; on the pretext of repairing the roof of the old one, one, two or three floors are added. Each year the bishop ordains thirty or forty priests. One of them, who is telling me the story, had arranged to make a pilgrimage to Rome, by joining a tourist group going there by bus. At the

Hungarian border, a police officer asks, "Does anyone have any religious books?" No one answers. They search everywhere. In the young priest's pocket, they discover a breviary, still in Latin. A discussion starts, which the young woman who is the official interpreter for the Polish group puts an end to by saying, "Can't you tell that it's a pornographic book? Let it pass!"

Some monasteries have been converted into veterinary schools, some churches into youth training centers. All the communities that I go to have been moved, one or more times, since their monasteries were destroyed. Some worker priests joined with the religious for the work of reconstruction. I have the joy of passing through the Carmel where Edith Stein had been and, in another one, of meeting one of her novitiate companions. There are vocations in the active religious Orders. Theology follows Western developments, although with some lag.

One of the limitations of this Church is that it does not nourish much esteem for monastic life of the contemplative type. Not only are monks not involved in preaching or in religious teaching, but it also happens that some oppose this kind of vocation, and discourage them. It is a useful trial, since there are many among the youths and adults who are outstanding and who have all studied, taught and labored. Cardinal Wojtyla, however, understood this life.

Moreover, all feel that they must pray to be freed and must help each other so as to maintain, despite everything, the greatest interior freedom possible. Even in this field it is appropriate to apply what is called the "Gierek method." It seems that, shortly before coming to power, this benevolent mediator between the party and the people would go to factories and, to appease discontent, would say to the workers, "Comrades, help me! You will see: the situation will soon improve!" In one school, a pupil is having difficulty at the chalkboard because he does not know how to find the solution to the problem that has been posed to him. He asks the teacher, "Can I apply the Gierek method?" "Of course! He is the party secretary." The boy turns toward the class and says, "Comrades, help me!"

3. On the Eve of Repression

During the summer of 1983 I had been advised, "You will find an atmosphere of resurrection." Everything was going a bit better. For the first time I did not have to acquire local currency with dollars ahead of time and then deposit it upon arrival. I immediately went once again on pilgrimage to the three great crosses erected in Gdansk in memory of the victims of the repression. At the airport a porter took my luggage and ticket and led me ahead of the passengers in line. I confessed my bewilderment, and was told, "He saw that you were a priest, and besides you were with a nun." Then, before getting on board the airplane, I was dispensed from the weapons check on my person: another chance for officials to show their esteem for the Church in the person of a cleric and their trust in it. Someone pointed out to me some people ostentatiously holding clandestine publications that at one time they would have hidden. A provocation? It was an affirmation of a recovered freedom; but for how long? It was foreseen that within a short time the prime minister and others would be changed, yielding their posts to "hard-liners." What would then happen? Upon arriving from Gdansk in Warsaw, a police officer, alerted by a nun who was waiting for me, went personally to call a taxi for us. Small signs of a liberalization of the antireligious system.

On the general level as well the situation has improved: the rich are less rich, and there are fewer of them. The poor are less poor, and have decreased. No one any longer believes in the grand words of propaganda; not even persons in power have the courage to use them any longer. The reforms of socialism have been adopted, leaving aside the ideology. As in all these regimes, there is a bit more justice but much less liberty. Here—but perhaps this is a temporary situation—there is at the same time more justice and more liberty, thanks to the courage of Catholics, who must be grateful to the Church.

Humor is reaching its peak. "What difference is there between the United States and Poland? In the United States you can buy everything with dollars and nothing with zloties." Again: "In Poland the constitution guarantees the right to speech before you have spoken; in the United States it guarantees it to you after you have spoken."

"In England everything that is not prohibited is permitted. In Germany everything that is not permitted is prohibited. In America everything is permitted, including what is prohibited. In Russia everything is prohibited, including what is permitted."

Many of these jests are based on puns and are untranslatable. The old jokes, which circulate in entire collections, are already forgotten, and new ones are found endlessly.

As a sign of internal renewal in the Church, there are some places where the phrase "first communion" is not used, but rather "first full sharing in the Eucharist." The number of working women is still increasing. This conforms, it is said, to a plan: perhaps that of reducing the influence of the family over children? In any event, the party has provoked a spiritual reaction, a need for prayer, manifested in groups bearing names like "Light and Life" and especially "Oasis" (the latter is very widespread). This kind of renewal seems to be developing especially among boys. Atheistic propaganda and immorality are particularly preying on girls, because of the influence they will have as mothers of families. Officially the sale of vodka is limited, but in fact it is fostered: it is yet another means for "de-moralizing." However, there is now more difference between those who decide to be Christians and those who are so out of traditionalism.

After so many years of atheistic indoctrination, the faith has deepened. Marian piety has increased, even in worker environments. Between this element and the Church there was no rupture in the nineteenth century: the Church did not "lose the worker class." Thus, strikes today are accompanied by Masses, rosaries and confessions. In all of this there is something that goes beyond the means for demonstrating against the authorities. Family tradition is joined by the Church's catechetical power. Moreover, it has always had the courage—generally alone—to speak the truth. For this reason, many atheists respect its authority. The newspapers have never spoken so much about the primate of Poland as in these recent times. At Czestochowa, a tunnel was planned for profaning the countryside. The local bishop fought against the project, and he won.

A new form of ascesis has appeared: praying and singing during the interminable waiting in line outside of stores, something that normally causes much annoyance. For hours people dream of a piece of sausage, then look at it when they get near the showcase. But if, before they are served, it has all been sold, then there is disappointment and even anger. Praying constitutes a way not to lose patience and to reduce aggressiveness. Charity is inventive.

In the monasteries of various Orders, life remains hard but joyous; it is enough if someone comes from outside so that they might laugh more easily. Every visit is appreciated.

The daughter of a police colonel has entered the convent. Her father goes to get her back and lays siege to the monastery. Yet at the moment of forcing entry, the grate and the keys block his way, and so the superior has time to call the police against the police. Are the grates therefore useless? We laugh, and then we talk it over. Moreover, they are a sign, and this is undeniable in a certain culture. The grates are perhaps more significant where freedom is missing: they have always been the symbol of a free and voluntary incarceration, of an imprisonment for love.

The legacy of the past poses certain problems, such as in those places where the church of the nuns coincides with that of the parish: there can be conflict between the schedules of liturgical functions, between the chaplain and the pastor. In one monastery, where I am lodging and where there is a nun who knows the archives of the Congregation well, a nun arrives from another house. Around her abbey a vast settlement has developed. The bishop wants to take possession of the church. Now, this has been the nuns' property since the fourteenth century. The historical sources are checked: so it is. Must this right be upheld? It is discussed. I quote the First Letter of St. John. What would the Lord have thought? Does the fact that a population of twenty thousand inhabitants is now there, for whom a parish church cannot be built, persuade the nuns to yield their rights? The final decision would seem to move in that direction.

As in other countries, monastery hospitality runs the risk of being secularized. Some students come in order to get ready for exams, others come for a vacation. This very question was posed at the monastic congress in Abidjan for Africa, and was answered in the negative. Is a hospitality without prayer and without the Word of God in conformity with the Rule of St. Benedict? Is the additional effort that it costs the community—already overloaded with work—proportionate to the bit of good coming from it? At any rate, the fact that this can be discussed is a healthy sign.

In addition, the nuns and monks make an intelligent effort to translate and publish monastic texts. The abbey of Tyniec leads in all this work. Monasticism is extremely lively.

I have always refused to go to Auschwitz, left as it was during the years of horror. The king and queen of Belgium, on an official visit to Poland, went there one afternoon. By the end they were sick. The rest of their program for the day had to be canceled. Yet before my return I have the joy of meeting Prof. Génicot, who came on the occasion of giving a conference, and some Belgian artists who gave a concert. For the first time during a baggage check, a young zealous police officer begins to examine my notes that I use for my talks. The other passengers wait and smile, and during the flight they will joke about it. A second officer came up to say something in the ear of the first one. Without doubt he must have suggested to him, "Let him pass. You can tell that he is not a dangerous sort...." Small mysteries of great surveillance.

On this as on every other sojourn, at the end it was obligatory to make a pilgrimage to the sanctuary of Jasna Gora in Czestochowa. "Our Lady, show us the way!" people cry, at least inwardly, when from afar on the road they see the spire of the church, as at Chartres. And yet the access to the heart of this country is not at all easy. Czestochowa, as a sacred place, officially does not exist. Everything has been done to leave the religious aspect of this holy city in the dark: limited trains, special transports for pilgrims that stop in mid-journey, because of a lack of gasoline or a breakdown. On the roads, before the last thirty kilometers, there is no sign that bears this famous name. And when one is found, it is written in small characters, while less important localities are very visibly marked. All that can be visited there is a "cultural center for national history." A tourist leaflet provides a purely secular version of this historic place. Since the fourteenth century, iron has been mined here. In the immediate environs, a king of Hungary founded a monastery for the Order of St. Paul. The locality received then the name of "Shining Mountain," Jasna Gora. A brief mention is conceded to the icon of the Madonna. There is no allusion to the miracle wrought by her during a war against the Swedes, which preserved Poland's independence. What is supposed to be admired here is the fortress, the library, the treasury and, above all, the arsenal. All of this was saved, thanks to the Soviets, from a Nazi plan of destruction. Much importance is given to the industrial center which, now freed from capitalist exploitation, is developing without stopping: metallurgy, cotton fabrics, plastic materials. Additions have been a polytechnic school, an academy of economic sciences and another for agriculture. Also, there is a theater and a philharmonic orchestra.

People come here for something else or, rather, for Someone else. For the first time are seen not just some buses of the official tourist agency, but also those of the transport enterprises that have put them at the disposal of *Solidarnosc*. Up until now it was impossible to buy picture postcards and slides that did not show the arsenal or the other tourist curiosities. Now, for the first time, the Primate has secured the rights for images of the sanctuary and of the pilgrimages to be sold in a separate secluded shop, but one accessible when discovered. In this city, officially with a permit to build a granary, some cells have been built for nuns. In three different chapels Masses are celebrated, communion is given, sermons are heard, hymns sung, confessions heard, flowers are carried to the sacred statues. Some people are sitting on the ground, others are kneeling or prostrate. There are people of every age: elderly, adults, children; many young people. The atmosphere draws people in. We are at the vigil of the solemn Marian celebrations held on August 28 every year. Gypsies are present—coming especially from the north of the country, where they are numerous—evoking their legends. One of these recounts that when Jesus was taken down from the cross, a gypsy stole one of the nails of the crucifixion. From that day they have had the right to steal. A rich country, in which faith and folklore are so joined.

What for me remains unbearable in Poland is the lack of liberty, and especially of information. Between Jasna Gora and Warsaw I get off at the airport and board a plane bound for Frankfurt. I am invited to return, but this time the request is, "Prepare for us now a message of consolation."

Vichy, July 7, 1984

Part Two

Memories from Overseas

8

Listening to America

1. INVITATION TO TRAVEL

Lent 1992. Once again I am devoting my efforts, since I have been asked to do so, to that special task of writing the Memoirs that I interrupted eight years ago. My aim is not to tell everything that has happened to me, or rather that has been given to me, nor all the anecdotes that have embellished this period; rather, it is to present the aspects of the mystery of the Church that emerge with regard to the problems of the Church itself and of monasticism. These new pages tell especially about some journeys, and this perhaps deserves a preliminary explanation.

In reality, the reason I was invited, by different people, to give such an account seems to derive from the contradiction that exists between the monastic ideal that I have exalted — that of a contemplative life — and the fact that I have traveled a great deal. I was introduced once, at the University of Tasmania in the south of Australia, as "the most traveled monk in history." The Dean of Theology at the Southern Baptist Seminary of Louisville, Kentucky, introduced me with these words: "I call him Abbot 707," since that was the number of a Boeing jet at the time. Recently an oblate of our monastery, who had been a sales representative for a large industrial concern, said to me, "I have traveled a lot, and have been in forty-five countries." It had never occurred to me to do a similar calculation. But a short time later, in a free moment, I tried to count my journeys, descending mentally from north to south of the coasts of the Pacific, the Atlantic and the continents, and I ended at fifty-five. I then happened to learn that an association exists of those — not very numerous, it seems, and generally diplomats — who have traveled to more than fifty countries.

I admit that this kind of contradiction between my ideal and its realization might cause some scandal and require me to explain myself. To state it in a few words, I would say it is due to abandonment to Divine Providence. This in turn is a phrase that may need explaining.

My first journey goes back to the years of early childhood. In 1914, while my father was a prisoner of war and later at the front, my mother and we four children were in the North of France, which was then occupied by the Germans and subject to very grave food restrictions and to disturbing alarms. Our health suffered from this. Through the Red Cross, I believe, my mother arranged, during the winter of 1915-1916 — which was very harsh — for us to go to "free France," as it was called. Avesnes is about 200 kilometers from Paris, but we were separated from it by the front. We had to travel around it, as I mentioned earlier. It involved a trip of eight days and eight nights on a train of refugees, through Belgium, the Netherlands, Germany, Switzerland and France, until we reached Paris. We lived miserably both there and, later, as wandering refugees between Lourdes in the Pyrenees and Normandy on the shores of the English Channel.

The consequence of all this for me was that my health was frail. When I was a postulant at Clervaux, I was always afraid that they would send me home for that reason. But they were kind and, to free me from that anxiety, the father master of novices had me read the work by a Trappist abbot, Dom Vital Lehodey, on *Le saint abandon* [*Holy Abandonment*]. This book left an indelible impression in me and since then I have never failed to let myself be guided by Divine Providence, since I felt that I was dispensed from all efforts in regard to how to direct my life. So it was, also, in 1959.

In that year I was invited to go to the United States, by chance and perhaps by mistake, but in any event by Providence. I had long dreamed about the United States without thinking that I would ever go there. In 1924, a delegation of Americans came to Avesnes to dedicate a monument to "Jesse de Forest and his companions, founders of New York." I kept the souvenir program from those festivities which included the speeches that were given. This French-speaking Avesnes Huguenot from Hainaut, who had lived under the domination of Catholic Spain, organized an expedition that departed from Amsterdam and founded a village that was called New Amsterdam before it got the name New York. This bond between Avesnes and New York was, undoubtedly, advantageous — after the wars of 1918 and 1945, the Jesse de Forest Committee helped to rebuild everything that had been destroyed in my home town. I had never imagined that I would be able to return the visit. But I understood why when, one day in California, I came across a long truck on which was written, "De Forest, The First America's Family." And in different university libraries I happened to find some works of one or another illustrious member of this family.

Now, in 1959 the Benedictine nuns of the United States had decided to create a "Benedictine Institute of Sacred Theology" (BIST). They had organized a summer session, with the program already planned. An eminent theologian from Sant'Anselmo's, Fr. Cipriano Vagaggini, was invited. He had accepted and prepared for his conference. Shortly before his departure, however, he had to undergo an operation. By chance, a young American religious had insisted on having the text of a talk that I had given in Rome published in the journal *Worship*. The directors of BIST had read this article and so came up with the idea of having me replace Fr. Vagaggini but I was already committed to speak in Paris at a meeting on "Separation from the World." No sooner did I finish that conference than I took the first flight to New York. From there a Benedictine oblate, who became a fine friend, took me to various monasteries. Then I left for St. Benedict's Convent, near the abbey in Collegeville, Minnesota. I spoke American English badly: when I would say "penance," the nuns understood it as "peanuts"; when I wanted to say "to weep," they heard it as "to sweep." Despite everything, the result was that I was invited to the next session of BIST the following year. And since then I have returned to the United States and Canada one, two or three times a year. I already had many friends there, and came to know many more religious, monastic, university and ecumenical settings throughout the States. I discovered this world, so vast and so varied, with wonder.

On the occasion of the first session of BIST, I had improvised a series of conferences on a theme that was dear to me since youth: friendship. The very positive idea that I had of it was confirmed everywhere. Recently I had occasion to make it the subject of a publication, in the United States and Canada. In these two countries some friends arranged all my travel for me. The articles that they asked me to write fell into three categories. I had left to serve a monastic cause. Yet soon other situations arose which made it necessary for me to take part in them. At the same time there were universities and many religious groups that began to multiply.

2. MONASTICISM IN MOVEMENT

The Benedictine life is widespread in the United States including both monks and nuns. So as not to have to repeat the words "monks" and "nuns" each time when I was speaking of one or the other, I soon developed the habit of designating them both with an inclusive neologism: "nunks." This referred to whatever is common to the vocation of them all. After teaching at the summer course of BIST, at St. Benedict's Convent, I was invited to preach the spiritual exercises at the nearby abbey, St. John's at Collegeville, which constituted the most numerous community of the entire Benedictine federation, with its four hundred members. For one week those who were usually away for reasons of ministry, teaching, or study returned to the abbey while others went to take their place. The exercises, in double sessions, thus lasted two weeks. I do not believe that they were very successful because of my difficulty in expressing myself before those vast audiences following upon one another, mostly in sites that were in the midst of being remodeled. Indeed, the part of the building that had been rebuilt in the nineteenth century in the Neo-Gothic style was then being replaced, little by little, with construction of a rather innovative kind, which did not fail to stir up some debate. For example, when a large statue of St. John the Baptist was lifted out of its crate, it caused so much astonishment in many of the older monks that it had to be put back temporarily in its covering. Now it adorns the baptistery of that extremely functional church.

In Minnesota they were kind enough to help me travel and visit the neighboring states, particularly the Indians; there were some villages of Algonquins in South Dakota. I had the opportunity to meet others, of different tribes, in many states, and this would one day facilitate my encounter with some of them on the occasion of inter-religious meetings.

Soon I was called to give conferences, meetings, and exercises to Benedictine communities, both traditional and of the newer type, which seemed very promising. I was in contact especially with Fr. Damasus Winzen, the founder of Mount Saviour, and with Fr. Leo Rudlof, of Weston Priory. I was also introduced to the monastery of the Benedictine nuns of Regina Laudis in Connecticut and I preached a retreat there. Later, like others, I would be excluded from this.

Ever since my first sojourn in the United States, I have been able to visit the Trappist community at Gethsemani, because of the connections that, for some time, had bound me to Thomas Merton. Later I was to visit all of the Trappist abbeys in the country. Because of the fruitful influence wielded by Merton's writings, the influx of vocations forced them to make new foundations. I always had cordial relations with the abbot of Gethsemani, Dom James Fox. It happened that they became a bit strained, but we remained friendly throughout his long abbacy. He continued to write to me afterwards with cheer and warmth. Merton was an exceptionally intelligent and cultured man, full of ideas, the foreseer of the renewal that his Order, perhaps more than others, needed in the fifties. His convictions in an early period came up against some opposition.

But Dom Flavian Burns, successor to Dom James, acknowledged later that Merton had had an important role, thanks to his influence over many novices, whom he had formed and who even became abbots, taking part in General Chapters. All this has been the subject of many publications.

I returned to Gethsemani once a year, from 1959 until the year that Merton died, that is, in 1968. Certain heralds of public opinion held me responsible for the disappearance of this great man, because I had suggested that he be invited to Bangkok, where he was accidentally electrocuted. Dom Flavian, however, made me promise that I would continue to come. I would also visit monasteries of Trappistines as well as Trappists.

The welcome was warm both in Catholic Benedictine monasteries and in the Anglican abbey of Three Rivers, Michigan. Contemplatives of every Order were in full renewal. I would also take part in two sessions of the Union of Contemplative Religious of the United States, and of those of Canada, then at meetings of the Carmelite nuns, especially at the Carmel of Reno, Nevada and of Roxbury near Boston.

At the Boston Carmel, young artists from the Opera and Theater Consortium of Boston had come to get information about the habits to be worn and the necessary demeanor to adopt in order to stage the *Dialogue of the Carmelites* by Bernanos, with music by Francis Poulenc. By way of thanks they came, on a day when I was there, to give a performance of it for the nuns in their chapel. They truly had entered into their roles.

The Carmel of Indianapolis, in the capital of Indiana, was built in the twenties by a very wealthy agnostic, a lover of medieval ruins. He wanted to leave a monument to posterity. He sent an architect to Avila to study the walls and to reproduce them, which he successfully reduced, for the Carmelites. When the building was constructed, the Depression came, because of which, it is said, the Maecenas committed suicide.

The Carmel of Baltimore is the oldest in the United States. A community expelled from England because of the Reformation, it took refuge in Flanders and was expelled again by Napoleon. It then took refuge in the city of Baltimore, still keeping its archives: in them there are documents in old English, French, Flemish and American English. During the early American period, the religious earned their living in the tobacco trade. One of the nuns had, as part of her dowry, a black slave with his family. When the Carmel had to be moved, leaving the slave on the plantation, great care was taken that his son, David, should receive a Catholic education. There is touching correspondence witnessing to this.

One of the problems under discussion at that time was that of the cloister. Since I was involved in the preparation of the document *Venite seorsum*, I was invited to participate in the debates. On the whole, the evolution of this observance and others was accomplished in a balanced way, except in some circumstances where an attitude prevailed either of rejection of everything that had come before or of preservation of forms that had been invented under the influence of various cultures, especially Islamic, that had passed through Spain. History helped to discern what constituted authentic tradition between innovation and immobility. The atmosphere of all these encounters was filled with real and joyful fervor.

One of these sessions left me with a special memory. It was held at the Trappist community of Oka, Quebec in 1971. I was one of the last to arrive. All the men and women were stunned: "What? You're alive? We thought you were dead. Masses were celebrated for you and a funeral oration was given as well." The illustrious Belgian writer, Msgr. Jacques Leclercq, had departed this world a short time before; the initial of his first name, the same as mine, had caused the mistake on the computer terminals of press agencies. I have a letter from an abbess telling another about my passing. But since it was only an anticipation, I was able to participate in the work. One afternoon, we went to meet some thirty youths from Quebec, who termed themselves ex-Christians, gathered around the venerable Rimpoché, a Tibetan Buddhist. Seated on the floor, with crossed legs, they offered *putjas* (sacrifices) and continuously repeated, "Nothingness! Nothingness!" We felt sorry for them and returned to Oka to talk about God.

Evolution continued its course in many areas. At Cuernavaca, Mexico, Fr. Grégoire Lemercier invited the monks of his Benedictine community to undergo psychoanalysis. This aroused much animated controversy. The initiative failed and Lemercier acknowledged that this method was not generally applicable. I spent a week with him; I saw him again in Rome during the Council and I had yet another occasion to speak with him at Cuernavaca some months before his death in 1989.

During the sixties, Fr. Winandy welcomed to his hermitage, in British Columbia on the Canadian Pacific coast, some monks who wanted to lead a solitary life, while the institution to which they belonged was not allowing it. I made a brief and useful visit to him and his colony, some members of which I had known well some time before. He was backed by the bishop of his diocese, Bishop De Roo, whom I saw again at the Council. Then, little by little, after eremitism had recovered its traditional place in Benedictine and Cistercian monasticism, this provisional institute lost its reason for being and Fr. Winandy went to pursue his hermit's life in Belgium, where he still resides.

Finally, an organization was created parallel to the one that existed in Europe under the name of DIM (Inter-Monastery Dialogue). It took the name that showed its purpose: NABEWD (North American Benedictine East-West Dialogue). The secretariat was entrusted to Sister Pascaline Coff and its central office was located in Sand Springs, Oklahoma, where I stayed more than once. All these efforts give testimony to an intense vitality.

The welcome I received was cordial everywhere. Since I have never been anyone's superior, and therefore was making a visit without being an ecclesiastical visitor, I was invited and welcomed as brother and friend. In the airports of New York and of other American cities, as in Europe, I lived in what I called an "airport cloister," within which I could make stopovers between flights in a religious context. I keep a special remembrance of the Poor Clares in the Bronx, near Kennedy and La Guardia airports, for having offered me this service so often. Such contacts with monastic and religious settings nonetheless constitute only a part of those that I had in North America.

3. MEDIEVALISM IN THE UNITED STATES AND CANADA

I had just arrived in the United States when some friends introduced me to several universities. The first one I was to speak at was Fordham in New York. Soon after, I met again at Harvard Giles Constable, whom I had known in England at the time when he was a student of Dom David Knowles, a historian of monasticism at Cambridge. He had come to meet me at Clervaux, and I stayed in contact with him as with many other former students of Knowles, such as C. Brooke and B. Hamilton. Constable and I had a common friend: Peter the Venerable. He in fact was working on the critical edition of the abbot's letters. He loved Cluny.

The first time that I went to Harvard to give a conference, a journalist was waiting for me at the airport for an interview. The first question he asked me was this: "What is the best century in history?" I answered without hesitation, "Our own." The whole order of the questions that he had prepared was upset. "Why?" he asked me. "Because historically, from the point of view of the facts, I do not believe that our century is worse than the preceding ones, and because, theologically, ours is the only time that God gives to us and that we ought to render to him, after seeking to improve it."

Thereafter I had other occasions to return to Harvard, and then to go to numerous universities in the States, from Burlington, Vermont, to Yale, Princeton, Rutgers and others in the Northeast, out to Los Angeles and to other campuses of the University of California in the Southwest. I was at the University of Washington on the day that the Soviet missiles were installed in Cuba. I had to give a conference there, to which the ambassador of Luxembourg had also been invited. At the last moment, he telephoned to say that, like all the chancelleries, he was in a state of alert, on the watch for a possible war. That same evening on the airplane returning to Rome, where the Council was beginning, I made the acquaintance of Raymond Brown, the great biblical scholar.

At the universities, depending on the situation, one or more courses were to be given, and sometimes I was a visiting professor for several weeks, as at Santa Barbara in California and at the State University of New York (SUNY) at Binghamton. There were also extension courses that consisted in accompanying students to Assisi or Florence. At Toronto the memory of Gilson, the founder of the Pontifical Institute for Mediaeval Studies, was evoked. The themes in question were at times religious, as at the University of Dayton, which specialized in Marian studies, or at Notre Dame in Indiana, where Christine Mohrmann and Father Louis Bouyer, long before Vatican Council II, had renewed studies on the liturgy. At the University of Dallas in Texas, ecumenical dialogues were being conducted with Orthodox and Protestant professors.

Some "festivals of medieval studies" had an extraordinarily large audience, although not as large a group as the spectators present for the annual football game between, for example, the team of the University of Tennessee and that of the University of Alabama. During classes, student rallies could be heard shouting, "Beat Bama!" Nonetheless, a certain public did exist that was interested in the Middle Ages and especially in its religious history. Indeed, one of the aspects of the culture that was uncovered in this country was that an agreement existed between the various data of knowledge—religious and profane—and the different religious confessions. At Chicago, after a talk at the Divinity School with theology students of different beliefs, I met an expert in the comparative history of religions, Mircea Eliade. After dining in a Chinese restaurant, we passed through a pagoda. He was very skilled in making parallels between elements of different traditions and would put his knowledge to the service of current causes: he had a lively interest in the encounters that were taking place among Christian, Hindu and Buddhist monasticisms and loved to keep informed about recent developments in this field.

Current problems were reflected in medieval studies. An allusion to what could be called an "unlucky victory" – a phrase of St. Bernard – if won at the price of unjust violence, was easily referable to the Vietnam War. Beginning with the sixties, the promotion of women – later at times transformed into what could be called "hyper-femininity" – began to stimulate research that later only multiplied. This happened especially at Barnard College of Columbia University in New York, which was limited to women.

A great interest in spirituality was nourished. In this field Ewert Cousins and Bernard McGinn, among others, initiated a wide array of publications: encyclopedias of spiritualities of the whole world, editions and translations in the series "The Classics of Western Spirituality," for which I was asked to write the introduction to the first volume, dedicated to Julian of Norwich. The great mystics of the fourteenth century and afterwards attracted the greatest attention, inasmuch as it was not necessary to know Latin to study them. Nonetheless, there existed in New York an Institute of Medieval Studies where Latin was taught in Latin. Everything there was medieval: plays, food, even Bishop's Whisky, an old brand brought in from Scotland.

The renewal of religious and monastic life took advantage of this research. At a time when there was the temptation to "liquidate" all the past, the recourse to history could help to discern what was possible to preserve. In a university run by religious, when I met the rector, he told me this anecdote: "A colleague, who had come to see me, was stunned that I had a dog. Yes, I told him, I bought a dog because, now that 'obedience by mutual consent' has been invented, I want at least somebody in this house to obey me." At the University of San Francisco, the whole problem of the relations between religions and cultures was to be explored during the course of an entire session, with particular applications to practices of monastic and religious life. At the congress of the American Academy of Religions, at Dallas and elsewhere, monasticism had an officially recognized place.

There were encounters with Jewish scholars at Dumbarton Oaks and elsewhere. One day, I was touched to see the surprise of an old rabbi, who had suffered greatly during the war, when he learned that the medieval monastic interpretation of the Song of Songs could be considered related to the Talmudic tradition. Beryl Smalley, in whose presence I had discussed this at Oxford, had encouraged me to follow this line of study.

Interdisciplinary studies went hand in hand with interreligious research. In particular, the utilization of various methods of psychology seemed to impose itself in the field of history. One especially heard much talk about Jung, and an American student of mine invited me for a brief sojourn with him at the Carl Jung Institute in Zurich, where I had useful conversations and was able to admire the vast documentary material that this scientist had compiled, drawing upon art, literature, imagery and archetypes of numerous cultures. Freud was certainly not unknown there. Rogers still had followers. Many were inspired by the Englishman Winnicott. All these scientific resources were at times applied to historical personages of recent times. With regard to the Middle Ages, I undertook an essay that I was asked to publish in *Speculum*, the journal of the American Medieval Academy. In the meantime I had been engaged for several years in the post of guiding a practical seminar at the Institute for Religious Psychology, recently founded at the Gregorian University in Rome. There we sought to interpret medieval texts according to the most recent methods. The participants were few in number, something obligatory for this discipline, but they came from many parts of the world, and many of them had already practiced their psychological competence in their own countries. They belonged to different schools. Some friends, who had been trained in Paris and Brussels, also collaborated with me.

Thus I had the chance to frequent various settings. Nonetheless from 1970 until about 1985, while I was teaching during the first winter semester at the Gregorian in Rome, I was asked to teach the summer course of theology at Fordham University. Shortly afterwards another university, Cornell, decided to establish, for the first time in its history, a "chair of Catholic doctrine." I was advised to accept it and so I did, until I learned that I would also have to examine, along with other topics, problems of contemporary bioethics, and this was enough to discourage me. The chair was awarded to Charles Curran, the moral expert.

Interdisciplinary studies were also spreading outside of America. Everything began when a group of American physicians asked to meet with historians. The meeting was set up and took place in Seville, at the Hotel Alfonso XIII, so named because it had been inaugurated by the Spanish king bearing that name. It was located very near the Alhambra. One afternoon I took two of the participants—an Episcopalian and an American Muslim of Iranian origin—to a monastery of nuns, situated on a beautiful square, where I was well known; we were received with all Oriental grace.

Spain had fascinated me since my childhood. When at about the age of thirteen I read *Le Cid* by Corneille, I was impressed by the chivalrous glory and the beauty of that country. Some years ago, when a session of the American Medieval Academy was scheduled in Albuquerque, New Mexico, I was invited to speak on a Hispanic theme, given the historical background of that state. Since the general theme was hermeneutics, I had elected to show in the treatise of St. Bernard to the Templars and in the *Cantar del mio Cid* two different models of interpretation of the same phenomenon, namely chivalry. Soon afterwards, another congress was held in Burgos, the city of El Cid, where I was to speak on the same topic, but from a different viewpoint. And, in 1990, I also had to go again to Galicia and Catalonia on the occasion of the "year of St. Bernard." These, I think, were my *ultima verba*. Thus did I spend my time. Finally, St. Anselm's Abbey, in New Hampshire, invited me in 1989 to award me a medal, as is done for old soldiers. As I was returning, this same medal, which was in a metal case that I had put into my suitcase, made the metal detector at the airport in London suspect a bomb, and it set off an alarm.

A special mention is due to Western Michigan University, in Kalamazoo. My first visit there occurred in an unexpected way. Not long before, Professor Sommerfeldt, the president of the Medieval Institute, had organized an annual congress of medieval studies to take place there at the beginning of May. It had not occurred to me to participate in it. One year, as I was traveling from a Trappist abbey in Oregon, on the Pacific, to another one in South Carolina, Sommerfeldt got me to make a detour and stay with him. *L'amour des lettres et le désir de Dieu* had been translated. I had just discovered, at a book and magazine stand in the Cleveland airport, that it was being distributed in a pocket edition at the price of sixty cents, thus less than a dollar. For my conference, added to the congress's program, the audience had to move to a larger auditorium than the one scheduled. From that time I would return every year for these congresses which became ever more crowded, until it now includes over two thousand participants. There too everything "tasted" medieval: science, art, folklore. Some spirited students, members of the Society for Creative Anachronism, simulated tournaments with horses, armor and swords.

Religion naturally found a place there with full scope, according to the organizers' desires, especially of the presidents, first Sommerfeldt and then Otto Gründler, with the amiable Rozanne Elder, the efficient executive director. From this there arose "Cistercian Publications," launched and for a long time guided by Fr. Basil Pennington, a Trappist from Spencer, Massachusetts. The Institute of Cistercian Studies organized some sessions that were held either there or at the Dallas abbey or in other Cistercian houses. Various specialists could be heard and questioned every afternoon on spiritual problems. Every morning was dedicated, for those who felt the need and the desire, to the teaching of Latin, given on two levels, one for beginners and the other advanced. Some time was dedicated to the liturgy or to initiation in other forms of prayer. In every case the meetings were characterized by seriousness and at the same time by freshness: erudition went hand in hand with a good mood and even humor. On the occasion of the great congress in 1990 that celebrated the ninth centenary of the birth of St. Bernard, a very rich program had been arranged of various events — scientific, liturgical, artistic, culinary, literary. I was asked to write a brief preface for the program and, so to speak, for the menu. There I quoted a phrase of St. Bernard, in which the abbot of Clairvaux said that he was God's cook, and the kitchen was his soul; he then gave a learned explanation of the meaning of this jest. Someone had the marvelous idea of making aprons for the members of the Institute of Cistercian Studies to wear during the whole congress, even during the banquet. At the center was pictured the head of St. Bernard and around it the phrase — written in Latin! — in which he defined himself as "God's cook."

4. Pluralism

The appeal of medieval studies and of monastic research has enabled the identification of one of the concerns that without doubt was then predominant in many American circles: that of giving fair space, in scholarship, to one or more forms of prayer, thanks to which people could remain free with respect to a growing material prosperity. At that time many new modes of feeling oneself to be Christian, with their possibilities and their risks, were becoming manifest on the part of Christian men and women who often had recourse to history and to spirituality to inject their effort into tradition and to guarantee their initiatives a solid foundation. This was the case, for example, in many institutions with respect to what were called "houses of prayer." Did not certain persons, convents and diverse established groups already carry out that function adequately?

Forms of Christian presence and action were greatly varied, and ranged from those academies reserved for the education of wealthy young people, coming mostly from countries where almost everyone else was poor, as in Latin America, to the apostolate among people living in apparently irremediable material and cultural misery. It was important in every case not to lose courage, in the awareness that one would not find it except by uniting with God and, through him, in him, and starting from him, with everyone. People wanted places, times and circumstances allowing them to intensify their relationship with the Lord.

Fr. Bernhard Häring, the Redemptorist then famous for his fervor and for his skill in communicating in different languages, was very much involved in the creation of these houses of prayer, at an early time destined especially for clergy and religious. There were invitations to lead such groups, sometimes in large empty novitiates. They also accepted people, young or not so young, who were studying the Vedas without having ever carefully looked at the Gospel. Much heat and little light, more fervor than formation, but also a desire to understand who one was and why, for whom one was living and expending oneself, and how to reconcile an interior life with intensive service.

Soon there appeared that other manifestation of the same profound need that became the "charismatic" movement. I had occasion to be present at, and to share in, prayer meetings which sometimes lasted a long while, with intercessions, witnessing, urgent pleas for healing, laying on of hands, all of it accompanied sometimes by a certain obsession with the "demonic." These forms of prayer were widely developed, for the good of the Church, without being necessary for everybody. I was able to be a witness of it in groups that were Catholic, Anglican, Episcopalian, and Protestant of various kinds.

Among the projects started by these different currents, there is the one of Sister Marie Goldstein: encouraged by many religious, she had the idea to unite not only Christians of every confession, but also Christians, Jews and Muslims by having them pray together. And indeed the organization that she established was called HOPE, House of Prayer Experiment. The project brings together representatives of the three great monotheistic religions — whose members are all children of Abraham — to have them live together for some time, so that they might know one another: by exchanging ideas and by being present to the mystery of each other, they understand the levels of their differences and can stop identifying each other as opponents. It is just a question of spirituality. An early session was held at the University of Notre Dame and was encouraging.

Later, a group of permanent members and sympathizers settled in Israel. It met in Jerusalem for conferences, excursions-pilgrimages, and to attend each other's prayer practices. In addition, sessions were held every summer for a number of weeks. For two years running, Sister Marie asked me to accompany her group.

I was already in the Holy Land at the time when, while doing research on manuscripts of St. Bernard, I was wondering if there was something I could find in Jerusalem and its environs. I then went as far as Petra, in the desert. Now, however, we were lodging at the picturesque Ecumenical Center of Tantur. As a point of departure and general theme for our reflections, I had proposed the Song of Songs. There were about twenty of us, all English-speaking, almost all American and British. Some devout and educated Jews and Muslims came to join us for the work meetings. A sheik came to tell us about and — it should be noted — to show us Islamic prayer. André Chouraqui came to talk to us about the Song of Songs, of which his new translation entitled *Poème des poèmes* had just appeared.

We decided to go over to Mount Sinai. I reread Exodus on the airplane while we flew over the Egyptian desert, and thought of the many biblical allusions in which that land was rich. I did not have the strength to go up Mount Sinai. Nonetheless, the experience was beneficial and enlightening for everybody. The following year we stopped at Ain Karim, in Jerusalem, and went to spend an entire week on the shores of Lake Genesareth, in a house made available to us by the YMCA. To read in this way the pages of the New Testament in the very sites where the holy history took place was truly enriching. But we began to perceive clearly that good understanding among Christians, Jews and Muslims in the Holy Land was not just a question of spirituality; alas, politics interfered.

In 1967, during the last session of Vatican Council II, some of those who had attended it on whatever basis had the idea of creating a group that would continue its work in the field of spirituality. Real progress in ecumenism could not be made unless we made the effort to unite ourselves on the level of spiritual experience. It was insisted that I become part of one group, of which the main promoter was Douglas Steere, whom I proposed to call "the pope of the Quakers" because he had visited Quakers throughout the world many times and represented them at the Council as their observer. In addition there was Fr. Godfrey Diekmann, Fr. Bernhard Häring and still others; we met during a dinner in Rome. The definitive group consisted of some twenty members, of whom almost all belonged to Churches and associations in the United States; among the Catholics, Jesuits, Dominicans and other spiritual traditions were represented. The whole was designated by the acronym EIOS, Ecumenical Institute of Spirituality.

Our first meeting was held at Collegeville and the proceedings were published in *Worship*. Thus we met every year in a different place, belonging to a different Church or confession. The second year we went to Pendle Hill, Pennsylvania, near Philadelphia, the cradle of American Quakerism. Then it was the turn of St. Vladimir's in New York, and of many other fascinating places, often laden with history. It was agreed to set the meeting for the beginning of January, a favorable time for everybody. Once it was in a convent of the Cenacle near Miami; many of our sessions took place, in the middle of winter, on the sunny beaches of Florida. In our discussions—and this occurred undoubtedly under the influence of Quaker tradition—the "bio," namely the biographical account of the past year, with one's own experiences and activities, was given much room; the ideas were injected into life.

Every year a theme was chosen, and experts were invited from a specific field—such as Fr. M. Williams on Buddhism—and two or three "guests." The group renewed itself little by little thanks to the entry of younger members, and this turned out to be beneficial for all of us. At the beginning of 1992, at Pendle Hill, in order to celebrate the twenty-fifth anniversary of EIOS and the ninetieth birthday of our elder brother "Douglas," he was presented with a volume of miscellany on historical, theological and practical topics, with some twenty contributions from us. There is no obvious reason why this work should not continue. The plenary meetings gave us the chance to program reciprocal exchanges: thus, I was invited to speak at the Episcopalian Seminary in Cambridge, MA at Harvard. Moreover, I was asked to give some courses at the Southern Baptist Seminary in Louisville, Kentucky, over many years, and finally to "lead a prayer service."

On the occasion of the twentieth anniversary of the foundation of the United Nations, Pope Paul VI had come to New York and had delivered a stirring discourse before the General Assembly. For the thirtieth anniversary, in 1975, a "Spiritual Summit" was organized, in the course of which representatives of all the world's religions were to present the constitutive elements of their own identity, emphasizing what everyone had in common and lifting up vows and prayers for world peace. The sessions were held in the Episcopal Cathedral of St. John in New York, and in the ample adjacent buildings. At the entrance to the choir, on a platform facing the audience that filled the nave, I was to speak on Christianity. American Indians with their plumage gave color to the assembly. We also listened to the sociologist Margaret Mead.

In the Grand Ballroom of the Waldorf-Astoria Hotel, where we were lodged, a banquet was held where we sat at tables for eight. The menu contained characteristic dishes of the five regions of the world. Religious taboos, however, prevented many people from eating one thing or another; so, at each table each of us could choose according to one's own membership, and different platters held what a Hindu, a Buddhist, a Jew or a Muslim could eat. The Christians were the only ones who could taste everything. Thus, at table as elsewhere, peace reigned.

The Summit was concluded in one of the sites of the U.N. compound with a solemn session, presided over by the Secretary of the United Nations, Kurt Waldheim, flanked by Robert Muller, the co-ordinator of the program. Mother Teresa of Calcutta had taken her place among the representatives of the world's principal religions. All of them were allowed to speak for not more than eight minutes, but the only orator who respected this limit was Mother Teresa.

The elderly nun had come to receive, in North Carolina, the Albert Schweitzer Award for charity. The selection committee, of which I was part, every three years would confer important awards on three persons who had been eminent in the three fields in which Schweitzer had worked: biblical studies, music and charity. Mother Teresa used the occasion to speak to us about the poorest of the poor and to tell us about some encounters she had recently had with them. She made such an impression that the next day on page two of *The New York Times* a large headline defined her as "The Living Saint...." When it was pointed out to her that she had already been canonized, she said simply, "Let me die first."

Later, and as a consequence of this "spiritual summit," Dr. Robert Muller invited me to speak about monasticism in the great hall of the U.N. that served as a place of interreligious meditation, under the care of a bonze. Dr. Muller, an avowed Catholic, had been strongly influenced by the religious attitude of the first great secretary of the U.N., Sithu U Thant, a Hindu, and he strove to keep religion present, in that immense world organization, in the specific forms of the various religions.

After the Second Vatican Council, the Roman Secretariat for the Unity of the Churches was given a special section dealing with the relations with the Pentecostal Churches, founded in California at the beginning of our century and widespread today. In them, a fundamental place is assigned to "speaking in tongues." A conference had been announced in Rome, at the convent of Trinità dei Monti. They had assigned me to give the opening report. Some experts in Sacred Scripture had come from the Biblical Institute; they did not leave much room for glossolalia.

Everything was cordial. When Paul VI received the group in audience, he lifted his hands toward heaven and said in English, "Praise the Lord!"

Following this meeting, some members of the group invited me to take part in some sessions that were being held at their "Centers for Biblical Studies" in different regions in the United States. In one of them it was even proposed that I be taught to engage in glossolalia. Later in Rio de Janeiro I met again one of the bishops I had seen in Rome. These bonds with Pentecostalism were maintained, so much so that in 1985, when the "Society for Pentecostal Studies" held its annual assembly in a community in Maryland, with a session at Catholic University in Washington, I came to it from Rome. I was asked to present an opening report on the relations between prayer and theology. Others spoke on the ideas of their own Churches, with their concrete applications in the various cultures where their movement had spread, especially among the Indians and the Blacks of Latin America. Everything was compiled in a very stimulating volume.

In 1982 the U.N. decided to proclaim a "Year of the Aged," after having given room to children, women, the handicapped and still others. Given that the aging of societies posed special problems of economic and political organization, the delegate of the Holy See, Msgr. Di Filippo, had the idea of attracting attention to the psychological, moral, religious and spiritual aspects, by gathering testimonies on the way of aging and of assisting elderly people in all religious and spiritual traditions. He asked me to write a chapter concerning monasticism. The whole thing appeared in 1982 under the title *Aging: Spiritual Perspectives*, published by an organization called "Opera Pia International." When the volume was presented to the competent commission meeting in Vienna, a representative of the Soviet government was surprised by the fact that, in discussing "aging," support had been sought from the "Opera people."

Thus there was no lack of occasions to work for the Church: in Montreal, on an adult-education television program; on a program of interdiocesan television in Newark, in the colors that the technology of the time still required, a broadcast on St. Bernard; in the Cloisters Museum in New York, an interview on Thomas Merton: the context was wondrously monastic, but nearly every minute a low-flying jet would pass above and force us to stop.

The Middle Ages helped. After a Sunday Mass at a prison near St. Meinrad's Abbey, and after a congress at which I had spoken about William of St. Thierry, I was asked to address the inmates. The day before at Pennsylvania State College I had talked about William of St. Thierry. I linked up with one of his favorite themes: the image of God in each of us, which can be obscured but never erased. At the exit, one of the inmates waited for me to tell me that that was what they most needed to hear, because the most painful thing for them was not the lack of privacy, of comfort or of freedom, but that of never being respected for their dignity as human beings.

Another evening, the founder of a new community, on the occasion of the vows of his first professed, wanted to celebrate the Eucharist on the tomb of Teilhard de Chardin, in the cemetery of the former scholasticate of the Jesuits, not far from New York City, now the Culinary Institute of America, where cooks in white caps have replaced the Jesuits. Someone suspected that we were preparing an orgy and the police, summoned immediately, rushed there while we were looking for Teilhard's grave among the others with a flashlight. However, they realized right away that we were monks and so we were able to celebrate the Eucharist.

One day, during one of the "cathedral conversations" in Louisville, I was to talk — as the dinner speaker — about psycho-spirituality. In the meantime, I had entrusted my health to a generous chiropractor in Wisconsin whom I called "my American electronic sorcerer," because he used machinery of impressive complexity with rays that benefited me.

Thus the welcome and the aid of the adoptive country of Jesse de Forest did not fail. Friendship was maintained, constant and delicate, from the day of my first arrival. Almost as part of the tourist attractions of the period, I was invited to dine with Bishop Fulton Sheen, an auxiliary bishop of Cardinal Spellman. He was then a preacher and pious author esteemed the world over, and was likewise known for his generosity toward all Catholic works. One of my friends, without telling me, had thus scheduled and organized, for the day after my arrival, a dinner with this prelate whose conversation was brilliant; all those invited were missionary bishops. At the moment of our departure, I was the only one not expecting, to Bishop Sheen's great surprise, an envelope containing a check. Nonetheless, his encouraging smile never failed and everything was fine in the end.

Thus in 1983, on the occasion of the 150th anniversary of the North American College in Louvain, when I was assigned two reports on *Les charactéristiques de la spiritualité américaine* and on *L'impact des États-Unis sur l'Église en Europe*, it was not hard to illustrate with varied examples the pluralism of this spirituality and to show how Catholics of this country have always been committed to reconcile an innate demand for democracy with submission to the authority of Rome. On many occasions they have not supported the most centralizing efforts of the papacy.

But, partly because the majority of their bishops were of Irish origin and thus coming from a country that had paid dearly for its own fidelity, they have remained obedient to the Holy See as well as generous. By reason of this double teaching that they have not ceased to give, it could still be said: *America docet* [America is teaching].

The few memories that have just been recalled allow one to perceive the intensity of the spiritual life that could be experienced in the United States. I have not thought it necessary to indicate all the places where I went nor to say what I did there. But what reemerged in my memory reminded me of the phrase: *Amica America* [America the Friend].

9

From Morocco to Madagascar

1. New Unexpected Invitations

I used to have many occasions to pass through Paris, or to stay there to work in the libraries. I always lodged at the Abbey of Sainte-Marie on Rue de la Source. One day, around 1960, Fr. de Floris, the chaplain of the Benedictines of Vanves, near Paris, made an appointment with me. Over a dinner at the buffet of the Gare de l'Est, between trains, he told me that the Benedictine nuns wished to see me to discuss something with me. So I went. Now Fr. de Floris was also, at that time, the director of a new organization, of which the secretariat was located at Vanves. Its name was changed about halfway through its history. At an earlier time it was known as "Aide à l'Implantation Monastique," particularly for Africa. Then little by little, as it extended its activity to parts of the world where monasticism had already existed for a long time, sometimes before Christianity, the choice was made to name it "Aide Inter-Monastères" (AIM). In reality, in the majority of Asiatic countries, where monks number in the tens of thousands—and in India perhaps in the millions—to attempt to "implant" monasticism would be like urbanizing Rome or Paris. Nonetheless, since Christian monasticism was the concern, the idea of implantation held true even for those regions. Indeed, the intent of AIM was precisely that of fostering foundations in the making, or those already existing. Among them all, at the national or continental level and even on a worldwide scale, AIM created, through a "Bulletin," the kind of bonds that would otherwise have merited it the name of "Amitié Inter-Monastique" [Inter-Monastic Friendship].

Now, Fr. de Floris needed a kind of mobile auxiliary, traveling salesman or liaison agent who could go to distant foundations as a friend and give some talks there. And it was proving difficult to find a monk who was available (useless and jobless) for this task. Thus little by little he invited me to work for AIM: it would consist above all in taking trips.

an article by Fr. Nwyia stating that "Islam is a religion of monastic nature," especially because of the importance it gives to prayer. Some historians have pointed out the similarities between the penances of ancient (and medieval) monks and the prostrations of Muslims, between the rhythms of ancient monastic prayer and Mohammed's first prescriptions on the hours at which daily prayers are to be said, between the "memory of God" dear to the spiritual tradition of monasticism and certain forms of Islamic prayer that utilize ejaculations or other methods. Thus when, why, where and how did the idea spread that the Koran excludes monasticism? It seems that the latter, at least in certain regions, had aroused opposition because it appeared as a fearsome obstacle to the expansion of Islam. Christians, at the time and in many areas, had become political enemies.

Some monastic realities within Islam and in the course of its history should therefore cause no wonder, given Islam's Christian premises on the one side, and on the other the enduring and often peaceful coexistence of Islam with Christianity in many regions. Indeed, various historians of Arab literature have pointed out that in the Koranic poems favorable mention is made of monks. Moreover, it is noted that a diversified Islamic monasticism did exist: hermits like those whose lives of piety and self-denial converted many Berbers; cenobites who continued to live as did those communities of recluses that had existed already for a long time in the deserts of Egypt, Palestine, Syria, and Arabia, where Islam was implanted. There were certain ascetics among the men and certain descriptions of life in some Sufi *coenobia* incredibly similar to those of Christian communities; there were also convents of nuns. Islamic monasticism has even seen bad monks who were called sarabaites, of whom Christian monasticism has provided some examples. Finally the gyrovagues, both in the worst and in the best sense of the term — fakirs or wandering dervishes, poor, similar to the *peregrini* of Christian monasticism — were the subject of Brunel's fine volume, cited above. This author dwelled especially on the Haddawa that Sidi Heddi (†1219) had founded. His way of life included the search for the presence of God, poverty, the rejection of vain knowledge, humility, celibacy. In his community there were some deviations, but also many fine texts on the search for God, and contempt of oneself and of the world. This maxim — "to despise the world, to despise oneself, to despise the contempt that this inspires" — is very similar to what I had published and commented upon following some manuscripts on the *Life of St. Malachy*, a bishop in Ireland, written by St. Bernard. Brunel had mentioned that, according to Asín Palacios, Muslim Spain of the twelfth century had experienced several kinds of monks: those who fast, watchers (who call to mind the Christian "sleepless ones"), the reproachables (who simulated faults in order to be humble), the voluntary poor, paladins, meditators or contemplatives.

One day I met a wandering hermit on the road; I was told that he spent all his time doing what I saw him doing: walking and pointing to the sky with his finger and repeating aloud the ninety-nine names of Allah. Historical research also has current aspects.

Within Christianity, in the East and the West, especially in southern Italy and even more in Spain, these Islamic monastic realities were known and accepted. I had heard about the case of two communities—Christian and Islamic—that shared the same building. Do not all these instances, which can only be mentioned in passing here, perhaps seem to invite Christian monks to be present in Islamic lands, not only with their prayer but also with their charitable activity? Such activity should require not only corporal aid, but should also include interest in the country, in its people and its tradition: charity of a cultural and intellectual nature that nonetheless does not imply doctrinal concessions nor facile agreement. Would the result not be to create a sympathy, an opening? And through this opening, grace would flow. Later, in Indonesia, I was to see the Cistercians of Rawa Seneng help their Muslim neighbors build their mosque. Was it not right to hope that this kind of attitude, wherever there were monks, could become mutual?

3. PROBLEMS OF AFRICANIZATION

The prospect of being invited into diverse regions of the immensity of Black Africa prodded me to attain a state of preparation that was not at all easy. Indeed, within its geographical unity, this continent offers an extreme variety. The problems differed according to regions, countries or groups of countries—Bantu and others—and according to ethnic groups. The diversity was due also to the large number of countries in Africa. I have before my eyes a volume, in English, called *History of Africa According to Geographical Maps*, which I was using then; in addition to the borders set by nature, by races, by ancient empires, there are also those going back to the colonial ages, from the sixteenth to the nineteenth centuries, with names that sometimes indicated what the non-Africans had come in search of, as for example: Ivory Coast, Gold Coast and even Slave Coast.

Recent political influences, especially socialist ones of the Marxist kind, tried to superimpose themselves on these already old realities.

Thus I acquired documentation on the movement of "Christians for socialism in Africa." I found myself in Benin and in the Congo soon after the installation of what was called "Marxism-Leninism" in the former country and "scientific socialism" in the latter. I came across vans and trucks of the "Soviet Ministry of Sports"; one wondered if only athletic or sports equipment was being transported.

People spoke readily about "African anthropology," but I maintained that this expression should be used in the plural. There were few works available for being trained in these anthropologies. For example, for the Bantu world, which is itself quite varied, there are the books by Fr. Tempels or *Bantu Humanism* by Fr. Nothomb, and the ones by Fr. Guérin Montilus for the Fons of Benin (this Haitian priest published brief works on the traditional religion, which was Voodoo, regarding the idea held about birth and about family). Within the family, aunts and uncles sometimes had greater moral authority than that of fathers and mothers. On that account I was to suggest that in monasteries superiors be designated by the titles Uncle and Aunt. The proposal was not taken very seriously, but later I came across a study in an African theological journal on the role of mediator played by an uncle, with application of this category to Christ.

At the Lumen Vitae Institute in Brussels where I taught, and which was attended by some thirty African men and women, I had heard African psychology discussed by two African specialists, a psychoanalyst and a physician. They confirmed my conviction that we whites must not be content with empirical knowledge deriving from the fact of living in Africa (what is called "experience"), but that it is useful to allow ourselves to be taught about Africans by those among them who are studying African anthropology and its consequences in every setting, especially those concerning monastic life: community, authority and submission, work, and the deep attitudes and reactions of blacks with regard to whites. A brief job with the commission that translated the principal texts of monastic tradition into "basic French," just as another commission had done into "basic English" to make them accessible and understandable for everyone, made the difference obvious.

For the sub-Saharan part of Africa, I used the documentation that was issued by the Missionary Institute of the University of Notre Dame in the United States. The art, in its rich variety, would become known thanks to some essays, catalogues and other publications. As regards customs and folklore, they had to be left to be discovered in each country. Fr. Liutfrid Marfurt, whom I had known very well at Engelberg

Abbey, produced interesting works on *The Pipes of Cameroon,* on a game of chance, *The Game of the Beti of Southern Cameroon,* and on the music.

All this allowed me to glimpse a fascinating world in which our monasticism should take root. Above all, it was necessary to find attitudes of prayer that were African, a spirituality — or more exactly diverse spiritualities — that could be expressed in psychological and cultural forms of the people of every region. Surely, a "black spirituality" existed. A Black American, Fr. Cyprian Davis, a Benedictine of St. Meinrad's Abbey in the United States, began writing *Black Spirituality*, which he later published in two volumes. Many people were seeking black-African forms of prayer. There was no lack of work.

"We are waiting for an African St. Benedict," some were saying. But that which could not be done by one person alone could be done by a group of representatives of monasticism, provided that they could meet with each other and share their own experiences. Hence the necessity for convening monastic congresses, for all of Africa or for one or more regions. And that was what began to be realized in a first assembly held at Bouaké, Ivory Coast, in May of 1964; its influence would be decisive.

There were about forty of us, coming mainly from Africa and Madagascar: monks and nuns, superiors, members of the Benedictine and Cistercian Orders; various abbots and abbesses had come from Europe. Some experts and observers were members of the local clergy or Europeans. Brother Daniel-Ange de Maupeou represented the Brotherhood of the Virgin of the Poor of Rwanda. A varied and very cordial group, it met for a whole week. I was assigned to open the session, and I had decided to do so with a speech on "Tradition as an opening to the present." Being traditional does not mean imitating the past, but rather transmitting to the present what were its permanent values — that present which, for us, was the Africa of today. Just when I was about to begin my contribution, a violent tornado struck unexpectedly. The noise made by the rain falling on the sheet-metal roof of our site completely prevented anyone from being able to hear. So we remained in silence, praying for about an hour. It was Pentecost Monday: was this not perhaps a symbol for us? Then I shouted out my report, the storm calmed and our debates could continue in peace and joy.

All the problems were faced: discernment of vocations, recruitment conditions, formation at every level — human, doctrinal, spiritual, professional — community life, hospitality, work, forms of economy. A preliminary question had been posed on the eve of the congress, that of the identity of monasticism. During a conversation with the Bishop of Bouaké, I had noted that much was expected, even too much, from the monks. The stereotype of the "well-educated," even "erudite," Benedictine led him to wish to entrust to the monks all the difficult tasks that no one in his diocese was in a position to take on in the theological, liturgical and social fields. Now he risked being disappointed. I tried to explain to him that, in comparison with religious in certain other Orders who specialized in these fields, ordinary monks would appear rather "underdeveloped." This was for him a hard blow. Therefore, the first day of the session, which I had been asked to lead, was dedicated to this theme. Suddenly the Bishop of Bouaké asked for a clarification, and also for a declaration of the assembly on what it thought about monastic life and about the vocation of a monk in the Church. In his judgment, it was necessary to avoid a misunderstanding among the bishops and among Africans who might become prejudiced against an intellectual monasticism in social service.

I insisted on the "mystery of charity," that is, monastic life, justified in itself, independent of any missionary role, nonetheless without excluding services and activities that did not compromise the primacy of the prayer life. The Archbishop of Cotonou, Archbishop Gantin, with whom I had a long friendship, expressed his agreement with these two aspects. Fr. Pierre Faÿe, a Senegalese Trappist, accented separation from the world—without prejudice toward some contact with the outside—and the humble, hidden, poor and stable character of life in the cloister. A "Declaration on the Fundamental Orientation of Monasticism in Africa" was drafted; I suggested that Fr. Champetier de Ribes, the prior of Keur Moussa, a foundation of Solesmes in Senegal, be asked to write it, which is what happened.

The debate on the liturgy, which also was my task to lead, was interesting and colorful. The discussion turned to the capability and even the need that African monks have of "gesticulating," so to speak, when they speak, sing or listen: when hearing some "dramatic" page from Scripture, such as the story of Susanna's victory over the elders who accused her (in the Book of Daniel) or the tale of the healing of the man born blind (in the Gospel of John) they become indignant or rejoice, they take sides for or against the person being mentioned. Participation in the liturgy can then admit expressive forms unknown to the founding monks coming from Europe. Language, formulas, rites, songs and music ought to conform to the requirements of each African environment. On this question, Fr. Otmar Bauer, a Benedictine from Engelberg, Switzerland, drafted a declaration that had the force of a master plan.

The whole Bouaké session proceeded in an atmosphere of authentic and joyous searching. It ended with a pontifical Mass preceded by a procession during which each of us, at least inwardly, danced in African style. The texts were published; people reflected on them and sought to put into practice the initiatives that they proposed. Two years later, in September 1966, the opportunity was taken to convene a new session on the occasion of the congress of all Benedictine abbots in Rome, since all the superiors of monasteries in Africa and their founder-superiors were gathered there. In the meantime, I had visited twenty-eight monasteries in fourteen countries. I understood much better the patience in the desired evolution which some African clergy urged upon us, like Fr. Pierre Faÿe, Fr. M'Wenge, a Jesuit from Cameroon and a talented artist, and others still. "There will be a sun again tomorrow," to quote an African proverb. And, according to an Irish proverb that came again to my mind, "when God created time, he created a lot of it." Over many days, divided into groups, we shared experiences and encouraged each other for the future.

Paul VI did so on the occasion of a public audience to which our group was admitted. We were placed a very short distance from the pontiff. Before the audience started, I had chatted amicably with Carlo Colombo, the pope's theologian, whom I had known in Milan, and met again at the Council. He accompanied the pope everywhere. I had forgotten to suggest to him that the pope come to greet our African group. At the end of his discourse, I asked the chief of the laymen in livery, who were part of the retinue, if I might have a word with Archbishop Colombo. He did not allow me to do so. Undoubtedly he had guessed my intentions and, seeing that it was almost lunchtime, all the personnel were thinking only of going to eat. I secretly prayed that something might happen. The audience was already over and the pope was seated in the *sedia gestatoria*. Suddenly he saw our group and, as if moved by an impulse, got up, came toward us, had each man and woman presented to him, and had words of encouragement for everyone. The gentlemen in livery could no longer manifest their disappointment. Everything then concluded with even greater joy.

Another session to which I was invited was held in 1970 at the Trappistine monastery of Obout, Cameroon. It had been organized by and for nuns, and some fifteen delegates took part, with the authorization of their superiors; they came from monasteries of different Orders scattered throughout French-speaking Africa. In addition, there were some African and European clergy. The Archbishop of Yaoundé, Archbishop Zoa, wanted to take part, as did Bishop Etoga of Sigmelima, the first of the black bishops ordained by Pius XI. The problems discussed were varied but, in general, they were part of the much broader question that I had heard formulated by the African group of the Seminary of Propaganda Fide in Rome: "Why impose on Africa the consequences of European history and, for example, those of the conquest of Spain by Muslims?" In Africa the condition of women had evolved, and was continuing to evolve, in a way that perhaps was anticipating what was happening in Europe. A delicate point was that of cloister. Each delegate explained why this or that prescription of the recent decree *Venite seorsum* was inapplicable in her own monastery. We did not have the authority to dispense them from it. But, with Archbishop Zoa, we verified the cases of impossibility, which still were no reason to put an end to cloistered life. Some of the conditions described were rather comical, but should humor be excluded from the interpretation of canon law? Indeed thereafter, with the aid of common sense, many difficulties were smoothed out.

Finally, a third great pan-African session, which interested all of monastic Africa, was convened by AIM at Abidjan, the capital of the Ivory Coast, in September 1979 in order to prepare for the coming Year of St. Benedict. About eighty delegates from seventeen different countries took part. This time the majority of participants, both English- and French-speaking, was composed of Africans. African monasticism had consolidated, and the number of communities had increased considerably; some communities were entirely African.

Africa had developed in two senses that at times seemed opposed to each other. On the one side, "authenticity" was demanded, namely, faithfulness to African identity; on the other, the influence of the West was growing, thanks to the spread of education, to industrialization and especially to urbanization. What could be done to reconcile, in our effort of inculturation, the traditional values tied to family, to village, to rural life with the new values, according to which young people were now growing up who, very soon, would also be monks and nuns? In the closing reflections, I thought it opportune to underscore the twofold distinction—Christian and monastic—of our communities. Christian, because the Church does not have the task of managing either the new needs created by consumerist societies or what remains of certain spontaneous expectations within the African soul. Monastic because, before the new demands of development to which we have the driving duty to contribute, we should not try to respond to all needs: monastic observance has its own imperatives, which exclude others from it. It was a useful occasion to recall the great ancient principle: *Non omnia possumus omnes,* "Not all of us can do everything." Monasticism existed in Africa. It had to become an African monasticism. Yet Africa itself was changing, not without difficulty. This is being observed in the political field. It should have been foreseen, even in hope, that the way of monasticism would not be easy; this too can now be observed.

4. DEEP IN AFRICA

With regard to the information that emerged from the preparatory research and then was formulated during the congresses, I was given the chance to "contextualize" it when I had to go, in three successive trips, to the countries where some monasteries were, namely from the northwest to the south: Senegal, Ivory Coast, Benin, Togo, Congo, Zaire, Rwanda, Burundi, Uganda, Kenya, Tanzania, Madagascar. During these journeys, as in all the others, I went from cloister to cloister, yet from each one of these I was led into the surrounding regions. Thus I had the opportunity to visit their cities, their monuments and their museums. I spoke only at two universities, that of Yaoundé, the capital of Cameroon, and that of Dakar in Senegal. The monasteries were generally located in the savannahs. Everywhere I was enchanted by the beauty of the places, and not just in the region of the Grand Lakes.

Every place I visited, I discovered how picturesque the people and their customs were: the lively and harmonious color of their clothing, both ordinary and liturgical; their exquisite gentleness, their signs of respect, their warm way of always clasping with two hands the one hand that a European extends; their habitual attitudes, different from ours, but which they had the right to introduce into their prayer; their gestures of welcome. I cannot forget the ceremony with which I was presented to a village chief who said to me, "The village belongs to you; when you come back, you will be its chief." I could only answer him, "When you come to Paris, the village will belong to you." Their celebrations of the first crop of rice or corn included symbols that were adaptable to the rite of religious profession. The funeral rites of a chief were preceded by a long procession that was also a dance. In assemblies, order was introduced and guaranteed by those "words" — or "discourses" — that make one think of the parables of the Lord. All the richness of "negritude" appeared in the markets, so important, so full of imagination, but also of very specific actions.

Nature was full of intense life, which still required a certain prudence. On the first day of my arrival at a monastery of nuns in Benin, I learned that their chaplain had been bitten by a snake the very evening of his arrival. The incident had not been taken very seriously, but he died the next day. So, I was taught how to kill a snake, and what the precautions were to take against insects. In Burkina Faso, I heard lions roaring. The bishop had the nuns' cloister walls built higher so that lions could not get over them. Does the bishop not have the task, according to canon law, to secure the observance of cloister? All the forms of holiness were present, there as in every other place. The Martyrs of Uganda had just been beatified. Upon my return from Africa, I sent from Rome to each monastery a poster featuring each of those beatified, with the totems of their respective tribes, with their African names under which young Christians were now being baptized.

It is impossible to recall all of the anecdotes that marked all these encounters with the spontaneous and deep Africa. Many memories are set in images: drawings, photographs, slides. The episodes were often touching and always edifying. At Keur Moussa, in Senegal, I was able to admire what the monks who had come from Solesmes had done to restore appreciation for old musical instruments, such as the balafon, the drum and especially the kora, which they had perfected and made known. They created new songs based upon indigenous melodies, in the two local languages and in French.

In Benin, Archbishop Gantin, whom I had known in Rome, where he later became a cardinal, helped me understand many things. The Benedictine nuns of Toffo, who had come from Vanves, and the Trappistines of Parakou had developed some very expressive rites, inspired by customs in the country, for investiture, profession and other occasions. In Cameroon, Benedictines, Trappists and Trappistines competed with a creative spirit in the same vein. The monastery of Mont-Fébé, located near Yaoundé, had become an ecumenical and intercultural center. The monks had established a rich museum of Bamiléké art, and they themselves were creating musical texts. The Poor Clares of Sigmelima were accompanying the liturgy with ritual dances. Among the Trappistines of Obout, during a Sunday Mass, some girls — including postulants — would dance after each article of the Creed and sing, "Yes, it is true! Yes, I believe!" This could go on for some time. During an early sojourn, when Obout was still occupied by monks, I had known there a Brother Pascal, the Jean Bourgoingt who had been one of the *enfants terribles* in the book by Jean Cocteau with the same title. I put him in touch with Bishop Plumey of the north of Cameroon, who sent him to a leprosarium, where he devoted himself and later met his death. Bishop Plumey remembered him in his book *La Mission Tschad-Cameroun* which he published and gave to me in 1990, shortly before he was assassinated.

The monastery of Hanga, in Tanzania, had only African monks, young and enthusiastic. Their priory had been built near a forest, and many Africans had chosen to come with their families to live near them. However, because of dangerous incursions by elephants, the monastery had to be moved and, with it, the village. Since the prior—called Baba, meaning Father—had been a student of mine in Rome, I was considered to be the Babou, namely the grandfather of this community that by now was very developed. I maintained a correspondence with Baba and many of his sons. Benedictine life in Tanzania had had its potential martyrs in the young nuns who had suffered persecution and had sometimes undergone imprisonment in order to follow their religious vocation despite the opposition of their own families and environment. Full documentation on this matter was sent to me, which was deserving of publication, written in German with the title, "They have suffered for their Lord."

Dar es Salaam, the capital of Tanzania, its name meaning "port of peace," is a port that opens onto Asia. From there, crossing that part of the Indian Ocean that constitutes the Mozambique Channel, in order to go to Madagascar, signifies entering a new world. But immediately one realizes that many of its traditional values are held in common with those in Africa, to which it is also bound by economic, political and cultural relations. This allowed me to travel with many presidents and ministers who were coming to Tananarive for a meeting of OCAM, the Organization of African States and Madagascar. The Benedictine nuns of Vanves had come to this country as early as 1934. Then came Benedictine and Trappist monks. Each one of their communities, composed of Malagasies and Europeans—and the same was true for Carmel—was the living manifestation of ideas expressed by some specialists on the richness of this island's civilization, which has gained contributions from Polynesia, from the Arab world, from Africa and from Europe. There were so many tales of vocations and so many testimonies about the prayer life and its benefits for community life, so important to the Malagasy soul! So much experience already accumulated by the country's monks and by those who came to live with them, like them, brings to mind this proverb of Madagascar: "Only the one who eats it knows what an orange is."

The nuns of Vanves, established at Ambositra, had already made a foundation at Mananjary. A harmonious balance had been found between the spirit of the Rule and native human and religious capabilities. Joy reigned, as shown by a demonstration of the country's dances, accompanied by local songs and instruments. Work allowed the nuns to provide for their subsistence and for their generosity: farming, cheese-making, gardening, livestock breeding, and manufacture of bamboo and textile articles. Finally, their influence was wide, thanks to their guest facilities where numerous groups of participants in spiritual retreats and trainees came to benefit from the spiritual and material aid which the community lovingly dispensed, without sacrificing anything of their own life of prayer and mortification. Another Malagasy proverb was quoted to me:

Flowers hidden in the grass:
if they are trampled
they breathe out their perfume.

A meeting held with Malagasy nuns, at which a Benedictine monk, a compatriot of theirs, was present, allowed them to discuss very frankly the problems raised by the progressive creation of a liturgy and a ritual of conventual life that corresponded to the country's psychology and customs. There, as elsewhere, the problem is complex but at least it is being examined. Better than any theory, the performance by Malagasy and European monks of a series of religious songs—called *zafindrony*—in which texts and melodies blend in a marvelous way, was able to reveal all the artistic and spiritual resources that the traditional culture in that kind of environment could put to the service of Christian worship.

Thus the monasteries everywhere contributed, in their way, to the emergence of African and Malagasy theology, liturgy and spirituality, especially in the realm of prayer. The liturgical use of the psalms was a great help. The Church had helped Christians shift from magic to religion, namely, to a living relationship with God, from fear to adoration. The problem remained to find for this new attitude an expression proceeding from each country's own culture. During a first phase, that of settlement, Christian faith and the cultures encountered each other. Then, in a phase of "acculturation," they began to know each other and understand each other. Now a phase of "inculturation" had to come, through which cultures could appropriate Christianity so as to express it according to each culture's own richness. Monasticism in Africa and Madagascar had to become African and Malagasy. It was a beautiful gift of Divine Providence that I could be the witness, even though in a very limited way, of this slow but definitive progress.

10

In Asia

1. CROSSING CULTURES

Since the monasteries of Asia had expressed the desire to have, as in Africa, congresses and series of conferences, I was sent to the following countries one or more times: India, Sri Lanka, Thailand, Vietnam, Cambodia, Indonesia, the Philippines, Hong Kong, Singapore, Korea, and Japan. Each of these countries is in its turn rich in different cultures. Yet there are more or less idealized images circulating around each one, and around Asia in general, such as that of the tolerant and peaceable India. What is the reality? It was important that these images be placed in correct relation to it.

I was fortunate to be able to discover something of the life of the real India, the real Vietnam and the real Japan. I was welcomed by a family like any other; I traveled by automobile over long distances, observing everything that could be seen; I visited with common people to compare idealized Hinduism and Buddhism with the religions as they are really lived.

In India I had wanted to see the Ganges and Benares, and to be present at sacrifices, *arti,* which are offered at the end of every afternoon in the temples. People had told me in Rome, "It is just a two-hour flight from New Delhi to Benares." But what would I have seen, from airport to airport, from hotel to hotel? I took a full day to travel the distance by auto, and then I spent a whole morning on the banks of the Ganges, the site of the sacred bath. I was welcomed by a modest family, and I observed their religious practices which I asked them to explain. All this —which I wrote down in some pages of "Impressions sur le monachisme en Inde," in the journal *Parole et Mission*—was very different from the images that I had seen earlier.

Upon arriving in India, the first—real!—images that one has are those of poverty. Crowds of children are seen begging, but the police chase them with blows of their sticks because their right to exist is not even recognized. People had advised me not to look around between the airports and the cities so as not to see the afflicted who lie along the roads: "You will get sick," they told me, "and it would not change a thing!" Alcoholism is a real problem, because there is an *Indian Whisky* of which I could see the sad effects. Violence, restrained by the police, is always lurking. After a night during which the American Express agency of Rome had arranged lodging for me in the Oberoy, the most luxurious hotel in New Delhi—about which Thomas Merton made some ironic comments in his *Asian Journal*—at the time of leaving by bus for the airport, a crowd of rebels were agitating in front of the door, demanding higher salaries. Another contrast between the people's misery and the refinements of the elite: one evening, I went to a lovely concert of Indian music performed on traditional and Western instruments. What place would Christian monasticism hold in this whole setting? There was at that time still not much talk about the "Christian ashrams" which later became more numerous.

I went down to Kerala and the South. In Kerala I stayed at the Kurisumala ashram, founded by Fr. Francis Mahieu, Swami Acharya, an experience of the Indianization of our monasticism. Fr. Bede Griffiths was also there; he later left to found his own ashram in Shantivanam, where Fr. Monchanin stayed. At Clervaux I had known Fr. Le Saux, Swami Abhishiktananda, at an earlier time, but I did not have a chance to meet with him in India. At Bangalore, one of the congresses organized by AIM was held. Raymondo Pannikar was present, along with a Jain monk, a member of the branch of wanderers, namely those who take a vow—so I am told—of not staying more than twenty-four hours in the same place. With Pannikar, we were welcomed in the city at the monastery of his Order.

At the congress in Bangkok, I had met a sadhu, a layman, named Ittiavirah, an itinerant preacher and the author of numerous popular small books of great benefit. We became friends and later I helped him win the Albert Schweitzer Award for religious literature, thanks to which he founded an institute for the agricultural development of his region. We are still in contact.

For travel in the South of India, and then in Sri Lanka, I had as a guide Fr. Aloysius Pieris, a Singhalese Jesuit. In his country, where we also had a congress, I went to admire the great stone Buddhas of Polannaruwa, which had made such a strong impression on Thomas Merton, as he mentions in his *Asian Journal*.

Bangkok was a stopover place where I stayed many times. There I was introduced by Fr. Pézet to a group of young Westerners who were studying Buddhism at the Buddhist University. I also met Fr. Verdière, a priest of the Foreign Missions of Paris, who was founding a Christian monastery adopting Buddhist customs. The nuncio, Archbishop Jadot, had come to meet me at Clervaux after his retreat for his episcopal ordination which he had made at Maredsous. He helped us greatly in Thailand, and I was glad to find him again in the United States, as nuncio, and afterwards in Rome. In Bangkok I had to give an interview for Italian television on a boat traveling through the city's canals; this gave me a chance to see the contrast between the misery of the common people and the luxury of the quarter with the grand hotels, situated near beautiful old pagodas that crowds of tourists were admiring.

Cambodia offered still another example of peaceful coexistence between the Vietnamese, who were numerous, and the Khmer. In the Benedictine monastery of Kep, many were preparing for martyrdom without knowing it. It was proposed to me that I should visit the famous temples of Angkor. I answered that I was not a tourist. However, at the end of the retreat that I preached, I suggested to the community that it organize a visit to this important religious site of the country, which the monks had never seen. They later went there and sent me a postcard.

Vietnam, in contrast, was in a paradoxical situation. I went there twice. The first time was in 1967: the war was then in its American phase, and victory seemed certain. It was a war of attrition, almost without battles, resembling a military occupation more than a series of combats. People seemed almost accustomed to it, in the hope of a better future. One of my American students in Rome had presented at Sant'Anselmo's a thesis on *St. Bernard and Teilhard de Chardin*. The professors, troubled by the title and the theme, had sought my opinion. The thesis was sent to me in Saigon through the American embassy, and I responded through the one in Manila in the Philippines. Everything seemed to be working. The Church was enjoying a "colonial" prosperity. They were building for an even finer future. Nevertheless, some young Vietnamese religious were looking forward to a decolonization of religious life. During one session that I was asked to lead in Hué, on the renewal of religious life, I noticed that many wondered about the Church's triumphalistic character.

Then the Tet offensive occurred; the military situation worsened. In 1970 I was invited to return to Vietnam, but with this perspective: "If the situation changes"—although others were saying, "When the situation has changed"—"will it still be possible to continue our monastic life under a socialist regime?" So I went back to exhort the religious to detachment and, if necessary, to courage as well. Indeed, this time one could feel the battle approaching. In the North the bombing was intensifying.

One day, at the Saigon airport, a Protestant pastor admitted to me his regret over the fact that Cardinal Spellman had come to bless the war. I talked about it in a letter to Thomas Merton, who alluded to it in one of his writings. In the South, bombs were exploding on the roads, blocking the passage of huge convoys, military and civilian, and this provided good opportunities for conversation and apostolic work. At the Benedictine convent of Thu Duc, at the gates of Saigon, we often heard machine-gun fire. One day, while we were singing vespers, a bullet that had come through the wall of the chapel without hitting any obstacles — where the cloister gates were open — passed within inches of my face. I kept it as a souvenir. In the meantime I had useful conversations with bonzes, both men and women.

On the day of my departure, the nun driving me to the airport thought that I should pay a courtesy call on the apostolic nuncio. I promptly told her that my visit in Vietnam was absolutely private in nature, but she insisted. The nuncio obliged me to tell him about my impressions. All this had some consequences.

While I was among the Montagnards or aborigines of Vietnam, I had a moving religious encounter with a village chief who was the leader of the Christians there, which I will relate further on in this chapter. I was not surprised by everything that happened thereafter: the collapse of the American offensive, the spread of Marxism, and the faithfulness of the Christians as a whole: "We are building a novitiate for one hundred future monks," they had told me. I had thought, "This will be a wonderful indoctrination site for the Communists." That monastery did indeed become the center for all the police in the country.

Indonesia had a completely different culture, since the country had been Islamicized in the thirteenth century. Still, Dutch missionaries had formed a solid Christian community. With the Trappists of Rawa Seneng, we visited the impressive ruins of the temple of Barabudur; Fr. de Lubac had once praised its sculptures. I sent him a picture postcard that pleased him greatly.

The Philippines were, in their turn, very diverse since they had been Christian since the time of Philip II of Spain. I stopped only once in Manila, but I went several times to the abbey, a very prosperous one, of the Benedictine nuns of Vigan in Ilicos Sur, two hours' flight from the capital. I kept some delightful souvenirs of the place. Vigan is one of the few "colonial" cities that was not destroyed by earthquakes or bombardments.

In Hong Kong, in the continental part of the Chinese territory bordering on that of the People's Republic, I found Buddhism again: near the Trappistine monastery there was also one of Buddhists. Even there, albeit over a long term, the future was worrisome. Some very elderly monks of the original community located in the People's Republic of China, were still in prison, subject to a harsh regime. Several, humiliated and tortured, had been heroic martyrs. I believe that their cause for beatification is about to be advanced. At the time of my departure, the novices and young people offered me an artistic ink drawing portraying a bamboo stalk standing tall—a symbol of the course of life—with nodes representing the power that makes bamboo grow. A Chinese inscription, translated for me, wished me "eternal youth" with everybody's signatures. They also gave me the book *Les Trappistes en Chine* that described perfectly the founders' colonial mentality. Mistakes are costly.

In Korea, Buddhism was accompanied by Confucianism. Benedictine monks and nuns had numerous settlements. There too some of the young people were beginning to pose questions about Korean identity. A Carmel of traditional European imprint had some property surrounded by a cloister wall built of stone. Someone told me, "With this wall, a village could be built for the poor." It fell to me to aid a Carmel of the new type; it had only Korean members and is now developing, yet it is built in the same way.

Japan, where I went three times, constituted a mysterious world. In 1968 I first stayed in Tokyo with the family of an industrialist who, upon returning in late afternoon from his high-technology job, would take off his shoes, put on a kimono and sit down on a low seat in perfect conformity with the archaic customs of the traditional culture. We were in a room with the walls crammed with electronic devices. A marvelous accord between modernity and the past. I met with some experts in Buddhism, in particular with Fr. Enomiya-Lassalle, the Jesuit. He had scheduled a conference of mine for Sophia University. However, a student strike that lasted several months blocked all activity of that kind, as well as access to the campus. Nevertheless, Fr. Enomiya taught me Zen meditation and had me visit the famous temple of Kamakura, where I was able to attend some meticulous and harmonious ceremonies celebrated by bonzes.

I had a great wish to visit Kyoto, the religious capital filled with Buddhist monasteries. They had advised me to seek the hospitality of the Carmel of that city. By chance, the prioress was Belgian, and she put me into contact with a compatriot of hers, an orientalist who was working, on behalf of the University of Louvain, on a dictionary of the languages of the Far East. Thanks to him, I was able to visit one of the monasteries, although it was difficult to gain entrance to it, and also was able to learn more about the life that they were leading there. Among other things, I took note of an exercise called *samu*, which consists in meditating while moving a broom according to a certain rhythm and swaying of the body. I had it explained to me; then I noticed in museums various images of bonzes with brooms. All this brought me onto a track of research on the significance and iconography of the broom and of its use not only in Zen but also in ancient and medieval Christian tradition and, in the contemporary era, in that of the American Shakers. Thus, when I was asked for a contribution to the *Mélanges* in honor of Cardinal Daniélou, I chose as my theme "The Broom in the Bible and the Liturgy."

When I returned to Japan in 1970, the huge World's Fair, "Expo '70," was being held at Osaka. I spent several days immersing myself in this mixture of advanced technology and traditional values. The result was an article that appeared in the *Japanese Missionary Bulletin* of Tokyo and in *Nouvelle revue théologique*. This extraordinary explosion of science, art and religion offered some points for reflection on the theme of the Expo, "Man in the World": progress, value, relationship with God and Christ. There were things there to praise and to be grateful for. On the keyboard of an immense electronic organ, on which anyone was invited to offer a theme, I played the first notes of *Regina caeli, laetare, alleluia.* And suddenly the room resounded with a series of rich and harmonious variations on this Marian and Paschal theme. Technology can help human beings to live more fully, but it can also kill them. However, it cannot revive them; yet we know that the Lord of the world, who truly died, is forever truly risen.

I was struck by the courtesy of the Japanese and often remembered, in other countries of Asia, their smile. I was pained when I learned that, in all the places they occupied during the war, they had behaved in a totally contrary manner. In addition to differences among the cultures, there were also the oppositions arising from recent historical memories.

2. A MEMORABLE EXPERIENCE

In Vietnam the aborigines, who correspond more or less to those whom Americans call "Indians," are called Montagnards because they live in scarcely accessible uplands where they have been confined. I had occasion to come into contact with them, and this permitted me to have a spiritual experience, the memory of which I still cherish deeply. I cannot fail to recall it again here.

The tribe to which I was introduced belonged to the ethnic group of the Rhades. I had read what had been written about them by Fr. de Lubac and others, and especially by Fr. Dournes, an ethnologist who specialized in the study of their culture and religion, to which he had dedicated several books. I had admired the very developed faith and morality of that population as well as their poetic expression: a large house is "as long as the wave of the sound of a gong," and so on. In the rare monasteries where there was a Montagnard monk or postulant, I loved to converse with them.

A missionary led me to two of their villages, not long ago reached by what we call civilization. Nonetheless, they have preserved all their ancestral traditions: their religion—they believe in a Supreme Being—their precise morality, their manner of comporting themselves, of dressing, of eating, and especially of building villages according to a rigorous plan and of constructing, with perfect use of wood and without any metal, those long houses—one for each large family—which, as I mentioned above, are compared to the echo of a gong. I will not tarry over details of hospitality, of visiting the village and then later the cemetery, so emblematic of a whole mental and spiritual universe. All these persons were able to grasp and appreciate the least sign of interest, and in all their faces a reflection of the mystery of God could be perceived.

The question arose about a monastic settlement intended for the girls of this tribe. The nun placed in charge by the bishop for accomplishing this project led me one morning to the village where she lived. When they saw me coming, they asked me if I was ready to accept the Montagnards' sign of hospitality that would give them the greatest joy and honor: "to drink from the pot" a liquid that I understood to be rice-based. After my answer, affirmative of course, someone ran to the spring down in the valley, to fetch fresh water which they immediately began to transform into that beverage. After a stroll through the village, we went back to the house where the meal was ready. Seated on the floor—set on piles—we ate rice, pineapple and a plate of banana leaves, to say nothing about all sorts of sauces and peppers. After eating, we moved to the house's great room, where guests are received. They brought in a bamboo mat and the rice juice ceremony began. A boy near the pot had the task of adding water as it was drunk. Then the head of the family began to drink and invited me to do the same; then it was the nun's turn. After us, he called upon all the other inhabitants of the house to perform this rite of friendship according to hierarchical order.

Suddenly the head of the house summoned a boy to take his place in directing the ceremony, because he wanted to approach me and tell me everything that he had in his heart. He asked me if I would accept, and then he started. The nun was translating. For twenty minutes I felt the Holy Spirit expressing himself through the mouth of a simple man, a representative of that elite that was not cultural nor economic but simply spiritual — *electi*, St. Gregory said, "those chosen by God" — that Fr. Dournes talks about. And everything that this head of family said corresponded to what Dournes had expressed in his theological language. Indeed this Montagnard was Christian, baptized, and all of his family were baptized or catechumens, some of whom had already received or were preparing to receive the first rites of the baptism of adults. I wish I could have written down every sentence of this witness of God, because everything he said was so beautiful and elevated.

He began by saying that he had a great desire and a great suffering. Every day he saw that the Montagnards were poor and weak in every respect. They were not humanly developed. They were especially dominated by Satan, who acted in them both through malign influences and through the wickedness of men. Only Jesus could help them out of their spiritual and material misery. He absolutely wanted to force himself — and he repeated the word several times, with insistence, as my translator made it plain to me — to force himself to do something. But he did not know what. He asked me to enlighten him. He asked me to pray and have prayers said for the Montagnards and for him, so that he and his family might always have the courage, the strength (he insisted again) to serve Jesus, to make him known and to do good to all the poor Montagnards. He could not understand precisely what God wanted of him. He only knew that he was very determined and that he needed help, because he felt alone before Satan and the world. At the end he expressed his wish to see the Blessed Sacrament kept in the village. A house could be built for It, It would be guarded, people would pray before It; indeed, he believed that there was no other hope than this victorious presence of Jesus among them.

I was deeply moved. I told him that I was going to answer him and the nun would translate. For about half an hour I talked to him about the death and resurrection of Jesus, and about the Spirit of fortitude whom He unceasingly sends; and then about the loneliness and the apparent defeat of Jesus — misunderstood, persecuted, rejected, condemned, killed — but who saves by loving and forgiving. All the young people of the village gathered around while he was speaking; they were now listening to my response as well. I added that Jesus has neither known nor promised success, victory or large numbers. But what matters for everyone, as for Jesus, is the desire, the courageous solidarity, the love that helps us to forgive, to do good to all, even to enemies. Jesus personally knows and loves every Montagnard like every other member of humanity. He wants to save them all and he does so if they practice faith and morality according to their tradition, despite the influence of Satan. Indeed, love is stronger than everything and Jesus is victorious: now he is in glory, and these few Christian Montagnards could not have these desires, this courage, this faith and this charity unless Jesus Christ was sending them the Holy Spirit. May they therefore have hope, regardless of what happens. Their life and their effort already had meaning, they were already a success and they were doing good for the Montagnards and for all of humanity. Let them extend their desires, their prayer, their love to all the Vietnamese, to all humans—Christians or not—of Asia, Africa, America, Europe, to the Communists of Russia, of China, of Vietnam (many of those present were refugees from the North, orphans, victims in one way or another). I spoke of the mystery of the whole universal Church, which is Jesus spread throughout the entire world, to which he and his own are really united through the faith and the sacraments, especially the Eucharist, through prayer and charity.... As for his wish to keep the Blessed Sacrament in the village, he could speak about it with the bishop who had the authority to take the matter into consideration. Personally I would be glad to see It present there, as soon as possible, at least for a while. He thanked me and said that he would try to keep all of this in his heart. All their faces were serious but relaxed, ready to smile.

Then I embraced every child, I approached all the adults—young people, women, elderly—I had myself introduced to each one. I asked their names, their ages (many said they did not know it), their progress in Christian initiation. This was true joy. They invited me to drink one last time at the pot of friendship.

Later, during the heroic years that followed, the village chief remembered our encounter and made this known to me through other persons.

3. CHRISTIAN MONASTICISM AND OTHER MONASTICISMS

Among the monasteries of countries with such different cultures in vast Asia, there were common problems: some cases were tied to the economic situation which in general was one of underdevelopment; others, to the fact that in almost all regions there existed non-Christian forms of monastic life. Christian monasticism was in the minority there and of recent implantation. Nonetheless, it had roots in ancient religions. How could it be placed in relation to them?

To discuss these matters, the idea was proposed of convening a pan-Asian and pan-monastic congress, to which representatives of non-Christian monasticisms would be invited.

Ever since my first journeys through Asia I had noticed, on stopovers in Bangkok or even simply passing through the airport, the great number of Buddhist monks recognizable by their saffron robes. And since I knew Archbishop Jadot, the nuncio in that country, and Fr. Verdière of the Foreign Missions of Paris, I suggested that the meeting be held in Thailand. The proposal was accepted, and in December 1968 the first encounter of monks of Asia opened, in the buildings of the Thai Red Cross near Bangkok. Afterwards there would be others in Korea, India and Sri Lanka.

I had also proposed to invite Thomas Merton, and so it was done. Indeed, among all the invitations and solicitations that he received, and the problems that he too was having, we had thought, with him and with his new abbot, Dom Flavian Burns, that it would be good for him and for many others, that he at last come out of his cloister and his country so as to go and share with others many valuable ideas that abounded in him. Thus it was granted — as he told me in one of his last letters — that once a year he should go out to hold retreats or conferences in monasteries of his Order outside of the United States. I saw him again at Gethsemani shortly before our common departure for Bangkok. We had also planned to travel together. However, he had to pass through California, Alaska and Tibet, while I, from Europe, flew to Japan. We saw each other for a short time in Bangkok. Although we had planned to have at least one long conversation, it was not possible to do so.

The congress had been carefully prepared by AIM. A questionnaire and some preparatory texts had been sent to all the monasteries of Asia and to their motherhouses in Europe and America. And so on the scheduled day, December 8, 1968, we were about seventy participants, representing twelve Asian countries, with various superiors of founding abbeys, and several experts and guests. Some monks also came from Australia and New Zealand. From Tokyo I had brought with me Fr. Oshida, a young Japanese Dominican, founder of a monastic community that took inspiration from Buddhism; he later became a traveling preacher. Recently I saw him again when he directed a series of conferences on Zen at a monastery in Belgium, where he would soon return. In a monastery in Indonesia I happened to notice in *Theological Studies*, published by the Jesuits, an article by a certain John Moffit, in which the author began by saying that for a long time he had been a Hindu monk in the Order of Ramakrishna. Upon returning from Martinique to Europe I made a one-day stopover in New York; I met with him there and secured his agreement to attend. He was invited and made a magnificent contribution. He was a renowned poet and a religious man. He was entrusted with the English edition of the proceedings of the Bangkok conference under the title of *A New Charter for Monasticism*. He did so well on it that he received a generous grant that enabled him to travel around the world and to write a book on his journey, no doubt very successfully. He remained a faithful friend to me and to AIM, until he died from a tumor.

The evening before the opening of the congress, I was asked to lead the session in which all the participants were to be introduced. I began by saying that the reason why this task was entrusted to me lay in the fact that I was "the clown of AIM and I have asked Merton to help me." He simply said, "We shall clown together." These were the last words that I ever heard him speak. The next morning, the solemn opening took place, in the presence of the apostolic nuncio, the Archbishop of Bangkok, the High Patriarch of the monks of Thailand, surrounded by a very colorful retinue, and other dignitaries. The Abbot Primate of the Benedictines, Rembert Weakland, presided with his customary skill. Then the first report was given by Merton. Given the growing influence of communism in Asia, I had asked him to speak about "monasticism and Marxism." He responded to me that the theme fascinated him, because he was just becoming familiar with the writings of Marcuse, a Marxist author now forgotten, but who was then very much in vogue.

The next morning I got up early and went outside for a bit of air. Not far from the site of the Red Cross where we were lodging, I saw a pagoda and went over there. It was the time at which the numerous community of bonzes was eating its only meal of the day, an abundant one that lasted for some time. A young bonze whom I had run into led me to the master of novices, who spoke English. He invited me courteously to sit near him and had food brought to me. After eating, he had me visit the whole monastery. Then I was present for the investiture of a young bonze. The fact remains that when I returned to the Red Cross at the end of the morning, Merton's conference was already over. So I was unable to listen to him. But since it had been recorded by several television stations, I had the chance to listen to it later in New York. It was truly remarkable.

We celebrated the Eucharist, and then a photograph was taken of some of us: it is the last one taken of him. However, that unplanned

morning visit to the pagoda had as a consequence the beginning of relations between that Buddhist community and our congress, which the
local bonzes were unaware of. During the following days we all went, in
small groups, to visit that monastery and to converse with both male and
female bonzes. We learned many things from each other. The pope had
sent us a telegram in which he expressed the wish that this congress be
for us the occasion of entering into contact with Buddhists. So, in the
afternoon I went to one of the Buddhist monasteries in Bangkok. When I
returned in the late afternoon, Fr. de Floris was waiting for me at the
door to prepare me for the upsetting news: "Fr. Thomas Merton is dead."
"Alleluia! Magnificat!" I exclaimed suddenly, content to know that he
had gone before us to where we are all heading. And I added, "A man
like him did not deserve a common death." Then in my room I wrote a
letter to Dom Flavian and began with these words: "At last, Fr. Louis
sees!" They had found him on his bed after his afternoon nap, with a long
burn mark on his chest caused by a short circuit: he had been electrocuted by a fan that had fallen on top of him.

The same evening I heard it said by an announcer on Thai television that this Christian monk had died from cardiac arrest, and I still
have the clipping from the newspaper *The Bangkok Post* of the following
day that confirmed this theory. After the solemn funeral, I had to give an
interview to a reporter of *The New York Times* who had been sent in and
who seemed to have great interest in this death. I conceded, as did
everybody, that Merton had died by electrocution. Afterwards a different interpretation circulated, according to which Merton had been
"liquidated" by the CIA, like Martin Luther King and others. I gave it no
credence. But now, in consideration of all the circumstances and knowing other facts that occurred afterwards, this sort of hypothesis no longer
seems to me to be excluded. Merton had spoken up in many of his writings against the Vietnam War.

The congress continued. The proceedings were published in
French in the journal *Rythmes du Monde*. There were two dominant
themes in the reports and in the exchanges of opinions. The first, constantly present, was that of poverty. What was generally favored was the
search for simpler forms of monastic life than those which were oftimes
customary in the great Western abbeys of recent ages: they ought not
serve as models. The other dominant theme was the necessity of finding
a way of inserting Christian monasticism into the forms of civilization of
different countries, taking into account the religions traditionally found
in each of them. One of the problems faced was that of the legitimacy of
the use of non-Christian texts in our liturgies. During the congress, a

positive solution was given, and thereafter this use was admitted, provided certain precautions were used in choosing the texts. Some rites were adopted that were of Hindu, Japanese, and Vietnamese inspiration, as was some music and some other elements typical of the different countries that were represented. The times of prayer, and especially that of the Eucharist, were the occasion of fervent spiritual experiences; friendships were formed and mutual encouragement was given. Indeed, in those times that were or were foreseen to be tragic in many regions, it was necessary to have a common hope and to practice it.

A "Union of Asian Monasteries," divided into four sections by different regions, was created. And two years later, in April 1970, one of them, the one of the Far East, convened a congress in Korea, a country then in full economic, cultural and religious development. I had documentation sent to me on its situation, that was the result of a broad inquiry conducted on the spot under the direction of Fr. Hutard, the director of the Centre de Recherches Socio-religieuses of the University of Louvain. We were twenty-five participants coming from five nations, in addition to the numerous members of the communities of Benedictine monks and nuns in that country. In Seoul, then in their monasteries and in sacred places of Buddhism and Confucianism, some eminent experts explained all the problems that were posed in every field. The poor, who are many, were certainly not forgotten. Dances, songs, games, and folkloric events abounded. We also visited historic and tourist sites and went to Buddhist monasteries. There we were able to engage in dialogue with the members, men and women, of those communities, to learn many things about them and to answer their questions.

The moment that remains most vivid in my memory is the one at which I entered a small sanctuary with a nun attending the congress, when we heard a voice coming out of it. There was a woman bonze in prayer. In unshakable recollection, as if we had not come to disturb her, she was reciting before the Buddha, or rather was singing some sutras with melodies that she was accompanying with a percussion instrument. By the end, her bows, her prostrations, her offerings and above all the profound calmness of her face and of all her gestures had left a vivid impression on us. Immediately afterwards she willingly made herself available for our questions. Other women bonzes invited the Benedictine nuns to return. On such occasions, beyond ideas, there was an encounter of hearts.

Then in 1973 a new great monastic congress for Asia was held in Bangalore, India. This time we had decided to examine all the problems in the light of a central and essential theme: the experience of God for the

Christian and the non-Christian monk. About a hundred participants had come from more than twenty nations. The Dalai Lama, at that time staying in Europe, had delegated two young lamas who made a fine impression. It was the time of the hippies and of "young people searching" for all sorts of things. Many of them were also present. There were two characteristics that marked the assembly: on the one side, many participants did not belong to the great monastic orders, but rather to those new groups, communities and ashrams under different names that were emerging a little bit everywhere, in India more than elsewhere, and which perhaps indicated one of the future ways of monasticism. On the other side, women were more numerous than they had been at previous meetings, and they had things to say. The desire was not to remain at the level of ideas, but the attempt was made to help each one gain some experience of what the others could offer. We were not disappointed, even though not everything was perfect. In particular, we regretted the fact that the representation of Sufis, and of Islam in general, was not really adequate. We also went to the temples of diverse religions and to the magnificent palace of the maharajah.

Still, we did not forget the poor and what Christian monasticism could do for them. We allowed ourselves to be questioned frankly by one another, and the dominant note was certainly not triumphalism! There was criticism of Westernization, of the preoccupation with activism and prosperity that sometimes has marked monasteries in Asia as elsewhere. In particular, costly buildings, sometimes built right when the people were being impoverished, was one of the most frequent targets.

Every day the three prayer gatherings, including a Eucharist, offered to Indian, Vietnamese, Korean, Japanese and Chinese groups the occasion to hold up for appreciation all the poetic and religious power of what had been done to integrate into Christian culture texts and attitudes derived from the Asian religions and civilizations, so ancient and so refined. Without understanding each other's languages, they could still participate together in the mystery of the presence of God.

Among these congresses were intermingled regional interreligious encounters, such as the one held in June 1977 in Massachusetts in the United States. All the new problems were concentrated there, from the Buddhist wave to feminism. Right at the first session, a religious was "mad" that she had again heard talk about *men* in general. One should always say: women, children and men. At the end of the morning, when I was invited to introduce the meditation, I conformed to this request and ended by quoting a bumper sticker that I had seen on the rear window of a car in California. It read, "Trust God, She takes care of you." Even those who were immersed in the immobility of a Buddhist meditative posture could not help but smile.

Finally, on the occasion of the "Year of St. Benedict" a new "monastic encounter of Asia" was held in Sri Lanka in August 1980. The site was Kandy, the country's religious capital, near the splendid temple that contained the relic of Buddha (a tooth) which, each evening during our sojourn, was carried in procession, accompanied by dozens of elephants, draped with festive ornaments, with members of the clergy sitting on them. There seemed to be more foreign tourists, especially Westerners, present there than actual pilgrims. Nonetheless I entered the temple many times to learn about the believers' forms of piety. One group of congress participants, including me, was received by the High Patriarch of the Buddhists. He told us of his regret at noticing among the people a decrease of what he called "devotion." This, we answered, is a matter of what we call secularization. The role of monasticism, Christian or not, is precisely that of giving witness to the permanent necessity of prayer.

Our entire congress had the theme of "the cry of the poor," material and spiritual poverty, the doctrine and the practice of poverty in Hinduism, in Buddhism, in Christianity, in Islam, with regard to lifestyle and all forms of worship. At the end, drawing conclusions, I recognized that we had not resolved the problem, because poverty is not first of all a problem or a set of problems. It is a mystery, which is realized in Christ once and for all. At the threshold of an era that is appearing new for many countries of Asia, Christian monks can remind everyone of a permanent reality: God himself become humble and poor in his incarnate Son. He looks to us not for prosperity but for faithfulness.

4. ASIA IN THE WEST

These many encounters gave me the opportunity to gather information that appeared in two long articles which appeared in different volumes entitled: *Problèmes du monachisme chrétien en Asie* and *Les leçons du monachisme bouddhique*. I was asked to have the second published in *Monastic Studies*. Indeed, while Buddhists ought to find out what Christianity is, we have something to learn from them concerning monasticism. This should be the aim of a true dialogue between us and them. Now, I have noticed quite often, especially in the United States, that there has been no dialogue: Buddhists would give soliloquies, often long, and Christians would listen without speaking. Buddhists generally are not interested in listening. It also happens that one or another of our missionaries, sent to the Far East to proclaim Christianity, returns from there to propagate Hinduism or Buddhism among Christians. Since the fifties we have seen a wave of Christian yoga inspired by Hinduism. It was followed by another, still spreading, consisting of both Tibetan Buddhism and — more often — of Japanese Buddhism and, in the latter case, of a practice that has always been in the minority in Japan: Zen. In the wake of AIM, an organization was created with the aim of fostering inter-monastic dialogue, under the acronym DIM. Its English-language equivalent, in the United States, was called NABEWD, North American Board for East-West Dialogue; it has since become an independent entity. Both have conducted fine activities.

In August 1987 an "international Buddhist-Christian congress" was held in Berkeley, California, given that the American Pacific Coast was considered to be half-way between what we call the Far East and the Far West which, for Buddhist countries, is Europe. There we admired the clarity with which both Asian Buddhists and Western specialists in Buddhism spoke. Mention was made of the "rationalism" which certain thinkers adopt, which leads to concepts that I have heard defined as "scholastic." In other, wider circles, the existence of a strong "anti-intellectual tendency" is emphasized. Many have acknowledged the recent and marginal character of lay meditation groups. The legitimate development of this non-traditional practice does not always seem to be accompanied, in the West, by other characteristic elements of Asian Buddhism, such as rites and ceremonies, devotional practices, and concrete support offered to the community. In Western Buddhism everything is concentrated on meditation, the aim of which is to reach a high level of consciousness (which can be the consciousness of a "nothingness") or, according to others, an elevated mystical state; but it always presupposes a state of psychological concentration.

On all these points, a great number of written reports were sent to us, constituting important documentation. Since I had to present Christian monasticism in a text that appeared in *Monastic Studies* in 1988, I tried to show that it realizes a kind of socio-religious archetype that is found in other traditions, with common themes such as that of the "assize" — now called "session" — in view of the unification of the person, and also to put into evidence what is specific about the monasticism of Jesus Christ, so rarely mentioned in this assembly, and the faith in a tri-une God, the perfect model of an interior and unifying session, after a phrase of a Father of the Church: "Sola tibi sedet Trinitas" (The Trinity sits for you alone).

Following upon this congress I reviewed, in a brief article that appeared in the journal *Buddhist Christian Studies*, the impressions that I had of these discussions and especially of the relatively vast American and European literature that concerned them. In particular, the traditional vocabulary of Christian spirituality was constantly applied to some interior states produced by the practice of Buddhism: for example, the word "contemplation," not long ago discredited in some Catholic circles, returned in force to designate the meditation and the exercises of mental pacification that Western Buddhism pursues, and in which important elements of authentic Buddhism found little room. I asked for a clarification of the semantics of the Buddhist-Christian encounter in order to avoid problems concerning some realities that are deemed identical that actually are not identical: the person in Christianity and the non-I in Buddhism; the presence of God and total emptiness; meditation and contemplation.

The appeal was heard and in view of an upcoming encounter, to be held in the summer of 1992, two commissions—one in the United States and the other the DIM—will strive to respond to them.

In the meantime, the religious forms of what some consider as the "Japanese invasion" continue to spread in different areas. In 1990, while I was at Cîteaux on the occasion of the "Year of St. Bernard," the father abbot, who had been invited to it, brought me to attend the inauguration of a Shintoist temple nearby—the Temple of the Cosmos—which bordered on a Japanese golf course. We were on the eve of the Gulf War.

In recent issues of the journal *Études bouddhistes-chrétiennes*, some comparative studies are beginning to be published with respect to not only the exercise of meditation and of other practices but also to doctrinal problems. These are what matter. Do not faith in God and the revelation that Jesus Christ has given constitute perhaps the difference between Christianity and other religions? And is it not desirable that Asians as well come to know them?

11

The Latin Americas

The title given to this chapter may raise some eyebrows. It calls to mind what others have expressed in works on *The Twenty Latin Americas* or even *Forty-eight Latin Americas*. This immense continent consists of at least two great zones: the one of *Hispanidad*, where Spanish is spoken, and the other which was and remains marked by Portugal, namely Brazil. The first comprises numerous nations which have in common the fact that at one time they were conquered by Spain. They owe a certain homogeneity to the influence coming from that country. But each one is different from the others. Even when there are border conflicts or other causes of opposition among them, they continue to ignore each other. Nonetheless, there is the Church which unifies them in a single faith and considers their problems on a continental scale.

1. MONASTICISM AND LIBERATION

From the beginning of 1965, in a letter of which a copy was sent to me, a Benedictine abbot in Brazil expressed the desire to give to Latin American monasticism a structure that it still did not have. He said that he was inspired by the meeting at Bouaké. He wished that, in that part of the world as well, meetings of the same kind might be organized, and he asked that I be invited to his continent. I went there alone in 1969 and 1973, visiting monasteries in Colombia, Chile, Argentina, Uruguay and Brazil. I returned to this last country in 1974 to give some conferences to monks and nuns of different nations in South America, at the abbey of Rio de Janeiro. Prior to that I had gone from the United States to Mexico and there my presence was once again requested during the winter of 1986-1987 for a series of retreats and conferences. The impressions that I still have of Latin and South America are, above all, of the situation in the seventies. After that everything changed.

For preparing to enter into contact with this part of the world that is so different from all the others, there was no lack of valuable works, both monographic and general. On the history of the Church in

Latin and South America, there were works like that of É.-D. Dussel. The customs and the thought of the pre-Columbian Indians had also been studied. I still recall having read on the plane while flying to that country the penetrating book by Unamuno entitled *Considérations sur la littérature hispano-américaine*. The monastic past had been the subject of a fair amount of research. There were more works on the history of particular communities than on visions of the whole. Nonetheless the research had started.

The Spanish that was spoken above all in the countries of the "Southern Cone" —Chile, Argentina, Uruguay—and which was called "Creole" abounded with charming diminutives. The original religiousness of the Indians had left traces in the culture and especially in the devotion: some residue of paganism had passed into the concepts and the religious practices of many. Theological production was abundant, a sign of intense vitality. Everything was being renewed: the synod of Medellín, in 1968, had given Catholic thought a new impulse. Moreover the presence of Asian religions, particularly Buddhism, was already becoming evident.

The first evidence that impressed itself was that of the contrast between the cities, especially in their old quarters and in the newer sections, and the immense misery of the majority of the people, in different modern suburbs. An example of this coexistence of two levels of life was found in Bogotá, the capital of Colombia. On the one side extended the "Bogotá of the Americans" —"Bogotá de los gringos" —with an abbey and its school, and on the other the Bogotá of the Indians, where a small monastery, Usme, had been for a short time; I went there. They had no car or telephone. But the monks from the other side were kind enough to put a bus at our disposal which allowed us to become acquainted with the real country.

In no way can I possibly forget, in a country cemetery near a monastery in Chile, the innumerable small graves with crosses bearing simply a name and then the legend, "Died at two (or three or four) years of age." Infant mortality was but one of the symptoms of the misery in which so many neighbors of our houses lived and died.

Upon arriving in one of these countries, one could not avoid being immersed in the great upheaval of Christian thought that has become renowned under the name of "liberation theology." In the south of Chile I met one of its pioneers, Fr. Comblin, a Belgian priest who had been expelled from Brazil for his subversive theology and who had been accepted by Bishop Larraín, a friend of Archbishop Helder Camara. He gave me many of his duplicated pamphlets, on account of which he remained suspect. Shortly afterwards, when I was leaving Argentina to go to Brazil, a nun warned me that, if I arrived there and the police discovered any publications bearing the name of Comblin, I would be risking imprisonment. She then pasted some decorative paper over all the covers, thus hiding the titles and the author's name. I still have them, with all the memories they bring back.

In Brazil I immediately purchased the most important book of Leonardo Boff, *Jesus Cristo Libertador*. The writings of Cardenal, about whom Merton had told me much, also circulated. The "theology of liberation" became for some a "theology of revolution." An entire "critical Church" provoked a reaction from a conservative angle. Some graffiti protested against "Marxist theologians." In every manner the importance of "politics" was affirmed; some said the word should be written with a capital "P" because it dominated everything. During my second sojourn in Chile, I was able to observe to what extent the socialist regime of Allende had changed the atmosphere that I had experienced before. Fortunately I did not have to take a position. Nonetheless, it fell to me to talk about "monasticism and revolution." The idea was that, by insisting greatly on the equality of everyone, nobles and serfs, and on the equity of distribution of everything among everyone under the governance of Christ, the Rule of St. Benedict was able to offer the elements of a theology of liberation in the sixth century. Gustavo Gutiérrez was, at that time, publishing his *Spirituality of Liberation*.

Near a monastery in Uruguay, in a very poor village that had been spiritually abandoned for some time, I happened to see at work one of the *Comunidades eclesiales de base* (CEB), base ecclesial communities, which were becoming numerous. I was also able to share a bit in its life: prayer meetings led by a local small businessman, a man both fervent and trained, a charitable aide with everybody, towards everybody. From time to time a religious missionary priest came, to give ministerial service. It all brought to mind the communities of the primitive Church. The Latin America Conference of Religious (CLAR) strove to have the teaching of the faith sustain all this fervor. The genuine people were unaware of the problems stirred up by the theologians working for them.

Some forms of authentically Christian prayer had to contribute to giving joy to all. Among Catholics a wind coming from the United States was blowing in favor of "houses of prayer" and of giving priority to the "prayer ministry." Hence the question that nagged me: "How can monasticism be placed in this whole context?" I had to go to some fifteen communities in the Hispanic zone and to about the same number in Brazil. This gave me the chance to observe life as it was led not only in the cities, large and small, but also in the country, where the people were also very diverse, as the proverb says: "When God creates peoples, he does not repeat himself."

No one evaded the duty of being involved in development. But it was known that this had to be an "integral development": not just material, but such as to enrich a human being in every sphere—political, cultural, religious. At what level would monasteries contribute? Should they dedicate themselves totally to immediate economic aid? Are they not perhaps the Church's "green spaces," so to speak, and on that basis necessarily less involved than other institutions in the task of evangelization and of liberation from poverty? It is a troubling theme, which we had debated in the United States during a session of EIOS; its texts appeared under the title *Prayer and Liberation*. I had written on "Jesus the Liberator."

Monasticism is liberation. Medellín had recognized the indispensable role of houses of contemplative life. Material development surely had to have a place in everybody's concerns, but not the only one. Many lay people pleaded for their faith to be nourished; some priests, more or less tempted to discouragement in the face of the immense task to be accomplished, had need of "green spaces" to recover their strength. For many, the most important problem was that of lived faith, of an encounter with God, of an experience of prayer. Certainly, as a slogan of that time said, "prayer is not enough." But without it nothing can be done that is lasting or profound. A permanent question, on which an inquiry was opened and about which it was necessary to write, was this: "Are our monasteries transparent to the Gospel?" Yes, to the extent that they do everything that can be done. Thus they should free themselves from the weight of the past without breaking with their authentic tradition. The country where poverty appeared to be the most burdensome—because it was the oldest in monasticism—was Brazil. From the time of the *Conquista*, Spanish-speaking areas had had some convents of nuns. Male monasticism was implanted only toward the end of the nineteenth century and especially in the twentieth. They were then inspired by the models provided by the great abbeys of Europe. In Brazil, Portugal had fostered the foundation of Benedictine monasteries since the sixteenth century: imposing monasteries were built in Rio, São Paulo and other cities, actual art museums of the Baroque period. The influence exercised by Beuron on Brazilian monasticism at the beginning of the twentieth century had ultimately reinforced the image of a grandiose past. In Spanish-speaking areas as well, they were also inspired at first by the great European abbeys.

Are our monasteries transparent to the Gospel? Without being the direct workers in the catechetical ministry and in social action, they can "think on" this action, encourage it, secure help for it. This is what the Benedictines of Los Toldos had done and continue to do for the Indians of the Auricanian tribe, who had come from Chilean Patagonia to settle in the Argentinian Pampas, not far from their abbey. And so as to give them not just the Word of God and bread, but also self-confidence, they had gathered in a museum all the mementos that they had been able to collect of the tribe's past and that remained dear to its members. One of the religious had written their history and the life of the chief who had led them to that place. In that monastery, as in others, after the Sunday Mass the community welcomed the field workers, some of them coming from afar, to an agapé that was greatly appreciated by the faithful, many of whom were undernourished. The temptation for the monks would have been to try to do everything, there where no one did anything in the face of the profound misery of all those who were not in a position to resolve human problems. One day, while I was at the monastery gate with the superior, a woman came to set at his feet, in a box tied with a cord, the body of one of her children who had died. She absolutely did not know what to do. They had to get a car, transport the rudimentary little coffin to the cemetery and bury it. The superior said to me, "As you see, here we must use all the *instrumenta bonorum operum* (instruments of good works) that St. Benedict mentions, including that of burying the dead."

2. In Brazil

I went to Brazil only twice. The first time I arrived from the south, from Argentina to São Paulo, right in the center of the old city, and I was immediately taken to the grand and beautiful abbey of São Bento. I said to the monk who picked me up, "Show me the São Paulo that nobody sees, the one of the majority of the people, the one of the poor." We took a taxi, so that we could get out at the perimeter of a *favela* and then walk in on our own. We did not have far to go. These shantytowns are found just a few hundred yards from the center of the large cities, with their banks and their luxury hotels. There stood a spectacle of misery that I would see again many times in this country, as well as in others: hundreds of thousands of peasants who come looking for work in the cities without finding any and who are left poorer than before. However, they keep smiling, without violence, and tranquilly express their faith with various gestures. And then there are the children with the swollen bellies, so characteristic everywhere of the undernourished, with faces bearing the marks of skin diseases, yet with a clear gaze, full of trust. Contact of this kind with the reality of the country was indispensable and preliminary to any active service of the Church and its monasticism.

From São Paulo I was to go to various monasteries, from Curitiba in the south of the country up to the Northeast. Then I went back to Brazil for a second visit to give a series of conferences at the abbey of São Bento in Rio de Janeiro, which was followed by another session of talks. Everything had been planned in Spain.

One evening in Barcelona, during a session of the Spanish Society for Monastic History, I took a long walk with a Brazilian abbot in whom the memories I had of the misery of his country seemed to have sparked a discovery. The next morning he said to me, "I didn't sleep all night after that brainwashing. It is absolutely necessary that you come back to Brazil." We settled the dates and I was able to go after first making a detour to the United States, where the meeting in Massachusetts was being held.

For me this was a chance to re-visit many communities of different Orders, from the Northeast to the South. A crowded session held at São Bento in Rio brought together a great number of nuns and monks from several Latin American countries. It was a relaxed and joyous atmosphere in which, privately or publicly, many problems could be faced. It was decided to do something special for me by driving me to Copacabana, the luxurious beach where every year the Rio Carnival harvests victims of all kinds. I also succeeded in getting back to the *favelas*, in one of which there was a group of Little Sisters of Jesus. But the air I was breathing in those zones, lacking in hygiene, became intolerable for me; an otolaryngologist in Rio advised me absolutely not to go back there.

Since I came from New York on a night flight, I was able to read a magazine put out by the American airline. How better to get prepared for landing in this country? Yet it did not discuss the Brazilians at all. The readers it addressed were businessmen going there to invest, to make the poor work and to make themselves rich. Brazilians do not matter to them. All that counts are the profits that they will make at the expense of the people of Brazil. They are given good advice about the regions where they can invest most advantageously. For example, where the people are poorest, the businessmen will earn more. Without doubt they will have to bring in some specialized workers from other areas; why should they ever have to help these wretches become trained? But since they will pay the laborers almost nothing, it will all be profit. All the photos show

Copacabana, the beach of great luxury, with its hotels, restaurants, bars and pleasure sites, as well as all of its night life. Naturally the *favelas* do not exist: they are not mentioned, nor are they shown. However, they do not forget to praise the beauty of Brazilian women: is that not another way of attracting businessmen?

After the stay in Rio, the abbot of Olinda brought me to nearby Recife to meet the bishop of that city, Helder Camara. I met him in a small room of what without doubt was a palace, at one time modest but now shabby. In another little room, a group of very simple men and women was there to assist him. Yet he found the time to speak a while with me. He was just as he appears on television or in newspaper photos: thin, spry, restless. His simplicity, in keeping with that of his people, contrasted with the luxury of other circles that shared his same faith, but not the same sensitivity to misery. I recalled that a short time earlier he had appeared to a crowd at the Parc des Princes in Paris, saying, "I am going to speak to you in the Camara dialect. Do you know what that consists of? Three things. First of all, I will speak to you in my bad French, secondly with many gestures, and finally with all my heart." In fact, he expresses himself well in French. But it is undeniable that he gesticulates a lot: he *lives* what he says. And it is also undeniable that he has a great heart and great humility.

He made no special revelation to me. He only said to me what he was saying to everybody everywhere: his protest against the fact that the poor are not helped and are despised, while the rich are honored: "To feed a normal family here, a worker would have to work twenty-seven hours a day." I then remembered what I had read during the flight from New York. And shortly beforehand, in Curitiba, I had seen a large plane of the American army landing, and out of it came a general surrounded by some soldiers and welcomed with great honors by a group of officials.

The "sign" of the evangelical spirit, Helder Camara had said, is that one has with the poor what he called "physical contact," meaning that it is not enough to love them from a distance, even through a bank check.

At Curitiba, a beautiful old city of colonial style, they asked me, "What would you like to see?" "The market," I replied, "since that is where the people can be found." Walking as much as I could, I met people, isolated or in groups, who were happy to be alongside a "Mister." Along the way I bought one of those illustrated leaflets, printed on low-grade paper, that shows the level and the centers of interest of those who prefer images to writing; simplicity, charm and sometimes Christian piety.

The most memorable experience I had was in the company of two Benedictine Oblate women in a small community located in the heart of São Paulo. They pray during the morning, then from noon until midnight they engage in a ministry that consists of showing to the poorest that they are always worthy of being loved. The stories that they told me were unbelievably sad and cruel, whether about the misery of the poor or about the corruption of those who are supposed to have the task of averting crimes and injustices. Children abandoned by or escaped from their families, who organize themselves in gangs to protect themselves from the police. When at night they see a patrol car arrive, they hide behind garbage bags. One time the police, not having noticed their presence, drove over them and one boy had his leg cut off. If they are caught, when they are released they torture cats in the same way that they had to suffer.

During an evening tour we pick up a boy numb with cold. They warmed him up with some tea poured from a thermos and with a sandwich. We stopped in front of a store and gave him some change; with it he quickly ran very proudly to buy some cigarettes, paying for them with money that for once had not been stolen. What a rehabilitation right before our eyes!

A little later we saw under the portico of a church, at the end of a blind alley, what seemed to be two human bodies entirely covered, since it was cold. We approached them. The noise of our engine awakened one woman with a prematurely worn face; she quickly told us, pointing to the other: "Let her sleep. She drank a lot...." She was amazed that we stayed to talk with her. We gave her some tea and a sandwich; she asked for more, and then she wanted a cigarette; she was used to begging, to depending upon others. She livened up and told us her life story without shame, not sparing any horrifying detail. At the age of nine she was sold by her father, who had killed her mother by blows with a stick, when she was bitten by a snake hidden in the firewood she was using for her cooking fire. Right after the burial, her father had her leave by another gate of the cemetery where someone was waiting for her. And after that, what horrors! But she, a woman of character, became the leader of a gang of other unlucky women who, like her, organized themselves in self-defense. The poor do indeed help one another. It was clearly evident that this woman was glad that someone was listening to her, was interested in her—something that she in no way understood—in short, that someone loved her as she is.

I learned that there are rudimentary refuges for taking these lost souls in. Some Christians expend themselves for them, with a sense of the Gospel that is proportionate to all this misery. There a young man whom I met discovered his vocation to monasticism. Indeed, caring for the poor, approaching them, loving them is something that changes them and changes us. Should we not give thanks for having found God in the least of his own?

3. MARY THE LIBERATOR

During the winter of 1986-1987 I was asked to preach a retreat in the large and beautiful modern Benedictine abbey in Tepeyac, near Mexico City, and to give conferences in some of the country's other monastic communities. I had not been there in over twenty years. In the meantime, there as elsewhere, many things had changed. The heritage of the pre-Columbian civilizations and of the Spaniards was always present in the archaeological, artistic and — it must be noted — religious fields, but in increased contrast with the technology that in many places assured a surprising development for industrialization. The people as a whole, whom I could find in the markets near their homes, maintained all their charm. The knowledge I had of the thought and customs of the ancient peoples, Nahuatl and others, was enriched thanks above all to the publications of León Portilla. Moreover, studies had been done on the forms of life, of an almost monastic type, of certain Indian religious groups.

Monastic communities had multiplied and organized into a Mexican Benedictine Union, of which the president was Fr. Gabriel Chávez de la Mora of the abbey of Tepeyac. An architect of great experience, he built marvelous churches inspired by the style of the old buildings of the Indians. Also at Tepeyac, a talented poet, Fr. Ezequiel Bas Luna, a native of Argentina, was preparing the foundation — which was later realized — of a simple monastery called "La Soledad" [Solitude].

The basilica of the Virgin of Guadalupe, wholly transformed and modernized, offered an example of art at once simple, majestic and functional. It is the most electronic religious monument in the world. Even the veneration of the miraculous image was carried out from a moving walkway.

Yet the greatest new element was the interpretation that studies by numerous philologists and historians have given to the apparitions of Our Lady of Guadalupe using the oldest text that recounts the facts of that time, through which God had wanted to give to humans a lesson in inculturation and liberation. After my experiences in Latin America, I could not give this literature a neutral reading without committing myself to a particular position.

In 1531, criticism began over the colonial regime and the spiritual conquest enforced by Spain ten years earlier: evangelization, to be sure, but imposed by the sword. The Nahuatl people had been oppressed many times by the Aztecs and the Incas. But now the dominant power was that of the Spaniards. In the zone of Tepeyac, similar to those artificial hills that are improperly defined as pyramids, a "poor Indian" catechumen, Juan Diego, saw in a bush the Blessed Virgin who appeared with Indian features and in the garments of an Indian woman, speaking to him in his native Nahuatl. He heard songs similar to those of his people and to those of Indian birds. The Queen of Heaven addressed him with a diminutive: "Juanito." He answered her, "Lady and my little one — niñita — I must go and listen to my priests, the Lord's ministers." He was, therefore, a faithful Christian. She told him about her wish to see a temple erected on that site in which she would show "all her love, her compassion, her aid and her defense": he must go tell it to the bishop!

Juan Diego went there; they made him wait a long time. Neither those in the curia nor the bishop — all Spaniards — could believe that God had chosen a poor Indian as a messenger. To confirm that he was truly sent by the Mother of God, she healed his uncle (the uncle was an important figure in the family structure of the Indians). He had contracted a virus borne by the Spaniards, which traditional medicine could not heal: another consequence of the domination. When Juan told the bishop about it, he refused to believe that an Indian was proclaiming the truth. Mary then performed a new miracle: in the middle of winter she made roses bloom and asked Juan to bring them to the bishop. At the moment that he opened his mantle where he had gathered them, upon it appeared the image of Mary. The bishop, now won over, had to accept the message and throughout the country these events were retold from village to village. Thus began the evangelization of the Indians by other Indians. What an advance for them, beginning with one of their own — a poor man besides — Juan Diego! In the oldest account the word "liberation" does not appear. Yet it is precisely about this: the whole text aims at showing that the bishop — a Spaniard — must acknowledge that the Indian possesses his own dignity and deserves trust. The temple that Mary, by the will of God, wanted to have erected would be a permanent testimony of the truth and the relevance of this message.

After having read the texts that explain its origin and its significance, one can no longer admire the basilica of Guadalupe as a mere devout tourist. There the Lord of the world calls upon all those in power to liberate those who have no power.

12

In the Caribbean and the South Pacific

1. IN THE ANTILLES

The list of missions given was determined by the geography of the monastic foundations. Now, there were some in different archipelagos of the Atlantic and especially in the South Pacific. In the former, there was the monastery in Martinique where I went in 1967. This island in the Caribbean Sea is part of the Lesser Antilles. The overwhelming majority of its population is black, the descendants of Africans. They have kept many of the traits of those indigenous to the Slave Coast. Their religion, which is very sincere, still includes certain Voodoo practices. One Sunday, after the main Mass, a book of prayer was found in the church that one of the faithful had forgotten. They showed it to me. Our Middle Ages were represented in it. One of the formulas invoked the "Great Saint Abelard," persecuted by enemies. It was asked of him to strike down (in Creole, "to make a pile of") our adversaries. It was almost always a matter of "praying against" someone, never on behalf of him. I admired even more the Catholic fervor of the monks and of all those who came to share their prayers and joys with them. They would express themselves in the delicious language that is Creole: Lamb of God, for example, is "mouton bon Dieu."

My schedule was interrupted by one of the hurricanes that sometimes break out violently and move swiftly across immense distances, causing destruction and death in the archipelagos which they assault from time to time. Fortunately some meteorological stations in the United States and elsewhere follow them with great attention and announce beforehand the itinerary that any disturbance, designated with a name, will take, thus allowing the needed precautions to be taken in homes and outside of them. It seems that people are almost accustomed to such unexpected events, thanks especially to the warnings offered by these forecast centers.

Before leaving the island, I managed to make a pilgrimage to the place where the monastery originally started, Mont Pelé, called such because everything on it was totally leveled (in Creole, "pelé") by a hurricane. In the monastery and in a friendly family, they wanted me to listen to Creole music, and to have me taste the punch made of rum and honey as well as other specialties of the island, bananas and fruits which, unfortunately, constitute the country's only wealth. I read everything that I could find in the monastery's library about the sorrowful past of the Antilles: those centuries of slavery caused by Europeans, all Christians, have left many recollections in the people's deep memory, many traces on a psychological level, and explain much of their behavior.

The superior of the community, Fr. Webster, was English-speaking and bilingual, originally from St. Lucia, an island in the Lesser Antilles which, over the span of a century, was under the domination of fourteen different colonial powers before recently attaining autonomy. Soon Webster would become archbishop of his country of origin. Each one of the islands had been annexed by a European power: England, France, Holland, Spain.... But the African base reinforced by the Holy Spirit assured the unity of them all: one and the same faith within one and the same culture.

2. IN OCEANIA

In the South Pacific, in New Zealand, there is a monastery which is the furthest from our European countries: Kopua. Its name is appropriately Our Lady of the Southern Star. I had to go there twice, and three times to the neighboring country, Australia. The journey itself was instructive in many aspects: across the whole Pacific, up and down this ocean, passed the International Date Line at which, from east to west, the change in time zones is twenty-four hours. Leaving from Sydney on the morning of St. Bernard's day, I arrived at a Trappist monastery in Oregon at the same hour of the same day. However, the Date Line is not a straight line: during the same night, one can go back and forth in flight between days several times.

In coming and going, stopovers allowed me to perceive something of the variety of the many lands of that immense part of the world which includes Polynesia and its inhabitants. It extends toward the south in Micronesia and then into Indonesia, from which many peoples traversed the Indian Ocean toward Madagascar and the nearby lands. How enormous is the cultural richness of Oceania! These territories have experienced the vicissitudes of colonialization since the end of the sixteenth century. Many regions have borne and still keep the names that evoke their conquerors who followed each other, as "New Holland" became the British Australia, or those countries which French and English have called New Caledonia or New Guinea. A museum like the one in Honolulu, capital of the Hawaiian Islands that are now American, gives rich evidence of Polynesian cultures and of their artistic and religious traditions. No wonder, then, that all kinds of curious people go there to learn, just as I did. But everywhere what is most interesting is not the souvenirs of the past but the people living now.

Everywhere, in the same way, one can perceive immediately the contrast which still exists between the world of the whites and the one that remains among the people whose roots are in these lands. In Tahiti, the "pearl of Oceania," during a stopover between two days that had the same date, I succeeded in making some very edifying contacts with people of the Church and specialists in ethnology and comparative religion. At the restaurant of the hotel where the airline had us lodging, I was listening to the conversation at a nearby table of some sports judges who had come for the Pacific Olympic Games: Polynesians could kick a ball only with bare feet, but international rules required shoes. Another day at the Singapore airport, I saw a group of young blacks passing by in colorful garments as they were about to board a flight to Rome. All the passengers waiting pointed out to one another that the young men were all wearing brand-new shoes, but were walking with difficulty. I went to ask one of them who they were. "We are Catholics from the island of Samoa, with the first bishop of our race, the one whom the Pope consecrated during his journey through Oceania. We are going to gather around the Holy Father and sing at his Mass for the Day of Missions." There they were shod like Europeans. Fortunately, inculturation has since made some progress.

This began to be encouraged by a journal entitled *Catalyst*, published by the Melanesian Pastoral and Social Service Institute of Papua-New Guinea. We were receiving it at Clervaux, and I had begun to read it carefully to prepare for my trips to those regions where the Church is lively and active.

Upon my arrival in Noumea, the capital of New Caledonia, in 1971, I was allowed to take part in one of the first sessions of the delegates of the religious institutes of that archdiocese which includes New Caledonia and the islands that depend on it. Two Trappists and their superior were there; he had prepared the meeting and led the cordial assembly in which different institutes, peoples and countries were represented. This first contact was already indicative of the specific function

171

that a small group of monks can carry out in the Church. Their monastery was in an area, on the top of a hill, from which the vista extended on the one side to the Coral Sea and on the other to the mountains — a harmonious landscape colored by every kind of flower, with some reddish patches in the distance marking the nickel mines, the exploitation of which would direct the country's economic and social future. The three members of the community constructed two modest buildings, one for the monastery and the other for the guest house: that too had been planned and was indicative of the wish that the monks have of sharing with others their life of prayer by welcoming them. In contrast to these two houses, which were modern, the chapel had been constructed by some Christians of the area, the Lifous of Graitcha, as a traditional hut with local materials — bamboo, mangrove roots, liana — and without any metal. The altar, the tabernacle, the statue of the Blessed Virgin and everything decorating this oratory made apparent the wish of those who had thought of setting it in the midst of this country. It was in rapid evolution, yet rich in an ancient culture that the wonderful museum in Noumea enabled people to understand and admire.

Everyone perceived this intention, as the stream of believers demonstrated who came to be present at the Sunday Mass and to sing. Although representing different races and circumstances, they felt themselves to be at home, and in God's home. There was a symbol of this synthesis and especially of this reconciliation of cultures and of faith which should mark a new era in religious history.

Moreover, there were many people helping the monks: while the monks dedicated themselves to prayer, anonymous donors of all kinds came to leave at the door of their house vegetables, fruits and other gifts; on weekends or whenever possible, some volunteers came to work with the monks on the construction site, in the garden, and on the plantation. The Sisters of the diocesan congregation, natives of New Caledonia or of New Hebrides, also offered their help; their novitiate was not far away from the monastery. There, as in the chancery, in the nearby missions and in their offices, one could hear expressed all the hopes for the future of this Church, in this monastic presence and in its peaceful growth.

Here there were several archipelagos and, in each of them, peoples are diverse from one island to another. This fact, which constitutes both an asset and a hardship, would not fail to have repercussions on the development of the community. Fortunately, it was not yet accustomed to monumental structures or to observances that could hinder its adaptation to the requirements of a changing situation and that would have involved some element of surprise. An enlightening detail: the monastery's small library already included a certain number of works on the country's history and civilization. One of these was a *Directory of Caledonians*. It told of explorers, traders, missionaries and many others — "cycling racers, adventurers, swindlers." Now a place must be reserved for those adventurers of God who are monks.

Some Trappists in New Caledonia and a hermit, who was part of their "communion," in New Hebrides were very few for the thousands of islands that constitute Polynesia, Melanesia and Micronesia. This vast part of the world, infinitely diverse, is still almost entirely without monasticism: one can only admire more the Trappist community of Sept Fons, because it had the courage to venture into what, humanly speaking, involved a huge risk. But cannot God, who has created so many different images of himself, also give the grace of adventure? Here communications are made difficult by distances, at times very great, that separate the islands from each other, and by the scattering of human groups, by their distance from the much larger continents where the Church has been able to organize best. That same year of 1971 followed the one in which Paul VI had consecrated in this part of the world the first Papuan bishop. And the journal *Catalyst* was trusting in the efforts realized for the creation of "a Melanesian theology and spirituality."

In the Cistercian monastery of Kopua in New Zealand, some Trappists from Ireland had brought monastic life to this extreme part of the world. Various novices from the country had gone there to join them, but also some from New Guinea, and this gave the community a special richness. Their welcome was all the warmer the more they felt isolated. This sort of situation and the tranquillity that reigned in the country could not help but favor a peaceful monastic life: the monks were far from the tensions and problems that perturbed almost all other countries.

Yet new problems were beginning to be posed for Christian opinion. For example, Hans Küng had just begun a tour of conferences and meetings with clergy; the major press was giving him rather broad coverage, and without doubt ecumenism and other fields of religious action would draw some advantage from this movement of ideas, even though at an earlier time it would have generated some confusion. The monks had to have a role to play in the evolution that had just begun, but whose progress was foreseeable; with much openness and courage, they consented to consider these future perspectives. The essence of their contemplative life could be safeguarded precisely when they had to modify this or that element of their observances or concepts. For example, they had adopted a schedule imported from Ireland, as well as certain forms of rural economy. Yet the young monks from Papua-New

Guinea found it hard to sustain this kind of life as well as certain activities typical of a climate totally different from their own. I made some comments on their behalf.

Shortly afterwards, the superior wrote to me that they had spoken in their chapter about all the points that had been brought up for discussion, and that they had decided to make the needed adaptations: "We have modified the schedule, and even the Irishmen are content." Before my departure they were so kind as to award me a diploma as "honorary member" of their Order, which at that time was still called "Order of Reformed Cistercians of the Strict Observance." I had accepted, on condition that I be dispensed from the observance: "Never strict, never reformed: it is too late!" They consented, and this gesture was the symbol of their being spiritually open to something that did not come from their Order, from their country of origin or from the heritage of recent centuries. On each of the islands on which monasteries existed, they absolutely did not run the risk of isolationism. Everything in them was being renewed thanks to a return to tradition. Medieval history could be a teacher of life.

3. IN AUSTRALIA

In a few hours' flight from Auckland, the capital of New Zealand, one reaches Sydney, a great and beautiful city situated on the south coast of Australia that, as it is said, is the smallest of continents but the largest of islands. All the quarters of this city bear the names of London suburbs, as in Toronto, and one sees all the prosperity that the British have brought.

Australia is an extremely vast and varied world, and is a kind of mystery. The impression that one could have when transferring from one religious house to another is that of an overdeveloped country and one spiritually without problems. Little by little, however, one realizes that behind this façade the situation is diverse. The secretary of the Benedictine Union of Australia and New Zealand presented me with a well-planned and precise itinerary. Not only was I able to visit all the monasteries in the country, but I also had contacts with people of the Church and people of science, specialists in pastoral work, catechesis and religious sociology. I was able to hold some very enlightening conversations with them before and after the conferences that I was asked to give at the national seminary in Wellington, at the scholasticate of the Fathers of St. Columban, at the theological faculty in Manly, where in addition to students there had also gathered a good number of priests and religious men and women, at the history department of the faculty of letters of Macquarie University in Sydney, as well as on other occasions. Everywhere the welcome was extremely warm. Some visits to the suburbs of the immense port of Sydney, and to the reception center in which members of the Society of St. Vincent de Paul provide lodging each night for free to four hundred homeless poor, as well as the questions that I was able to ask here and there, revealed to me certain aspects of this country that do not appear at first glance.

The National Library in Sydney holds a rather rich collection of manuscripts which have been registered in an excellent catalogue. When I went there and introduced myself, the librarian said to me, "Oh, you are the French prelate that the newspapers are talking about!" I thought she was going to throw me out. "No," I answered, "his name is Lefebvre; my surname is different." The schismatic Archbishop Lefebvre was due to visit Australia where, it seems, one of his sisters was the prioress of a Carmel, and he had already been challenged by the press in this Anglican-majority country. I was then able to work peacefully.

The monastic life had been introduced more than a century ago, when a member of Downside Abbey in England, Fr. Bede Polding, was sent there; he would later become archbishop of Sydney. In 1857 he had founded a congregation of Benedictine Sisters whose name was a program: Sisters of the Good Samaritan. His intention, according to the authentic sources that I examined in the archives of the general house of St. Scholastica in Sydney, was to have religious women "who would concern themselves with the humblest classes of society, especially women, girls and children of the poor class," in short, those whom no one was caring for. Hence the name he gave to these religious. Because of the historical circumstances determined by the evolution of this former British colony, their principal activity became teaching in schools. Today some of them are involved in a "motor mission": they go in car to teach catechism in some country schools.

Thanks to a sensible plan and to the collaboration of all the Sisters, I was able to meet most of them during two weekends, festively gathered in the houses of several states in Australia and in the novitiate at Pennant Hills; only the day planned for Canberra was canceled because of an initial attack of laryngitis, nor was I able to visit the convents located in the country's extreme north. Everywhere a series of questions had been prepared which the Sisters had posed.

Other monastic communities had also been founded in this country: at Manly, a quarter of Sydney, there was the one of the Benedictine Nuns of the Perpetual Adoration who had come from Tyburn in

London; at Pennant Hills, that of the Benedictine nuns who now have been transferred and have made a foundation; at Arcadia, that of the Sylvestrine Benedictines; at Tarrawarra, that of the Trappists from Ireland. All these communities, just as those of distant Western Australia and the one in New Zealand, were united with each other by an information center that published a "Letter," now become "an Australasian Benedictine Review" with the title *Tjurunga,* from the name of a sculpted stone which the Aborigines of this country venerated. There were also other houses of contemplatives; one of them had for its livelihood the manufacture of beauty products both for women, called "Monastique," and men, "Cardinal."

The cultural level was high, as could be seen when a congress was held in 1977 in Sydney to celebrate the centenary of Polding, as well as on other occasions, such as a well-organized conference that took place at Tarrawarra. There in particular the prioress general of Tyburn gave a talk, accompanied with slides, on the Rule of St. Benedict interpreted according to Jung's psychological categories. This presentation, with fine nuances, constituted an enlightening example of psychohistory. Nonetheless, considerations of this kind astounded those for whom psychology suffices for everything. It was necessary to take up the prioress's defense.

The fact that South Australia was a "rest and recreation" — R&R — zone for American soldiers on duty in the Vietnam War created some problems that brought back some of those that existed at the time of the foundation of the Sisters of the Good Samaritan; it opened broad areas for pastoral ministry and for prayer. A balance had to be found between action and contemplation.

I was invited twice to the University of Tasmania, on the island located to the south of Australia; its capital, Hobart, for its part lay on the southernmost part of the island. Because of its extreme distance from Europe, Tasmania was chosen by the English in the nineteenth century as a place of confinement and as a penitentiary. At that time most of the prisoners were Irish Catholics. Through the influence of certain pietist movements, it was thought that a period of prolonged "solitary confinement" would enable them to repent. Many became crazy or else injured themselves permanently while attempting suicide, made impossible by the kind of cell in which they were confined. Now people were visiting these "historic prisons" become museums of horror; illustrated books are published about them. The descendants of the survivors are now proud of them. A lovely culture has developed. At Hobart I met with Archbishop Young of that city; I had met him when I worked for the post-conciliar liturgical *Consilium*, in which he also took part.

At the university, after one of my conferences on a theme of medieval history, a group of female and male students recited in Latin one of the dramas that the abbess Roswitha had written in the tenth century in Saxony; she believed that her nuns — at least so she says — were reading too gladly the comedies of Terence.

Crossing enormous distances, I went to Perth in Western Australia and thence to the Abbey of New Norcia. I found myself affected by a loss of voice a second time, but it was treated and I healed; still, I had to stay in that region longer than I had planned. This trouble recurred with the same symptoms exactly one year later. Probably I had contracted a virus on one of the Oceanic islands. I went to a specialist in "colonial diseases," who prescribed for me a remedy found only in military hospitals: indeed, it was used by soldiers serving in the Vietnam War. So from city to city in the United States, this doctor continued to follow me and to heal me.

From New Norcia I canceled, by telegram, some commitments already made for Brussels and Paris, and this prolonged convalescence gave me all the time needed to look over this kind of monastic town with its church, its chapels, its two orphanages in which the majority of children are Aborigines, its two schools for boys and girls, the buildings that serve for the farm, the vineyard and for raising a large amount of livestock, the residence built for the personnel of the schools, for the Aborigine families and, at the center, the abbey that dominated everything. It, like the church, was in that "colonial" style that was created in the first half of the nineteenth century, and of which there are still some rare examples in the rest of the country. Some architectural elements inspired by English residences of the Victorian era join together with some traces of Spanish influence. I also had time to learn in depth the history of New Norcia thanks to the works, published or unedited, that were written about it, and thanks to its archives, its library — for the country, exceptionally old and rich — and its two museums, one of works of art and the other of historical relics. I was able to share in the community's life, to be present at the parish Sunday Mass, to have some meetings with teachers and students of the two schools and with members of the three religious communities who work in the place: besides the monks, there are the Sisters of St. Joseph who operate the girls' school and the Benedictine Sisters in the orphanage. For two evenings they all came together to socialize joyously.

There were two characteristics that gave this settlement a unique interest. First of all, there was its long and tormented history, sometimes dramatic, often heroic, also tied to that of Catholicism in Australia and to that of the Benedictine rebirth in Europe during the nineteenth century. At New Norcia they expended themselves ceaselessly for the good of the black-skinned Aborigines (the natives) who constitute one of the oldest races of humanity. During the nineteenth century, and sometimes even later, they were called "savages" and were victims of what can be defined as true genocide. Some now remain, of different branches, in Sydney and in the cities, in the country and especially in southwest Australia, and even more in northern Australia.

New Norcia had been founded among them and for them with a missionary aim. The implantation and then the development of the monastery had presented huge and nearly continuous difficulties. Later a distant mission was begun in the far part of the territory on Australia's northern coast at Kalumburu, about 1,800 miles away. I did not manage to get there for lack of good health and time: there was only one regular air flight every fifteen days one way and fifteen days later for the return. Nonetheless I had the greatest possible number of contacts with the Aborigines of the schools at New Norcia and with those of the families who live on a hill not far away, where I could go. One evening a festival organized by the Benedictine monks and nuns brought together whites and people of color who shared the same simple joy: it was a great experience and a magnificent demonstration of charity.

One name dominates the whole history of New Norcia: that of Dom Salvado, the Spanish Benedictine founder of the monastery and of the mission in 1846; he became bishop in 1849 and animated everything for fifty years. From his arrival in Australia, he had believed that he could recruit monks from among young Aborigines. Not long afterwards he took two of them to Europe and presented them to Pius IX. Passing through Paris during the revolution of 1848, one of them, upon seeing some men preparing to fight in the streets, asked, "Why do you not take away their weapons, like you did to us?" Salvado's answer is supposed to have been, "Because they are civilized." Later a successor to Salvado, Father Torres, also become a bishop, but died prematurely in 1914 worn out by his efforts. Other monks had been victims in different ways— sometimes by violence—of their dedication to the Aborigines. In 1943, Father Thomas, the superior of the mission of Kalumburu, was killed point-blank by Japanese soldiers when he rushed to help some children who were being massacred.

The impressions left by a place so rich in great memories as New Norcia cannot be summarized without impoverishing them; but it can be hoped that its future will follow in the line of its past.

Then from Perth across the Indian Ocean I returned to Europe, rejuvenated in twenty-four hours as at every new turn of the world.

13

Before the End

1. CONTINUITY

Parallel to my life as a traveler, I was continuing my life as a scholar, something that I had been asked to do and that had been made possible for me. It was enough to respond to the requests that came to me from different places concerning questions of monastic culture. This "monastic humanism," about which I had published a kind of manifesto in 1953, under the form of a prologue to some *Analecta monastica*, continued to arouse interest. I was invited to speak at universities in Macerata, Ascoli Piceno and elsewhere. Thus I could revisit for one last time two cities that I had loved so much: Venice, where I talked on "Monastic Themes in the Work of Petrarch," and Naples where the title chosen was "Contemplatives in Life." Old themes were becoming current again, such as that of friendship: this allowed me to make a charming sojourn in Oxford in order to evaluate a doctoral thesis in theology. Many times my companion then was my young namesake Jean Leclercq, a native of Liège, still a student and destined for a brilliant future. The author of the thesis in question, E. Carmichael, showed that the positive concept of friendship, obscured by an attitude of diffidence after the end of the Middle Ages, had been given new value in our century by the personalist philosophy of the thirties — the period in which I discovered friendship.

These "minor texts" which had occupied me for so long now appeared as the witnesses of a simple literature, I dare say popular, that responded to the needs of the majority of monks and nuns, unable to draw benefit from the difficult tracts that the great spiritual authors had written. I would need another whole lifetime to study the popular monastic literature that now I can only propose to the attention of medievalists. Nonetheless, the *Parabolaire* of Galand de Reigny, which I had made known in 1948, was finally edited and translated in the series *Sources Chrétiennes* in 1992. The integral history, which includes what is now defined as the history of "mentalities," presupposes that not only the works of authors be considered who have become famous for being elevated, but also works of everybody.

One of the sets of documentation not yet exploited that I have available has as its object the history of imagery. I had occasion to speak about this in 1989 during a congress organized at St. Anselm's Abbey in New Hampshire to celebrate St. Anselm, and recently to return to the same topic for a congress on phenomenology that was held in Luxembourg in June 1992 on "Allegory." Even such a speculative and sometimes subtle author as Anselm of Aosta made wide use of figures and parables in his systematic writings and left a whole collection of *Similitudines*. This remains a whole field to be explored, about which we should be more careful insofar as that language of the biblical, patristic and monastic tradition, in which the images and resonances take up so much space, is close to that of today's media, composed of a "mix" of slogans, sounds and images. To know the past, it is not enough to identify and date documents and to know their authors; it is very important to know something about the reactions of their readers and listeners or, more exactly, of their readers who at the same time were listeners.

Even interpretation raises new problems: must all psycho-history be suspect in the eyes of historians seeking absolute objectivity? For some, the mere word "psychology" evokes that of psychoanalysis, with all the diffidence that it arouses, especially in certain clerical circles, along with Freud, his work, his influence, his followers. Both in establishing facts and in interpreting them, it is necessary to be able to risk opinions, to have some bit of humor regarding the judgments of scholars. One time I wrote down the wise advice given by a Carthusian of the seventeenth century, Dom Bruno Malvesin, who paraphrased two Latin verses of an unidentified author:

> *Oblecter, animum plebs est morosa legendo*
> *Ille bene de te dicet, at ille male.*

"One should work only to enjoy oneself.
A pedant who will read the most beautiful story
will criticize the author, even if he is most faithful.
Another, in reading it, will prove it right."
(Analecta cartusiana, 82, 1 [1980], p. 45)

2. ON MARRIAGE

It must seem strange that in my old age I have written articles and books on love, marriage and women. This was indeed not planned: once again it was due to circumstances and requests that were made to me. Medieval monastic authors and especially St. Bernard had given me occasion a long time ago to approach the interpretation that they had given to the Song of Songs, where amorous relations are spoken of so extensively. I had been invited to speak about it several times in various places. Beryl Smalley had also advised me to publish the text of an interpretation that I had given on this subject at Oxford. In Paris, at the seminar that Georges Duby conducted at the Collège de France on medieval societies, I gave a one-hour report on love and marriage during which I alluded to the Song of Songs; this professor and friend then had me speak for another hour on the interpretation of this biblical text, the object of so much suspicion in our generation. He also asked me to return to deal again with these themes. I had occasion to participate with Duby in a series of conferences organized by the Maison française of New York University in 1986 on "Chivalry" and during a congress held at Maubeuge in 1989 on "Woman in the Middle Ages."

At the center of everything was the "problem of love," so important in medieval spiritual literature; its examination has not been overlooked since the Jesuit Fr. Rousselot first began to do so, in the years immediately preceding the First World War. Gilson had moved the study along. When in 1977 I was invited to Oxford to give some university classes on medieval culture, I chose for my theme "Monks and Love: Considerations on Comparative Amorous Literature in Twelfth-Century France." At the end of the course, Prof. Wallace Hadrill expressed the desire to have the text of the classes compiled in a volume and published at Oxford, because it was there that they were held. The book was translated into French with the title *L'amour vu par les moines*. Two years later, invited again to Oxford, I went a step further: the result was *Le mariage vu par les moines*. In the meantime there appeared *La femme et les femmes dans l'oeuvre de S. Bernard*, in which I subjected to historical criticism the opinions circulating about the misogyny of the abbot of Clairvaux. Bernard, it is true, had written two satires on a theme already dear to classical authors: women dressing. Now, the few times that he spoke ill of women was in connection with men, specifically the custom of two of their categories: bishops and certain knights. Within a short time there will appear in Milan a collection of studies published in various languages on love, marriage and women.

Did I have the right to address these topics without direct experience? I posed this question to some medievalist friends and they reassured me. It even seemed to me to be a duty because there was a "blank space" in the range of medieval studies. Marriage had been amply studied within social history, courtly literature and canon law. It remained to build a bridge between these fields and that of spiritual literature, which indeed above all was a monastic literature. In reality, beyond the "problems" of marriage — or rather before them — there existed the "mystery" of marriage. Contracts, chronicles and decrees informed us about the economic, juridical and political aspects of matrimony as an institution, but they said little or nothing about the person-to-person relationships in the conjugal union. When love was studied, it was above all a love — outside of marriage — testified to by romances, and limited to the "courts," society's aristocratic circles. For their part, canonists and theologians concentrated their attention on the characters of the sacramental bond, on the conditions of its validity, but not on conjugal love.

Long before becoming the object of "law" (which was established only later on, especially during the time of feudal society) and from the beginnings of the Church, matrimony was considered as St. Paul had defined it: a "sacrament," namely a mystery. It had assumed the character of a "covenant," with all the significance that this word had in the Old and New Testaments: a commitment to mutual faithfulness. Numerous texts presented the idea, not a utopian one, of marriage contracted out of love, in which the spouses sanctify one another by loving each other: an ideal that could be attained without leaving traces in chronicles or in trials, since happy marriages make no news. And the examples in a contrary sense, those about which many documents speak, clearly show the limits of the efficacy of this Christian plan, infractions of which are never considered as normal.

The examination of the texts that speak about love within marriage should contribute not just to progress in anthropology and in the knowledge of human feelings; it could offer remarkable interest to pastoral theology. Judging by medieval sermon collections, at least once a year — the Sunday on which the gospel of the wedding at Cana was read — the faithful heard the praise of Christian marriage and of the grace of fidelity that this sacrament confers, as I had occasion to point out in Luxembourg and elsewhere. In the 1988 conference in Maubeuge, I insisted on the beneficial role that, beginning with St. Paul, was acknowledged for wives with respect to their husbands. Later the labors of various American historians on Judaism showed that this tradition had only continued the Jewish one.

3. St. Bernard Today

The critical edition of the works of St. Bernard was finished in 1977, after thirty years of research and of sifting through compiled documentation. Now we were working with an established text. Inevitably St. Bernard had to be "computerized": this fulfilled a plan I had conceived in the early fifties and which IBM was ready to undertake. Nonetheless, during a meeting held at the IBM offices in Milan in 1953, Christine Mohrmann was completely opposed to it. The other philologists present favored it. However, at the abbey of Achel in the Netherlands, a concordance was drawn up manually. Just when it was about complete, although not yet published, the Centre de Traitement Électronique des Documents (CETEDOC) of the University of Louvain, under the direction of Prof. Paul Tombeur, began to set up, with the help of a computer, a vast *Thesaurus* of all the words of St. Bernard. It was published in 1987, accompanied by microfiches; a short time later we were able to present it to the Sorbonne. Even though it is not yet completely finished, since the variants of these data have not yet been inserted, nonetheless it confirms the validity of the text: one isolated voice did speak up to challenge its quality, on the basis of certain personal ideas concerning the Latin language and the utilization of the Vulgate. Will computerization really contribute to a better knowledge of St. Bernard? Will automation be able to dispense with careful reading?

In Spain, in Italy and in the United States translations of the critical text of St. Bernard had already been started; I had to write some introductions for them. A similar project began to be realized also in France and in German-speaking countries. Meanwhile, patient studies continued that gave much hope for the future of Bernardine studies. In a thesis defended at the Catholic University of Milan, Monica Sala presented with extreme precision the method that had been followed to establish the text. A Milanese priest, Fr. Claudio Stercal, professor at the Theological Faculty of Milan, presented at the Gregorian University a thesis on the development of St. Bernard's thought with regard to a principal problem: that of the presence and action of Christ in the Christian, in view of the "intermediate Advent," the interior coming, which St. Bernard had added to the "two Advents" that prior tradition had known— the one constituted by the Incarnation of the Word and the one that will be his eschatological return. This work was published in 1992 in a very fine volume. Everything in it is based on a minute examination of the variants that the manuscripts presented according to the edition's critical apparatus. In another field, my young friend and namesake, Jean

184

Leclercq, from Liège, presented at Louvain in 1991 a masterful study on *Blondel, lecteur de saint Bernard* [Blondel, Reader of St. Bernard]. The fact that the very next year this work won a prize makes one think that St. Bernard is being seriously considered today as a philosopher and master of thought.

In 1990 the ninth centenary occurred of the birth of the abbot of Clairvaux. Therefore that became the "year of St. Bernard." For that purpose I was asked to write *Bernard de Clairvaux* which the publisher Desclée issued in 1989, and translations of it into several languages were planned right away. Naturally the celebration of this centenary was the occasion for many television interviews, for example, the one for Munich television, where they posed questions to me including some insidious ones: "Would St. Bernard again send to Pope John Paul II his "De consideratione" in which he reproached Eugene III and the Roman Curia of his time?" Cardinal Danneels summoned me to Malines in order to help him prepare to speak about St. Bernard. The awareness of the holy abbot among the broad public thus received a new impulse.

Some congresses on St. Bernard took place in different countries of North and South America as well as in Europe, calling for both oral and written contributions. One of the most important was the one in Kalamazoo, while one of the most significant in terms of the progress of ideas was that of Lausanne where, in the cathedral that had become Protestant and for the first time since the Reformation, Catholics and Reformed — mostly Calvinists — prayed together. I had arranged to have the English theologian A. Lane invited to speak on "Calvin and St. Bernard"; he was the author of a thesis, yet unpublished, on this theme. I was assigned to conclude it, and so I sought to place St. Bernard in the past and present evolution of Europe. After that, the *Salve Regina* was proclaimed in a unanimous voice. On a high level, there was the conference in Lyons; its proceedings serve as an introduction to the translation of St. Bernard in the series *Sources Chrétiennes*.

On many of these occasions, which included the results of truly new research on historical facts and on texts, some interpretations were presented in the light of Marx, Freud, Jung and even of Indian Tantrism, and on the basis of contemporary literature. At Kalamazoo I had tried to use general sociology, but then in two recent articles I proposed an approach to the beginnings of the Cistercian Order according to the "sociology of groups": Bernard, a leader at once natural and charismatic of a group of knights, imposing on a not very old abbey, but one already threatened with extinction, his program of economic reform and making it prevail, not without some failure, in what became the abbey and the

Order of Cîteaux. Indeed, one can read the rare dated documents that are available through the eyes of a canonist inspired by more recent mental categories. Here we limit ourselves to conjectures, like archaeologists who reconstruct a whole inscription starting with the few letters or the few words that have been preserved, whereas the history of human groups, which today has at its disposal very precise methods, allows us to obtain more coherent results. A certain number of "myths" that burdened—and embellished—the Cistercian protohistory are thus brought into discussion. Nonetheless, a similar change in habitual ways of thinking inevitably arouses some criticism. St. Bernard thus has not stopped making himself talked about.

For the moment, it would remain to do a detailed and—insofar as Bernard's giant personality would allow it—impartial study of what his character really was. Was his *Vita* written because he was not a saint and to make people believe that he was, or else is his mystery not within the historian's scope?

4. LAST CHRISTOLOGICAL PROJECT

André Gide, whom I read in my youth, had written, "One is sixty years old for twenty years, and then all of a sudden one is eighty." In fact, a decline for me is becoming more noticeable and will bring me to heaven perhaps only after a period of deterioration which doctors' competence and brotherly devotion have the art of prolonging. To the extent that some reasonable project is still legitimate, it will be limited without doubt to the two fields that constitute the Christian-Buddhist dialogue on the one hand and spiritual gerontology on the other. Moreover, there are connections between them.

Indeed, in the publications relative to the first, one cannot fail to note all the importance that is attributed to the theme of nothingness and emptiness. Is this then the last word on it all? In Christianity we often speak as much about fullness as about destruction, and since there was an emptying of self—a *kenosis*—in Christ, this occurred in order to lead to that fullness that was for him and will be for us, thanks to him, the Resurrection. It is worthwhile to ask ourselves about the "non-I" exalted by some proselytes of Buddha. Is it really a "non-being" or else does it offer some enlightenment concerning our human condition that is lacking in traditional Christianity? In any case, St. Bernard possesses a theology of totality that a certain renunciation of the spontaneous ego has the purpose of preparing. "From nothingness to totality": this could be the title of a future study.

On the other hand, does not the experience of old age perhaps offer the occasion to reflect on what will follow it? A congress is to be held at the University of Lille on the theme: "Monks and Nuns before Death." A great number of communications will be presented there. It is easy to describe the organic and psychological manifestations of a tormented death. But should this be considered normal? What does the spiritual tradition of monasticism have to say about it? It displays many cases of tranquil and even happy deaths. Thus I have chosen as a title "Dying and Smiling," a formula more than ambiguous, because it suggests not an alternative but a threefold possibility, according to whether one smiles before, during or after dying. One time I found myself in a monastery in which they were praying for an abbess already far gone. One day a sign was put up which said, "The worst can be expected." The worst, it seemed to say, was that she would be going to heaven. Without doubt, one should not joke about the death of others, nor about what one will be up against when the organism defends itself in a final struggle. It is when one is still, if not in good health, at least fully lucid that one accepts one's own return to God.

A publisher had planned at one time to create a series of which the title, taken from the liturgy of the dead, would have been *Ossa humiliata* [Humbled Bones]. It would have consisted of a compilation of articles which had been discarded or forgotten in some journals, even recent ones. The idea was suggested to me to collect, by completing them, some studies on Christ presented just as certain medieval monastic authors had contemplated him. In teaching the history of christology, it happens that a direct leap is made from the age of the great councils to that of the scholastic masters, or in the best of cases to that of St. Anselm, as if in the span of seven centuries no monk or nun had tried not just to know who Christ was, but even to discover what he had experienced so as to join with him and share with him. Or else, after having affirmed that before St. Francis spirituality was based exclusively on the fear of God and on disdain for the world, one proclaims that at last in the thirteenth century the saint of Assisi discovered the infancy, the passion, the humanity and the humility of the Man God.

Thus there too is a "blank space" to be filled, as attempted by the little volume *Regards monastiques sur le Christ au Moyen Age*. In this kind of testament by an octogenarian, some flashes, so to speak, on the Lord Jesus are asked of the monastic tradition, to which I owe everything.

July 1992

Index of Names

Abelard, Peter, 59, 61
Abhishiktananda, Swami *see*
  Le Saux, H.
Acharya, Swami *see* Mahieu, F.
Alain-Fournier, 45
Alighieri, Dante, 59
Allende, S., 161
Alverny, M. T., 60
Anawati, G. C., 130
Anselm, St., 59, 60, 181, 187
Ansgar, St. 6
Apollinaire, G., 51
Arquillière, F. X., 33, 36
Asín Palacios, M., 131
Augustine of Hippo, St., 8, 9, 36,
  39, 50, 59

Baillet, L., 18
Baron, A., 73
Barrault, J. L., 53
Barré, L., 50
Bas Luna, E., 167
Basset, P., 46, 47, 53
Baudelaire, C., 51
Baudouin, L., 52
Baudrilart, A., 11
Bauer, O., 135
Beaulieu, E. M. de, 99
Benedict of Nursia, St., 24, 77, 91,
  134, 137, 156
Bernadette Soubirous, St., 15
Bernadot, M.-V., 39
Bernanos, G., 113
Bernard of Clairvaux, St., 59, 61,
  69-75, 76, 80, 85, 98, 117, 119,
  120, 121, 125, 131, 158, 182,
  184-186

Biala, H. de, 99
Bischoff, B., 72
Bloch, Marc, 37, 56
Blondel, M., 185
Boff, L., 161
Bolkos II, 94
Bonaparte, Napoleon, 113
Bonaventure, St., 49, 59, 61
Boniface VIII, Pope, 33
Bonsirven, J., 36
Borromeo, Charles, St., 55
Bouärd, A. de, 37, 49
Bourgoingt, J., 139
Bouyer, Louis, 116
Brezhnev, L., 97
Brillat-Savarin, A., 21
Brooke, C., 115
Brown, Raymond, 116
Brunel, R., 130, 131
Burns, F., 113, 151, 153
Butler, Cuthbert, 26

Caffarel, H., 38
Calvin, John, 185
Camara, Helder, 160, 165
Capelle, B., 52
Cardenal, Ernesto, 161
Cardijn, J., 24
Carmichael, E., 180
Casaroli, A., 76, 95
Cassian, John, St., 8
Castelli, L., 14
Catherine de Bar (Mechtilde of
  the Blessed Sacrament), 86
Cayré, F., 69
Cecilia, St., 66
Chaillet, P., 51